ΕΚΔΟΣΕΙΣ ΣΑΚΚΟΥΛΑ

Ioannis SARMAS

The Fair Balance

JUSTICE AS AN EQUILIBRIUM SETTING EXERCISE

SAKKOULAS PUBLICATIONS
ATHENS - THESSALONIKI

Nomos

Nomos

© 2014 ISBN: 978-3-8487-1825-2

http://www.nomos.de
nomos@nomos.de

SAKKOULAS PUBLICATIONS S.A.
ATHENS - THESSALONIKI

Athens

• 23, Ippokratous Str. - 106 79 Athens

Tel.: (+30 210) 33.87.500, Fax: (+30 210) 33.90.075

Thessaloniki

• 1, Fragon Str. - 546 26 Thessaloniki

Tel.: (+30 2310) 535.381, Fax: (+30 2310) 546.812

• 42, Ethnikis Aminis Str. - 546 21 Thessaloniki

Tel.: (+30 2310) 244.228, 9, Fax: (+30 2310) 244.230

http:/www.sakkoulas.gr • e-mail: info@sakkoulas.gr

05-22-337 ISBN: 978-960-568-067-1

To Stella, to Dimitris and Iakovos

CONTENTS

PART I

Justice as Equilibrium throughout History

PART II

Case-Studies on Justice and Equilibriums

PART III

The Shaping of Fair Balance Solutions

General Introduction

1. This book presents the means and the process by which fair balance solutions are shaped. Readers will find in it no recommendations to policy makers on social arrangements to be established, or proposals for solutions to social conflicts. Normative theories of justice, such as *egalitarianism*, *utilitarianism* or *contractarianism,* will be addressed here, but not for promoting the ideas of justice which are advocated by them[1]. They will be treated as material to be analysed for a better understanding of justice[2]. Justice in this book is regarded as an observable phenomenon consisting of the satisfaction provided to individuals involved in a social interaction when they are convinced that their interests have received the best possible treatment, having regard to the treatment of the others' interests. This conviction can be effective when it actually occurs, or hypothetical, when the individual in a position to judge considers that the treatment received by the interests in interaction may be regarded as being the best possible. It is about justice conceived in this way that we intend, in this book, to procure a study that is simultaneously descriptive and operational: descriptive in the sense of covering the whole phenomenon and built on accurate and verifiable knowledge; and operational, in the

1. See RAWLS 1999, SHAPIRO 1999, WALZER 1983, MOLLER OKIN 1989, GAUTHIER 2006, BINMORE 2005, BARRY 1989.
2. See BRIGHOUSE 2004, KYMLICKA 1999, FARAGO 2002, BESSONE 2000, SEN 2010.

sense of establishing the laws that govern the phenomenon, thus providing a sound basis for predicting the circumstances that may generate it.

2. The study presented here aims at bringing together three apparently unconnected worlds: jurisprudence, the science of social behaviour and rational decision theories.

The study is based on the case-law of the European Court of Human Rights and the Supreme Court of the United States, which, for a ruling that no violation of competing rights or freedoms submitted to their jurisdiction has occurred, require a fair balance to have been struck between the legitimate interests involved[3]. The Courts' case-law incorporates within it contemporary ideas of justice and offers the researcher prime raw material for a positive exploration of what justice is[4]. The conception of justice presented here will also rely on the lessons drawn from studies into the regulation of behaviour in animal societies[5] and, generally, on the emergence of order in the world of living and non-living beings by way of a self-organising process[6]. Living beings display complex strategies of cooperation and reciprocal altruism, within systems of distribution of roles and functions, ensuring the best possible satisfaction of their needs. And the whole world, as it is presented to us by the recent advances of science, is based on laws regulating interactions in such a way as to produce equilibriums permanently exposed to the risk of disruption[7]. This study will, finally, be based on rational decision theories, such as game theory[8] which promotes equilibrium as a solution concept for the strategic games it deals with. Depicting common social situations, the games in question

3. See *infra* §§ 72-86.
4. See *infra* §§ 74, 77, 80, 83, 86.
5. See *infra* §§ 105-113.
6. See *infra* §§ 115-117.
7. See *infra* §§ 121-124.
8. See *infra* §§ 118-120.

present players pursuing the maximization of their own utilities, face-to-face with other players animated by the same objective. Strategies initially conflicting, are stabilised, following the implementation of a harmonization dialectic, and eventually reconciled to an equilibrium position ensuring the best possible treatment of the respective interests involved.

3. This work is not original in its intention of presenting a descriptive and operational study on justice. To limit ourselves to contemporary publications, at least three works may be mentioned, whose authors set themselves the goal of exploring the structure of justice, even if they finally draw conclusions with a normative character. The first of these works is *Theories of Justice,* by Brian Barry[9]. Published in the 1980s in defence of *A Theory of Justice* by John Rawls[10], the book classifies theories of justice on the basis of impartiality, a concept which the author tries to portray as the very nature of justice. The second work, *Morals by Agreement,* by David Gauthier, was published during the same period[11]. While promising a normative theory of justice, the author studies the structure of fair balance solutions, and proposes a theory of justice based on the idea of consent. Finally, *Natural Justice,* by Ken Binmore, published much later than the previous two, has been explicitly designed, according to its author, to explore the deep structure of justice[12]. From knowledge gained from game theory and recent advances in the field of biology and of animal behaviour, Binmore builds up a conception of justice as fairness, akin to what was presented in *A Theory of Justice* by John Rawls. The authors of these

9. BARRY (Brian), *Theories of Justice*, University of California, 1989.
10. RAWLS (John), *A Theory of Justice*, Oxford University Press, 1999.
11. GAUTHIER (David), *Morals by Agreement*, Oxford Clarendon, 2006.
12. BINMORE (Ken), *Natural Justice*, Oxford University Press, 2005; see also BINMORE (Ken), *Game Theory and the Social Contract, Playing Fair,* (vol. 1) MIT Press, 1994; BINMORE (Ken), *Game Theory and the Social Contract, Just Playing,* (vol. 2) MIT Press, 1998.

books acknowledge David Hume as their master thinker for having founded justice on men's mutual interest[13]; the raw material that is behind their reasoning is game theory applied in the fields of economy, politics and biology[14]; and they constantly comment on the views expressed by John Rawls in his book on justice[15].

The originality of the study presented in this book, in comparison to the above works, is this: this study is a companion for justice's practitioners and users intended to provide its readers with operational knowledge they can use in dealing with issues of justice. To be effective in so controversial an area as justice, the analysis contained here is deepened and extended in order to create sufficient assurance for its readers when they try to find what a fair balance solution could be. This is the reason why this study recognizes as its key components the case-law of the European Court of Human Rights and of the United States Supreme Court alongside game theory and lessons learned from biology and animal behaviour, while including within its scope, not only the most influential theories of justice in the West, but also conceptions of justice, drawn from outside the Western world.

4. Ancient civilizations had the intuition that the equilibrium which establishes order, justice and prosperity in a society was the highest good and that this equilibrium was global, at the same time social and physical[16]. In such a worldview, men, animals and plants, the whole earth and the sky, even gods, were all linked in the same system, and charged to assume a role in keeping it effective[17]. Hinduism is based on the belief of an initial loss of balance,

13. BARRY 1989, pp. 145 *et seq.*; GAUTHIER 2006, pp. 1-2; BINMORE 2005, p. 4.

14. BARRY 1989, pp. 12-24; GAUTHIER 2006, pp. 14-15, 129-130; BINMORE 2005, pp. 58-75.

15. BARRY 1989, pp. 8, 146, 147, 214-215; GAUTHIER 2006, pp. 245-254; BINMORE 2005, pp. 15, 33, 125, 166, 170.

16. See *infra* §§ 12, 13, 15, 18, 19.

17. See *infra* §§ 23, 65.

a global outbreak that included the souls and the effort of the broken universe to return to the initial harmony[18]. In China, Taoism saw in the reconciliation of two opposing forces the path to global harmony[19] and Confucianism taught the internalization of the cosmic law of equilibrium in a morality of social harmony[20]. The Greeks had invented democracy to reconcile the will of the stronger with law and moderns used in this respect the fiction of the social contract[21]. Immanuel Kant, streamlining political liberalism, identified justice with a universal standard of behaviour imposed by reason and conceived as a tool to reconcile individual freedom with the freedom of others[22]. And utilitarians reverted to an empirical approach of justice, by teaching that justice is a matter of calculating the benefits and costs of actions[23].

These ideas of justice reflect the conflict concerning its sources. Some conceptions of justice identify its roots in the physical laws that govern the world, and use analogical thinking to draw standards applicable to human society from the laws governing the entire universe. The point of equilibrium, as an indicator of justice, is obtained, according to these conceptions, when humans come to be in compliance with the laws from which universal harmony emerges[24]. A second school of thought sees the source of justice in an immutable world of eternal ideas, and employs deduction as a method of learning the rules of justice. On that view, the point of equilibrium is stated axiomatically, and justice is identified with the correspondence between the requirements of the transcendental world and the material reality[25]. A third category, finally, of

18. See *infra* § 43.
19. See *infra* § 40.
20. See *infra* § 41.
21. See *infra* §§ 32, 50-53.
22. See *infra* § 131.
23. See *infra* § 136.
24. See *infra* §§ 65, 67.
25. See *infra* § 37.

conceptions of justice sees its sources in the world of contingency, and uses induction as a method of setting the rules of justice. Under this approach, nothing is immutable; everything is prone to reconstruction and modification[26]. By means of freedom of information, discussion and criticism, democracy enables equilibrium solutions to emerge which combine competing interests and which, by undergoing successive improvements, become more integrative and less conflicting[27].

5. The most elementary concept, from which this study proceeds, is the idea of interaction. Interactions are everywhere: entities, charged with their own power, interact with one another, to be neutralized or mutually absorbed or to coexist in a rather stable manner[28]. The world of living beings is characterized by a constant search for equilibrium under conditions of intense competition[29]. Natural selection has favoured structures enabling adjustments and cooperation in which animals of the same species develop a social life bringing comparative advantages to them in relation to their competitors[30]. To avoid internal conflicts and facilitate common endeavour, social animals, subjected to natural selection, distribute roles and functions and become integrated into hierarchies or systems of territorial priority, characterized by the law of the strongest[31]. Human beings also have the need to coordinate their behaviour to avoid mutual harm and also have to cooperate to make themselves stronger, thus increasing their chances of survival[32]. Their rationality helps them to realize that, on balance, they have more to gain by avoiding conflicts with others than by sy-

26. See *infra* §§ 66, 67
27. See *infra* § 182.
28. See *infra* §§ 115-117.
29. See *infra* §§ 111, 114.
30. See *infra* § 113.
31. See *infra* §§ 108-110.
32. GIBBARD 1996, p. 20.

stematically seeking them and that they can maximize their profits by being engaged in common endeavours than by undertaking activities alone. But the big problem they have to solve is the division of burdens and the distribution of benefits among those who are involved in coordination or cooperation ventures[33]. Avoid conflicts with others, why not, but *who is going to give in*? Undertake activities with others, why not? But *how will burdens and benefits be divided*? Thus, the question about justice arises. Each one of the parties, acting rationally, will seek to maximize their own benefits and minimize burdens, whilst minimizing the benefits of the opposing parties and maximizing their burdens. But, each one is sufficiently intelligent to understand that their own strategy is also the strategy of the counterpart. Should they exclude the use of force or fraud, there is no other way for them to resolve their problem than that of agreed mutual concessions.

However, justice is not defined here as the mere agreement of two individuals who, being of equal force, promise at a given moment to resolve their problems peacefully. We expect of justice a solution[34] which will allow people mutually to adjust their behaviour, within a general regulating system that decreases conflicts to a minimum. Justice, as understood here[35], seeks the stabilization of human behaviour, under conditions creative of order, in which benefits and social acceptability are maximized. This is why it is not enough for it to find, as in game theory[36], a point of equilibrium at which interactions between rational agents are simply stabilized. Justice seeks standards of behaviour which are consistent with a universal order of behaviour, acceptable to all who are subject to them as the best possible solution for regulating human interactions[37].

33. See *infra* § 147.
34. See *infra* §§ 159-161.
35. See *supra* § 1.
36. See *infra* §§ 118-119.
37. See *infra* § 125.

6. In this study, an inductive approach is applied initially. There is a core concept of justice which may readily be grasped on the basis of daily experience: the justice delivered by the courts under rules enacted by the legislature. This idea of justice, based on experience, will be applied to the facts of history to assist in understanding what mankind, throughout the various civilizations, has conceived as right or wrong in human interactions[38]. Historical research will allow us to make an inventory of the great ideas on justice in order to reflect on what they contain in common, despite their differences. More detailed work will then be necessary to shed the light of reason on the evidence gathered. Description of facts will thus give way to the induction of concepts from information garnered. When we deliver justice, when we reflect on right and wrong, do we follow an identical path in every case? How can we draw a line between what is constant in our way of thinking in this area and what is contingent? The inductive method will not enable these questions to be answered with sufficient certainty. Accumulated experience will bring us however to the position in which plausible assumptions may be made on what is required to be confirmed[39]. Thus we will move from the description of reality to the establishment of laws to which reality is subject. This is the heart of the project underpinning this book, namely to build an understanding of justice which can rise above experience in order to design a rational formula capable of explaining the phenomenon of justice and thus offering practical knowledge on how to deal with it[40].

7. This book is in three parts: Part I, *Justice as Equilibrium throughout History*, presents the conceptions of justice that have animated mankind, from its origins to the present day. This will be an essentially historical research designed to deal with the con-

38. See *infra* §§ 8-64.
39. See *infra* § 65.
40. See *infra* §§ 163-164.

cepts of justice that have governed or are still governing human societies. The reader will see that, despite the great diversity of conceptions emerging, there are yet some common elements running through them, which will enable us to start thinking about the structures common to the human mind when it deals with matters of justice[41]. Part II, *Case-Studies on Justice and Equilibriums*, will contain reflections based on materials as diverse as the judicial solution of conflict situations, plausible ways of harmonizing social interactions, and scientific evidence on self-organizing entities which will enable us to establish, across the cases studied, some constant parameters. Our research will lead us to identify the concept of equilibrium as the element common to all solutions, a conclusion which will give us the curiosity to answer the question why this idea, encountered in the hard sciences, is so useful also in morality and law. It is precisely the need to answer this question that will compel the method of approach of our study to change from an inductive to a deductive one[42]. Part III, *The Shaping of Fair Balance Solutions*, will take up the idea of equilibrium as a stabilizer in social relations, and will inquire further into situations where protagonists realize that they have received the best possible treatment in a social interaction. Equilibrium, as the indicator of justice and stabilizer of interactions, in fact has its own laws whose origin, interrelation and scope we need to scrutinise in order to integrate them into a structure offering a solution concept for justice's issues[43].

41. See *infra* §§ 65-68.
42. See *infra* §§ 121-124.
43. See *infra* § 183.

PART I

Justice as Equilibrium throughout History

8. Political organizations and social institutions, revolutions and wars are all, directly or indirectly, related to a question of justice either in the sense of defending a way of life which ensures good and eliminates evil or of searching for guidance in differentiating between right and wrong. It is, however, out of the question to be so comprehensive, in the first part of this book, as to trace a complete history of mankind. We will instead present here a selection of themes intended to encapsulate the main axes around which the imperative of justice has throughout history been articulated. Thus, the presentation will be configured according to a vertical structure, from the origins of humanity to the present day, intersected by a series of horizontal topics developed at each stage. Three such topics will more particularly draw our attention. We will consider, first, how the legislative rules, which may be presumed to be rules of justice, are formulated, by whom and according to which criteria. We observe, in the second place, how societies in producing an effective order assign to each one who lives under their jurisdiction patterns of behaviour predictable to the others. Finally, we will focus on the ideas which cement the unity of a society, making it possible for its members to share common views on their surrounding reality. These three themes relate in fact, at different levels, to one question only: how the competing interests of the members of a given society are subjected to a discipline, generating a sustainable controlling order.

There is an answer to this question that mankind, from its origins, has tried to avoid: that order is generated by the introduction of priority rights based on the rule of the strongest. Justice, in order to prevail, needs a global power capable of limiting the particular powers which, in their own interest, try to create priority rights.

The allocation of regulatory power to a superhuman being, the divine, has in this respect been a great invention. Two consequences arose from the introduction of a divine regulator: first, that the norms of justice should be revealed by those who claimed to act under his authority; and, secondly, that, as the divine regulator had full power to punish or reward the sinner even after her earthly life, the scope of a human being's vested interests was extended to areas beyond her tangible interests on earth.

9. In the following pages, we will present the forms that the conception of justice has taken in different civilizations, the contradictions that emerged and the limits to which those forms have been subject, as well as the real alternatives that humanity has explored. *Justice as Equilibrium throughout History* is made up of three chapters. In the first, *Emergence of the Requirements of Justice,* we trace the beginnings of humanity in its quest for justice, observing the emergence of justice as a need for equilibrium. Starting with primitive societies, whose traces are still identifiable in Africa, Oceania, Siberia and the Americas, we will collect primary ideas on order in society, the proper place of each individual in it and the principles of distribution and retribution. In the second chapter, *Justice's Major Platforms,* we present the idea of equilibrium in the major platforms of justice. These platforms are not philosophical conceptions or sacred books or, in any event, are not only that. They are particular models of justice applied in societies and which continue, even today, to govern societies, raising a claim to universality. Finally, in the third chapter, *Justice within Human Rights,* we will follow the path of the West toward universality, addressing equilibrium as an idea of modernity for resolving social conflicts. There is currently no greater claim to universality than the one raised by human rights, rights produced, however, within European societies or in societies that have come about as a consequence of European expansion.

1

Emergence of the Requirements of Justice

10. Humanity's first steps in search of justice are taken within nomadic communities. Members of the community established cooperative links based on reciprocity. Ideology emerging in the form of religion reinforces the primary order. Totemic thinking promotes exogamy and the taboo on incest is established; the father's sublimated figure is instilled in the son's mind who, even when he becomes stronger than his father, is subject to him. Animistic thought unifies man with nature in a relationship of mutual respect the infringement of which involves supernatural punishments. Between these primary societies and the great empires of the Nile and Mesopotamia there is no break, only an evolutionary progression. The clergy was set up as a repository of knowledge and directed its learning to legitimizing the power in place. The innocent idea of a balanced relationship between humans and nature, maintained by the shamans of primary societies, gave way to integrative constructions which transformed humans into servants of gods, the guarantors of the world's equilibrium, and kings into the intermediaries of gods, mediating to humans the divine will. The people obeyed, convinced that it was in their interest to support a powerful authority which was needed to contain the waters of large rivers and thus to facilitate the irrigation of the fertile land. The sovereigns, however, knew that there was within the people a tolerance level not to be exceeded. Their power rested on the approval of their subjects and an ideology, spread by an official clergy, was not enough to justify everything. Indo-European clans are federated in such a way as to found the power of the state on a pyramidal structure. In these societies, state power is legitimated on utilitarian considerations or popular consent. In the Americas, the elderly, children, the disabled, sick, and women are enclosed within family protection structures. State power protects people against uncertainties by arbitrating between present and future.

Primitive Societies: Keeping the Balance

11. Between three and one million years ago, in the southern part of Africa, some primates definitively became bipeds and began to manufacture objects which facilitated their life[44]. They become human[45]. To ensure, in such conditions, stable access to sex, the human male can no longer ignore the fate of the child that his partner has to raise. Family solidarity is born. Hunting is done by men, whereas women do the gathering. Fair sharing, cooperation and mutual respect are rooted in this social entity[46]. In sharing food amongst her children, the mother divides it according to the needs and the merits of each one. The old become educators. Their experience helps in predicting the succession of seasons, in healing, and sometimes in averting disasters[47].

Primitive society was probably composed of about thirty individuals. With more members, its movements would have been difficult; with fewer, it would have been less effective against enemy attacks. Dangers lurked everywhere and to survive, humans

44. WILSON 2012, p. 33.
45. BOESCH 2001, pp. 170 *et seq.*
46. CLASTRES 1974, p. 56.
47. DE LUMLEY 2007, p. 19; DEPUTTE, VAUCLAIR 2001, pp. 242 *et seq.*

had to cultivate their intelligence, extend the scope of their memory, build new materials, and reinforce their social relationships. By improving the stonecutting process, man could make lighter and more effective hunting tools. He was able more easily to travel to and from the place which his group had chosen for settlement. By using fire, humans could cook their food, preserve it longer, chew it and digest it easily. The use of fire came to enhance social links. Humans could spend a good part of the night around the fire and thus develop new sociability that led to the growth of language[48]. Primary cannibalism gave way to the burial of the deceased, surrounded by objects[49].

The first permanent settlements appeared at places where water was available[50]. The man who cultivates land, domesticates animals, builds his house and stores supplies, subjects himself to a new social discipline, different from that to which he was subjected at the time of his life as a nomad. He must henceforth work laboriously and organize his timetable with a previously unknown sense of responsibility[51].

12. Primitive man makes no distinction between physical forces, plants and animals. He sees no radical differences between inanimate objects and living beings, between nature and culture[52]. The wind, thunder and fire all have souls, in the same way as the plants, stars or sun. There is a living being behind the rain and the clouds; the forest, rivers and sea are intelligent beings[53]. Humans and animals have equal status in the community of life energy, and

48. LEWIN 1991, pp. 358 *et seq.*; REICHHOLF 1990, pp. 211 *et seq.*

49. LAFFORGUE 1998, pp. 100 *et seq.*

50. MEULEAU, PIETRI 1971, p. 15.

51. CAMPS 1982, pp. 302 *et seq.*; CLARK, PIGGOT 1990, pp. 148, 150; CLASTRES 1974, pp. 161 *et seq.*

52. CLASTRES 1974, p 91.

53. DESCOLA 2005, pp. 63, 65, 183 *et seq.*

their exchanges help in maintaining the equilibrium of nature by a strict equality of transfers[54].

Primitive societies are attached to the idea that our world coexists with an invisible world, the world of the spirits, with which it is in perpetual exchange[55]. Totemic thinking binds a family with a physical force, a living being or an object[56]. Misfortunes that strike humans are caused by spirits which act to punish them when they obtain more than they need. Humans should not needlessly kill animals. A spirit protects animals' lives and supervises hunting in the forest. The pact of mutual respect between the invisible beings and humans is broken when humans deviate from the principle of balance of trade[57]. The shaman performs, within primitive societies, the function of explaining the principles of peaceful coexistence of the two worlds and teaching the standards governing their peaceful relations[58]; he restores the balance when humans go beyond the sphere assigned to them by the order of nature[59]. By the explanations he gives, he offers to the tribe a reassuring image of the physical phenomena[60]. Shaman is also the great judge: he indicates the individuals held responsible for the misfortunes of the group and restores justice by introducing the remedy for the wrong caused. He is the agent who reminds his people of the laws of the world's equilibrium, and who by his advice points out how to restore it[61].

---

54. DESCOLA 2005, p. 475. See also p. 31: *"Each individual would thus be aware of being an element of a complex network of interactions unfolding not only in the social sphere, but in the totality of a universe tending to stability (...). It gives to all responsibilities of an ethical order, in particular not to disrupt the general balance of this fragile system and not to use energy without restoring it quickly by various types of ritual operations".*
55. DESCOLA 2005, p. 460.
56. FREUD 1965, pp. 11 *et seq.*
57. DESCOLA 2005, pp. 433, 441.
58. MALINOWSKI 1933, p. 76.
59. PERRIN 1995, p. 66.
60. DESCOLA 2005, pp. 32 *et seq.*
61. DESCOLA 2005, p. 32.

In primitive societies, the role of social power is to balance centrifugal and centripetal forces that develop in the community[62]. All institutions are means to strike such a balance[63]. From birth, the primitive learns to respect social norms with which he must comply. The chief of the village monitors social life so as to maintain each individual in his appropriate rank, denouncing and morally condemning any dangerous innovations, any turbulent, arrogant or ambitious behaviour[64]. He is the elected head of families and warriors, who all see him as a peacemaker, a man who can convince by the proper use of words, while by his generosity he shows that he derives no personal benefit from his function[65]. In case of war, such a leader is replaced by a war chief, dominant and heroic. But once the war has ended, the villagers restore their leader to the limited power he used to have in peaceful times[66].

13. Primitive man feels vested with interests which are personal to him and which he tries to defend or promote. Determined by his sex, his rank, and his capacities he is nonetheless fundamentally equal to his peers. His human dignity, founded on his capacity to take part on basis of equality in the tasks shared with others, pushes him to defend his position: *"You aren't worth less than the others, you aren't worth more than the others, you shall have no desire for power, and you shall have no desire to be submissive"* [67].

62. CLASTRES 1974, pp. 133 *et seq.*
63. MALINOWSKI 1933, p. 88.
64. MALINOWSKI 1933, p. 82.
65. CLASTRES 1974, p. 33. According to CLASTRES, p. 107: *"If exchange as the essence of social life can take the dramatic shape of a competition between those who are exchanging, it is condemned to remain static because the durability of the social contract requires that there is neither winner nor loser and that the gains and the losses balance each other constantly for everyone".*
66. CLASTRES 1974, p. 27.
67. CLASTRES 1974, pp. 108, 159-160.

Primitive man has an effective weapon for the respect by others of his individuality and his honour: reciprocity. Exchange and retaliation are the basis for social relations[68]. Each individual is involved in common tasks according to his rank, his age and his talent, and he derives from his work the individual's share which he deserves[69]. Reciprocity governs the relationship between husband and wife, between families which offer their children for marriage or exchange their goods, between communities which have a surfeit of certain goods and lack others[70]. Often, though not always, gifts conceal a relationship of reciprocity: a chief who makes gifts to his people, or the gifts which are offered on the occasion of a marriage, are hardly made in a gratuitous manner. In the same way as sacrifices offered to the divinities, these gifts aim in fact to obtain in return the recipient's benevolence[71].

Cooperation takes place between individuals who are not bound by emotional ties as narrow as in the case of family relations. It presupposes a kind of agreement aiming to produce mutual benefit by joint effort. Within the group, cooperation characterizes the relations among women in taking care of the children[72] and among men in hunting, or combating predatory beasts[73]. Cooperation for political purposes strikes a balance between opposing forces based on the agreement of a plurality of individuals against tyrannical force. Its objective is the more equitable satisfaction of the elementary needs of those who make up the group by eliminating a leadership which works in an egoistic manner[74].

---

68. JACOBY 1984, p. 5.
69. MALINOWSKI 1933, pp. 22, 43 *et seq.*
70. CLASTRES 1974, p. 103; MALINOWSKI 1933, pp. 35, 37.
71. MALINOWSKI 1933, pp. 26, 31. According to MALINOWSKI, p. 40: *"The system is based on a very complex* do ut des *and, in the long-run, reciprocity is achieved".*
72. WRIGHT 2000, pp. 19 *et seq.*; CLASTRES 1974, pp. 99-100.
73. CLASTRES 1974, pp. 97-98.
74. CLASTRES 1974, p. 176.

Egypt of Pharaoh: Submission to a Cosmic Equilibrium

14. Established throughout the Nile Valley, around the third millennium before Jesus Christ, the Pharaoh's empire was at first subjected to the authority of Horus, the god of discipline and co-ordination, to pass, thereafter, under that of Ra, the god of the sun[75]. Local hegemonies in the 42 prefectures that made up the empire caused the collapse of the central state[76]. Local entities were gathered again into a single state in the second millennium under the kings of Thebes. The Theban god, Amun, god of male fertility, was then associated with Ra, god of the old empire, and amalgamated into the official theological composition of the god, Amun Ra[77]. The clergy of Thebes, all-powerful, cultivated the idea according to which the Pharaoh *"finds his pleasure in justice"*, and advocated the king's intervention in society in order to ensure stability and prosperity[78]. The invasion of Hyksos, warriors on horse-drawn chariots, caused the loss of the delta and the contracting of the kingdom towards the south[79]. The restoration of the Pharaoh's authority in the entire country was accompanied by an extension of the powers of the clergy devoted to the worship of Amun Ra[80]. Pharaoh Akhenaton tried to establish Aten, the god of the solar disk, as an official single deity[81]. His doctrine was to secure the unity of the empire, diminish the influence of the clergy and provide equal dignity to all men regardless of their origin, education or wealth[82]. The failure of his

75. GRIMAL 1988, pp. 76, 116-117; MEULEAU, PITRI 1971, pp. 41-42, 52.
76. MEULEAU, PITRI 1971, p. 42
77. MEULEAU, PITRI 1971, p. 43
78. MEULEAU, PITRI 1971, p. 53
79. GRIMAL 1988, p. 245 ; MEULEAU, PITRI 1971, p. 43.
80. MEULEAU, PITRI 1971, p. 43
81. GRIMAL 1988, pp. 291 *et seq.*
82. GRIMAL 1988, p. 290.

attempt drove Egypt into decline. The lack of iron weakened any warlike attempt by the Egyptians vis-à-vis the peoples of Mesopotamia. The latter, by the use of iron weapons, had a contrivance similar to the chariot of the Hyksos which, more than a thousand years before, caused the loss of the delta[83].

15. The religion of the Egyptians was their science, their way of understanding the world. Each new physical discovery was physically invested as a new divinity. If fertility was represented by a woman at the beginning, it evolved later to be represented by an ithyphallic man. When the Egyptians realized that it was the sun which, by its light and heat, fertilized nature, it was set up as a supreme god[84]. For the Egyptians, the world resulted from chaos by the action of a powerful god, the demiurge. The forces of chaos, however, remained alive and aspired to replace the created order with the primitive disorder. The gods created by the demiurge, had a duty to maintain order in the world[85]. They were nourished by Ma'at, a primordial deity, who imposed on chaos an organization based on the balance of forces, the harmonization of wills, the reign of truth, the reward of good, and punishment of evil[86]. Ma'at was the goddess of the equilibrium, physical and social, the goddess of cosmic and human justice. Pharaoh was her servant, as were all Pharaoh's subjects, from the high clergy to the humblest peasant. Everybody was obliged to do what was appropriate

83. MEULEAU, PITRI 1971, p. 45.

84. MEULEAU, PITRI 1971, p. 63.

85. DERCHAIN 1970, p. 85; MEULEAU, PITRI 1971, p. 47. According to GRIMAL, 1988, p. 63: *"Ma'at holds a special place in the pantheon: she is not strictly-speaking a goddess, but rather an abstract entity. She represents the equilibrium to which the universe came about through the creation, that is, the compliance to the truth of the nature. As such, she is the measure of all things, from justice up to the integration of the soul of the dead in the universal order at the last judgment.(...) She is also the food of the gods, bringing to them her harmony."*

86. GRIMAL 1988, p. 63; MEULEAU, PITRI 1971, pp. 47, 53.

87. MELEAU, PITRI 1971, pp. 47, 53.

in order to maintain the equilibrium desired by the goddess[87]. A living god, Pharaoh, established by his decrees the social order, as a reflection of the divine order[88]. Humans contribute in maintaining order by doing good in their daily lives. It was their duty to help the hungry, the thirsty, the naked and needy, and to respect the lives and property of others[89].

Alongside the knowledge-based religion, another kind of religion emerged. Osiris, the god consoler, the giver of eternal life, the god of the dead, is its representative. On him was projected, not an explanation of the physical laws, but the hope of mankind in a life after death[90]. Egyptians conceived the idea of the *Last Judgment*, delivered by a court assessing the deceased's ability to live forever in heaven according to his deeds on earth. Ra and Osiris, scales in hand, presided over this court which comprised as many judges as there were provinces in the empire[91]. It is through this invention that the daily life of Egyptians revolved permanently around the idea of preparation for death. This preparation consisted of two parts, firstly, a material element, in order to secure what was necessary for the preservation of the body[92], and, secondly, a moral one, to ensure that one conducted oneself on earth in accordance with the preferences of the supreme judges[93].

16. The idea that the Egyptians were made to strive for good corresponded to their general conception of the factors of stability in their settled civilization. Egyptian society was based on a strict discipline which ensured the necessary order facilitating irrigation, culture and distribution of crops. Food supply was the fruit of the coordinated work of men, and depended on the proper application

88. MONTET 1970, pp. 28, 48; MEULEAU, PITRI 1971, p. 41.
89. MONTET 1970, pp. 51, 172.
90. DERCHAIN 1970, p. 82; MEULEAU, PITRI 1971, p. 42.
91. GRIMAL 1988, p. 199.
92. MEULEAU, PITRI 1971, pp. 49-51; GRIMAL 1988, p. 199.
93. GRIMAL 1988, pp. 142 *et seq.*

of the precepts suitable for agriculture[94]. In order to benefit from the order of things, the Egyptian had to harmoniously integrate himself into it, collaborating in the cultivation of the soil, and, in a word, had to respect the cosmic discipline which was also a social discipline. The action of the government, which enacted the beneficial regulations and ensured their application, was identified with the idea of good. Major works were undertaken by drudgeries imposed on farmers when they remained inactive during the Nile's high waters[95]. The royalty had set up a monopoly of exploitation of careers and mines[96]. The tenants of lands were obliged to offer a part of their crops to the temple, the local dignitaries and the central government. Individuals paid taxes in labour, cattle, or cereals[97]. The sentences were severe, such as mutilation or death[98].

Though the lands all belonged to the Pharaoh or to the clergy, the Egyptians had a rather concrete idea about the rights on which individuals could rely in respect of real estate[99]. Everyone was entitled to a piece of land that would guarantee to him and his family a decent standard of living, and everyone had the right to defend his land against any excessive exaction. The equitable distribution of land, even if farmers were regarded as mere tenants of the king or the temple, forms part of the eternal order in which Egypt is believed to live[100]. People accepted the established order[101] provided that this order was able to offer them the subsistence minimum[102]. There were, however, times in the history of the

94. MEULEAU, PITRI 1971, p. 53.
95. MEULEAU, PITRI 1971, p. 53.
96. MEULEAU, PITRI 1971, pp. 53-54, 57.
97. MONTET 1970, p. 91.
98. MONTET 1970, p. 86.
99. LAFFORGUE 1998, I, p. 252.
100. MEULEAU, PITRI 1971, pp. 54-55.
101. Social mobility could be provided either by the army or by literary or priestly functions: MEULEAU, PITRI 1971, p. 58; MONTET 1970, p. 83.
102. MEULEAU, PITRI 1971, pp. 60-61.

country when social upheaval occurred, especially due to a series of bad harvests. Satirical tirades, subtle social criticism, a secular wisdom teaching the joy of life, and pessimism before death are enough evidence to demonstrate the vitality of recalcitrance toward the heaviness of the civilization of temples[103].

Mesopotamia: Cooperative Behaviour to Maintain Prosperity's Order

17. Mesopotamia had a multitude of small towns whose centre of gravity was the temple. They were federations of clans, coordinated by the temple, whose means of production and goods were subject to distinct property rights[104]. The clergy, by its moral authority, imposed the rules of respect of property and, in general, the standards of community life. Members of the clergy, intermediaries between the divine and the human world, gathered knowledge and implemented it in order to organize agriculture, channel water, and avoid famines[105]. Settled communities were subject to attack by warriors raiding their food supplies. Warriors were initially limited to plundering. Once settled, they formed themselves into civic nobility, against the clergy, and claimed the right of commanding the city[106]. Several war leaders challenged authority over the valley, and a continuous mass of immigrants added instability to the political imbalance specific to the country[107]. Cities put themselves in conflict with each other mainly over irrigation. The winners found it hard to subject the defeated to a system of government capable of assimilating them. Revolts broke out and new invaders emerged to upset the established

103. MEULEAU, PITRI 1971, pp. 65-66; MONTET 1970, pp. 209 *et seq.*

104. LAFFORGUE 1998, I, p. 265; MEULEAU, PITRI 1971, p. 68.

105. MEULEAU, PITRI 1971, p. 69, 71.

106. MEULEAU, PITRI 1971, p. 70.

107. MEULEAU, PITRI 1971, p. 68.

order[108]. The period of Sumerian Mesopotamia, in this respect is no different from the Babylonian period that took over. The former conquerors, reduced to the rank of the humble, merged into the mass of the people[109].

18. Sumerian religion is structured geometrically according to a pyramidal order of the divinities. Its great god, An, god of the sky, is the fertility god who reigns over the Pantheon[110]. En-lil, second god in order of importance, is the Lord of the atmosphere, the part of the world that links heaven and earth. He is the god of the good natural and social order[111]. Implacable legislator, protector of sovereigns, dispenser of justice against the trouble-makers, he implements purges to ensure the harmonious development of the terrestrial world. En-ki, the third in the Sumerian triad of great deities, is the god of the water and of the ground, close to men, offering them his assistance to face the difficulties of life[112]. God of accuracy, balance and harmony, he bound men to gods in a spirit of collaboration to maintain global order. The remaining deities were responsible for the maintenance of order in specific areas of reality.

Water for irrigation is the instrument of reason and order[113]. Evil exists in the world in the form of irrational forces that constantly threaten the world's order. Identified in the image of a great serpent, the forces of chaos are those of waters not channelled by human science. "Me" is the constant development and the eternal

108. MEULEAU, PITRI 1971, p. 72.

109. LAFFORGUE 1998, pp. 302 *et seq.*

110. JESTIN 1970, pp. 190 *et seq.*

111. JESTIN, 1970, p. 192: *"The god En-lil possessed the aspect of a terrible warrior and a relentless legislator. He was the god who, in the company of men strives to maintain good order and strikes mainly those whose actions present the greatest danger to proceeding the right way".*

112. JESTIN 1970, p. 193.

113. JESTIN 1970, p. 162.

return, the force of progress and decline, of creation and destruction[114]. The gods are predestined to establish order and justice, while the power of evil seeks to destroy civilization and to restore chaos[115]. Destiny, experienced by both gods and humans, is that point of equilibrium between the opposing forces engaged in an unceasing fight[116].

Babylonian religion is an extension and, at the same time, a transformation of the Sumerian religion. A great god, Marduk, takes the place of En-lil by delegation; the part that demonic forces take in the process of universal evolution shrinks and finally disappears[117]. Misfortunes are not explained by the forces of evil, but as divine sanction striking the sinners[118]. Gods of good reign in harmony in the universe and monitor the behaviour of humans. The role of man is to help the gods so that good prevails in society and the man who is struck by evil must seek in his previous behaviour the causes of his misfortune. The innocent are not spared, but in their case evil is a kind of test and they will soon have their reward[119]. The believer seeks to know god's decrees, to envisage his will, to prevent his bad temper. He believes that by his prayers he will manage to contain his misfortunes and that he can, by magic or divination, provide for himself a more certain way of life, or even control the course of events[120]. Regarding themselves as creatures of gods made by them in order to be their servants, Babylonians saw no reward after death, whose darkness haunted their imagination[121].

114. JESTIN 1970, pp. 165, 178.
115. JESTIN 1970, p. 185.
116. JESTIN 1970, p. 165.
117. NOUGAYROL 1970, p. 219.
118. BOTTERO 1992, p. 295; NOUGAYROL 1970, p. 210.
119. NOUGAYROL 1970, p. 211.
120. KRAMER 1994, p. 133.
121. NOUGAYROL 1970, p. 87.

19. Mesopotamia possessed, thanks to trade and industry, cities which quickly evolved into great urban centres[122]. Work and classes became differentiated[123]. First is the warrior nobility occupied with the external and internal safety of the state and responsible for command and administration. The clergy provides moral authority to members of the dominant class by offering them a divine legitimacy in the eyes of the people. There is a mass of specialized workers, composed of metallurgists, ceramics manufacturers and others. Farmers and pastors come next in the social hierarchy followed, finally, by the immigrants, who, together with the slaves, perform society's most menial tasks[124].

The king, strategist and at the same time chief priest, ensures his authority by divine delegation and governs to make men work together in order to collaborate in the divine plan of maintaining universal order[125]. The sovereign is the dispenser of justice among men. The duty of the human in the face of the gods becomes a legal obligation to respect royal decrees by which divine will is carried out[126]. Whenever misery became extreme, revolts were likely to break out which, without having a concrete political goal, threatened the established order[127]. The kings, feeling the poor's exploitation by the strong, posed as arbitrators, seeking a reputation of restoring equilibrium between the strong and the weak within society[128]. The defence of the widow and the orphan became a real program of governance. King Hammurabi instituted a common unquestionable doctrine on justice in a code issued around 1780 BC[129]. In this code, the King declares himself the protector of the weak. Its

122. MEULEAU, PITRI 1971, p. 69.
123. MEULEAU, PITRI 1971, p. 81.
124. MEULEAU, PITRI 1971, p. 82.
125. MEULEAU, PITRI 1971, p. 81.
126. NOUGAYROL 1970, p. 241.
127. MEULEAU, PITRI 1971, p. 83.
128. MEULEAU, PITRI 1971, p. 81.
129. LAFFORGUE 1998, I, pp. 306 *et seq.*

Articles 196 and 200 set out the law of retaliation, *"an eye for an eye and a tooth for a tooth."*

Indo-European Societies: Searching for the Common Denominator

20. The Indo-Europeans, semi-nomads living on the plains, were organized in large families and in tribal confederations[130]. They handled horses, which allowed them to move fast. Iron weapons made them irresistible in battle. From the beginning of the second millennium before Jesus Christ, they settled in the Hellenic peninsula and Asia Minor[131]. State entities were built there on a practical basis[132]. There was no question of communion between man and god, but of relations of good neighbourliness. Relations were established among them on a basis of reciprocity, the prayers and the sacrifices of the men being balanced in return by the favours of the gods[133]. The rulers were exercising a power based on their own warlike and organizing capacities[134]. The Greek king, the *Basileus*, was in fact the first among the clans' leaders. The political organization was a confederation of clans, all equal in dignity and rights, with the exception of the royal clan. The clans had a good social discipline based on obedience to their chief, priest of the family worship, and head of the small army composed of members of the clan[135].

Justice began as an internal matter for patriarchal families, whose chief performed an intermediary function between the protective souls of the dead ancestors and the living members of the

130. GLOTZ 1968, pp. 14 *et seq.*
131. LAFFORGUE 1998, pp. 295-297.
132. BURN 1988, pp. 63-66.
133. VIAN 1970, p. 503.
134. VIAN 1970, p. 516.
135. VIAN 1970, pp. 516 *et seq.*; BURN 1966, pp. 45 *et seq.*

great family. He was the keeper of the rules of *Themis*, the sacred justice, whose origins dated back to the divine ancestor of the family[136]. When cities were formed by the unification of the clans into communities established in a territory, justice passed to the *Basileus*, chief of the confederation of the families, who had the religious authority to lay down the law, and the military authority to impose it. He was often assisted by a meeting of heads of patriarchal families, and he discussed his decision with all the people meeting in the agora[137]. Surrounded by the Council of Elders, he could not, however, invent the rules at will[138]. Subject to the mood of the agora, he sought a broad popular consensus around his decisions[139]. When the aristocrats took power, they continued to dispense justice that also referred to ancestral traditions[140].

21. Hittites considered that between men and gods there was a kind of contract: according to the principle of reciprocity, piety was balanced by divine favour[141]. Their sovereign played an intermediary role between men and gods. He was at the same time priest, legislator, supreme judge and governor of the country[142]. The dignitaries delivered justice in the name of the king and received from him instructions to be impartial, to check the facts well and to satisfy requests for justice from the humble[143].

The sovereign enacted laws gathered together in a code which was not considered of divine origin and non-compliance with

136. GLOTZ 1968, p. 30.

137. VIAN 1970, p. 516.

138. GLOTZ 1968, p. 58.

139. POSNER 1983, pp. 128-129; FUKUYAMA 2011, pp. 69-72; GLOTZ 1968, pp. 27 *et seq.*

140. GLOTZ 1968, pp. 108, 240 *et seq.*

141. MEULEAU, PITRI 1971, p. 152.

142. GURNEY 1990, p. 54; MEULEAU, PITRI 1971, p. 148.

143. GURNEY 1990, p. 75; MEULEAU, PITRI 1971, p. 149.

which was not considered a sin[144]. Collective responsibility in criminal cases was not allowed except for the crime of offending the sovereign[145]. Manslaughter caused by negligence was treated with a light sentence. Murder by premeditation was punished according to the discretion of the parents of the deceased. The sanctions were in general of a financial character[146]. However, incest, bestiality, rebellion against the authority of the state entailed the death penalty. The law punished crimes committed by slaves more severely. Nevertheless, it regarded them as human beings[147].

22. Mesopotamia, Egypt, Palestine, and Asia Minor were parts of the Persian empire[148]. The empire was ruled by a Persian sovereign who, at the same time, was declared successor to the sovereigns of each country conquered and protector of the specific cult of each such country[149]. The satrapies, administrative units of the kingdom, required their subjects, vassals and princes to respect the same laws and pay the same taxes[150]. Expended to finance new wars, or to build new palaces, taxation was the target of constant criticism by the different subject ethnic groups[151].

With so many different peoples living under the umbrella of the same state an opportunity arose for the advancement of synthesis and the mingling of cultures. There was no absolute truth in this empire except the unquestionable authority of the Great King. Ionia was living under the same royal authority as Egypt, and the Greeks of Asia Minor were to refer to the same central government as the Palestinians or the Babylonians. Channels of communication were to be a

144. MEULEAU, PITRI 1971, pp. 65-66
145. GURNEY 1990, p 82 *et seq.*; MEULEAU, PITRI 1971, pp. 149-150.
146. MEULEAU, PITRI 1971, p. 150.
147. GURNEY 1990, pp. 72 *et seq.*, 77 *et seq.*, 82 *et seq.*
148. MEULEAU, PITRI 1971, pp. 65-66
149. MEULEAU, PITRI 1971, pp. 137 *et seq.*
150. MEULEAU, PITRI 1971, p. 136.
151. MEULEAU, PITRI 1971, pp. 65-66.

commonplace[152]. The Ionians and Egyptians often headed for the Persian capital, where all ideas, religions, or knowledge of the occupied countries converged. The Jewish Diaspora became the source of new ideas about the divine[153]. The struggle between good and evil and man's moral duty to have a pure soul, are ideas that began to gain a universal audience starting from the Persian empire[154]. Zoroastrianism taught the existence of a single god and placed man in the centre of a divine plan in the struggle between the forces of good and evil[155].

The Americas: Arbitrating between Present and Future

23. In Lower Mexico, Guatemala and Honduras, the Maya civilization bloomed over a long period. The basic social unit was, throughout the territory, the patriarchal family. A certain number of families, worshipping a common ancestor, gathered in a village[156], while several villages came together to form a small state that had at its head a governor[157]. The concern of Maya was to make their land productive. They had to cultivate either on flat ground and fight against the jungle which asserted its rights without flexibility or on the slopes of the mountains and there create farmland in areas that were not conducive to such use[158]. The knowledge of time was held by the clergy[159]. A class of large landowners lived with the constant concern to keep hold of its wealth, hence the em-

152. MEULEAU, PITRI 1971, pp. 65-66.
153. ATTALI 2002, pp. 74 *et seq.*
154. DUCHESNE-GUILLEMIN pp. 625 *et seq.*
155. DUCHESNE-GUILLEMIN p. 656 *et seq.*; MEULEAU, PITRI 1971, pp. 65-66.
156. PIETRI, VENARD 1971, pp. 349-350.
157. PIETRI, VENARD 1971, p. 35; ELIADE 1990, p. 42; BELLINGER 2000, p. 597 *et seq.*; BELLINGER 2000, p. 602.
158. PIETRI, VENARD 1971, p. 349.
159. BELLINGER 2000, p. 600.

phasis on the clergy, as the repository of the knowledge of the solar circle, essential to agriculture[160].

The Aztec empire was formed by the union of a multitude of these small states[161]. At its head, the monarch was selected by a great council from the imperial dynasty. The upper class was composed of members of the royal family, the commercial and military nobility, and the higher clergy. The class of great traders had reserved for itself the major trading monopolies[162]. The Aztec society was living under the constant threat of an imminent collapse of the world into chaos due to the exhaustion of the god who guaranteed the world's equilibrium[163]. To maintain cosmic order, their god needed human blood. Aztecs had thus to fight constantly to capture prisoners and offer them as sacrifices to their god[164]. This idea of a god who needs human lives to live and maintain the world's equilibrium constituted the basis of their moral universe. Man had to fight to help his god to stay alive; he who is killed in battle becomes the companion of the god[165]. Any soldier capturing during war four prisoners became noble and could be allied to the royal court[166]. This conception of the world's order as a fragile equilibrium which needs human blood to be maintained drove the empire to expand steadily in order to maintain a continuous supply of human flesh. Imperialism was a state policy, supported, or perhaps inspired, by the great merchants, who thus saw their influence extended to new markets.

160. ELIADE 1990, pp. 41-43; PIETRI, VENARD 1971, p. 350.

161. PIETRI, VENARD 1971, p 350-351; FAVIER 1998, pp. 635 *et seq.*

162. FAVIER 1998, p. 637.

163. ELIADE 1990, p. 44; BELLINGER 2000, p. 59.

164. PIETRI, VENARD 1971, p. 351: *"The god is insatiable; what is more, his horrible appetite does not stop growing, he always needs more victims, which are obtained by war and levies. The Aztecs are condemned to conquer, to prevent their god from dying and thus annihilating the world".*

165. PIETRI, VENARD 1971, p. 351.

166. PIETRI, VENARD 1971, p. 351.

24. In South America, small tribal societies were structured in a pyramidal order rising from simple federations of chiefdoms to true kingdoms[167]. The basic unit was the Ayllu, a village made up of members of the same family and their allies. The Ayllu had a common ancestor, deified, called huaca and represented by a statue which all members of the Ayllu worshipped and for which a portion of the property of the village was reserved[168]. Each Ayllu held land whose pastures were in common use. The cultivated land was divided into lots each one of which, according to its fertility, made it possible for an individual to live for one year.

Curaca was the village chief, usually chosen from among the members of a certain family. He performed duties of regulation of social life. He distributed the land, organized collective work and settled disputes as an arbitrator. He helped the poor, the orphans, the old men and the widows[169]. The Curaca had a piece of land, ready to be distributed according to the needs of the village. He also coordinated the clearing of new land. The whole village owed him a number of working days for the formation of social capital of livestock, food and clothing to face future calamities. The Curaca preserved these goods, drew a profit for himself, but he had at the same time the obligation, where necessary, to come to the assistance of the needy. In fact, his function as regulator included a particular task of redistributing wealth to members of the village who, struck by the calamities of life, were excluded from the average prosperity that the Ayllu guaranteed to its members[170]. The Curaca had to respect the susceptibility of persons to whom he had recourse for works linked to the exercise of his duties. He recruited this personnel equitably, nourished and housed them, provided them with the necessary tools for work and, at the end of their service, he released them

167. FAVRE 2003, pp. 5 *et seq.*
168. FAVRE 2003, pp. 32 *et seq.*
169. FAVRE 2003, pp. 34 *et seq.*
170. FAVRE 2003, pp. 40 *et seq.*

with presents taken from his goods[171]. He incarnated a function of institutionalized solidarity[172] which in fact, was the reflection of a generalized network of reciprocities tying the members of the Ayllu[173]. The neighbours helped each other on the occasion of sowing and harvesting. Widows, patients and old men profited from collective work performed to cultivate their fields[174].

25. The Incas, conquerors of a wide range of peoples in South America, established a theocratic and authoritarian empire. The emperor ruled through a pyramid-shaped administration. There were four regional governors, the governors of departments and, finally, the governors of towns and villages. Homogeneous ethnic entities were broken up and transported by force to different parts of the empire where they were received by settled populations[175]. The misfortunes that hit Incas in their private and public life were due, according to their beliefs, to the sins they had committed[176]. They then had to be expiated either by sacrifices to the gods, or by identifying the wrongdoer and punishing him. The sacrifice of humans and, in particular, of children was regarded as the best remedy[177].

The Inca emperor, identified with the sun, whose unifying worship was imposed on all the subjected people, incarnated on earth the ultimate intermediary between the supra-terrestrial world of gods, the terrestrial world of living beings and the underground world of the dead[178]. He governed to hold in order the universe of humans. His political power was soon confused with his divine power. He was the head of a state extending over almost a million square

171. FAVRE 2003, p. 41.
172. FAVRE 2003, p. 43.
173. FAVRE 2003, pp. 36 *et seq.*
174. FAVRE 2003, p. 37.
175. FAVRE 2003, p. 27.
176. BELLINGER 2000, pp. 430 *et seq.*
177. BELLINGER 2000, p. 436.
178. ELIADE 1990, p. 60; FAVRE 2003, p. 67.

kilometres and ten million inhabitants[179]. As with his army he kept the peace among humans, so he established, by his supernatural capacities, the equilibrium of forces in nature[180].

The Inca empire assumed social functions in the event of a food crisis[181]. The property was divided into three parts: a third belonged to the divinity, a third to the Incas and the last third to the people. Public warehouses were placed at the disposal of the needy in the event of famine[182]. Clothing and feeding the people were regulated. The emperor held farmland and livestock throughout the empire and local leaders were to ensure that they bore fruit. Each Curaca[183] went once a year to the capital[184] to give the emperor the wealth he had been able to collect on imperial property[185]. Wealth held in the imperial warehouses[186] was intended to be provided for the maintenance of the imperial services, but also to provide the needy all over the empire with the goods necessary for them to survive[187]. As Curacas within their group corrected social irregularities, so the Emperor corrected social irregularities[188] occurring throughout the empire which could not be settled by the interplay of traditional solidarity[189].

179. FAVRE 2003, pp. 72 *et seq.*

180. FAVRE 2003, pp. 65-66: *"The sovereign was the link between the natural and social order. Located at the intersection of cosmic forces, he channelled their strength and kept them in balance".*

181. FAVRE 2003, pp. 41-42, 50, 52, 84.

182. FAVRE 2003, p. 38.

183. See previous paragraph.

184. FAVRE 2003, pp. 75 *et seq.*

185. FAVRE 2003, pp. 74-75.

186. FAVRE 2003, p. 67.

187. FAVRE 2003, p. 59.

188. BUCHANAN, TULLOCK 2004, p. 186: *"In order to prevent the possibility of his falling into dire poverty in some unpredictable periods in the future, the individual may consider collective organization which will, effectively, force him to contribute real income during periods of relative affluence. Such collective redistribution of real income among individuals, viewed as the working out of this sort of 'income insurance' plan, may appear rational to the utility-maximizing individual at the stage of constitutional decision".*

189. FAVRE 2003, pp. 37, 49-50.

2

Justice's Major Platforms

26. In the case of most major platforms of justice, God is confirmed as the supreme legislator and judge. All-wise, he sets the standards for human behaviour and, all-powerful, he punishes humans who do not respect his will. The holy alliance between God and men is preached in the pages of the Old Testament, the sacred book of the Jews, where the rules of justice are given to men directly by God. In Islam, the holy Koran delivers the word of God, including the eternal norms of justice. After their death, God distributes to humans rewards and sanctions, the scales of justice in his hand. In China, the emperor was the delegate of Heaven with the mission to implant the rules of the cosmic order into human society. If he could not guarantee peace and rice to his subjects, he could no longer claim to represent the divine order on earth. Brahmin India was living in another intellectual universe. Earthly life was a punishment that humans should suffer patiently in expiating their sins, and thus be able to find after death eternal peace. In Greece, the conditions were met for a pragmatic conception of justice, purified of religious considerations and limited to the satisfaction of the terrestrial interest of the individuals concerned. The political regime that the Democrats in Athens set up could not tolerate eminences of any kind. Law, expressing the will of citizens gathered in *ecclesia*, and not derived from any divine will, sought to maintain the democratic order by advancing the welfare of citizens. Rome, formally, had set itself the same goal, but in fact, the democratic elements of its regime were a mirage. Through a series of institutional manipulations, the Roman oligarchy always managed to avert insurrectionary movements by the non-privileged by granting them the minimum necessary to placate them.

The Hebraic Law: Social Equilibrium by Mutual Honesty

27. Hebraic history begins when Abraham[190] started moving his tribes from Mesopotamia to Canaan. Away from any local divinity, they practice the worship of only one divinity. Following the invasion of Egypt by Hyksos, they move to Egypt, where they live without merging with the local population[191]. Moses, their charismatic leader, brings them back into Canaan, after the reign of the monotheist Pharaoh Akhenaton[192]. They arrive in Palestine, at the end of great adventures in the desert, with the Hebraic belief in a single, powerful and wise God, incarnation of justice. With this God, the people enter into an alliance. They promise to respect his Law, and, in return, they obtain from him the promise of his blessing[193].

The Hebrews were divided into big families and recognized only the patriarchal authority of the eldest in each one of them. The need for statehood appeared, when the territory where they lived came under the control of the Philistines who withheld immunity from taxation[194]. The Judges, by the evocation of God,

190. POTOK 1992, p. 39.
191. MEULEAU, PIETRI 1971, p. 104.
192. POTOK 1978, pp. 100 *et seq.*
193. CAQUOT 1970, pp. 380 *et seq.*
194. MEULEAU, PIETRI 1971, p. 108.

conferred royal dignity on Saul, noticed for his qualities as a warrior[195]. He became the first king anointed of God, chief of the army and the state. David and Solomon, great kings, succeeded him. After the death of Solomon in 931 BC, the Northern provinces seceded. The southern kingdom, around Jerusalem, became the kingdom of Judaea and the Hebrew people living there were henceforth named Jewish[196].

Their deportation into Babylon by Nebuchadnezzar transformed them into the missionary people of God[197]. Subjected by force to the political authority of the country where they lived, they were nonetheless still subjected to the moral authority of their sacred Law. Cyrus, king of Persia, conquered Babylon, and gave to the Jews the freedom to decide on their own fate. They obtained the right to return, their temple in Jerusalem was restored and an autonomous Jewish state entity was established in Palestine. They also obtained from Cyrus the right of religious self-organization wherever they lived within the Persian empire[198]. From a national centre in Judah with Jerusalem as the capital, a religious authority operates, enforcing the sacred Law over all Jewish subjects of the empire[199]. The priest constituted the element unifying the dispersed people[200]. The Jewish territorial base disappeared, under the successive blows of the Romans, but the people, bound by its faith and obedience to the Law, no longer require such a base. The Jewish Diaspora grew and flourished[201].

28. The essence of justice that God revealed to his people is summarized in the *Decalogue*, otherwise known as the *Ten Com-*

195. ATTALI 2002, p. 50.
196. ATTALI 2002, p. 60.
197. ATTALI 2002, p. 66.
198. MEULEAU, PIETRI 1971, p. 117.
199. ATTALI 2002, p. 70.
200. MEULEAU, PIETRI 1971, p. 118.
201. ATTALI 2002, pp. 101 *et seq.*

mandments[202]. Belief in a God, anchored in the people's history and as part of people's identity, is a paramount obligation: *"You shall have no other gods before me"* (Exodus 20, 3). A sacred obligation is enacted for kinship: *"Honour your father and your mother, so that you may live long in the land the LORD your God is giving you"* (Exodus 20, 12). General mutual respect is required by four basic rules: *"You shall not murder"* (Exodus 20, 13), a commandment which seeks to preserve bodily integrity; *"You shall not give false testimony against your neighbour"*, a prescription which deals with the moral integrity of the person (Exodus 20, 16); *"You shall not steal"* (Exodus 20, 15), a requirement for the protection of the material goods of others; and *"You shall not commit adultery"* (Exodus 20, 14), a prohibition on the intrusion by third parties into family autonomy. By the last of his ten commandments, God speaks to the conscience of the Israelite: *"You shall not covet your neighbour's house. You shall not covet your neighbour's wife, or his male or female servant, his ox or donkey, or anything that belongs to your neighbour"* (Exodus 20, 17). This commandment is clearly an incitement to all bound by God's alliance[203], to observe, by strict self discipline, peaceful social coexistence.

The Decalogue constitutes only the preamble to detailed legislation, decreed by God and prescribed to Jews in their holy book[204].

---

202. The text starts with an assertion by God to the people of Israel: *"I am the LORD your God, who brought you out of Egypt, out of the land of slavery"* (Exodus 20, 2). Hebrews must not worship idols *"You shall not make for yourself an image in the form of anything in heaven above or on the earth beneath or in the waters below"* (Exodus 20, 4). The name of God is sanctified: *"You shall not misuse the name of the LORD your God, for the LORD will not hold anyone guiltless who misuses his name"* (Exodus 20, 7).

203. FARAGO 2002, pp. 74 *et seq.*

204. ATTALI 2002, p. 149: *"The Hebraic language indicates moreover an inequitable price by the word ona' ah, which refers to lie or wound. In other words, selling to an inequitable price means lying or oppressing"*.

Respect for God, parents and wife, respect for bodily integrity, honour and property of others and, finally, respect for the dignity of man, as the image of God on earth, are moral obligations, as well as legal burdens for the people of God. Respect for all human beings in a situation of weakness is emphatically required: *"You will not skew with the right of an emigrant or of an orphan"* (Deuteronomy 24, 17); *"You will have only one legislation: the same one for the emigrant and for the natives"* (Leviticus 24, 22). *"Never take advantage of poor and destitute labourers, whether they are fellow Israelites or foreigners living in your towns"* (Deuteronomy 24, 14). The infringement of these prescriptions is sanctioned by a series of punishments which vary according to the importance of the value attacked and the disapproval caused by the act of infringement[205]. However, collective responsibility is denied, a person is responsible only for his own acts: *"The father shall not be put to death for his son, the son will not be put to death for his father, it is because of his own sin that everyone will be put to death"* (Deuteronomy 24, 16).

29. Hebraic justice is the justice of the objective rule. Law must be interpreted and applied correctly: *"Do not pervert justice or show partiality. Do not accept a bribe, for a bribe blinds the eyes of the wise and twists the words of the innocent"* (Deuteronomy 16, 19); *"When people have a dispute, they are to take it to court and the judges will decide the case, acquitting the innocent and condemning the guilty"* (Deuteronomy 25, 1). Judges must be

205. In general, the principle of equivalence is enacted: *"you will pay (...) life as life, eye as eye, tooth as tooth, hand as hand, foot as foot, burning as burning, murder as murder"* (Exodus 21 , 22). Offences to certain goods or values, however, are punishable by death: *"who blasphemes the name of the LORD shall be put to death"* (Leviticus 24. 13); *"who insults his father or his mother shall be put to death"* (Exodus 21, 17); *"When a man commits adultery with his neighbour's wife, they will be put to death, the adulterer as well as the adulteress"* (Leviticus 20, 20).

impartial and independent: *"Do not show partiality in judging; hear both small and great alike. Do not be afraid of anyone, for judgment belongs to God"* (Deuteronomy 1: 17). Nothing else should be taken into account only what is relevant for the application of the Law: *"You will seek justice, only justice"* (Deuteronomy 16, 19). *"Eye to eye, tooth to tooth"*, the rule of retaliation, is but a tool by which objective justice works, imposing a limit on compensation and indicating the means by which it should be achieved.

The *Ten Commandments*, by requiring men not to envy the possessions of others, actually require them to obtain the goods through their work. *Work* rewards honest effort and pacifies society by its unlimited potential to create wealth, *trade* at fair value produces a society of respect for others in which violence has no place, whereas *compensation* according to the importance of the value offended, restores balance after the disturbance inflicted[206]. Hebraic justice is a justice of non-violence, of pacification by respect for the dignity and the goods of others. Wealth has a social function of seeking pacification and therefore ceases to be legitimate when it becomes a source of conflict and violence. This is why the rich have a duty of charity towards the needy and the totality of their goods is subject to a moral obligation of solidarity[207]. Thus, the Jews who work to enrich themselves must be honest in trade, even if they are operating in conditions of extreme competitiveness. Retaliation has little place in such a conception of justice. In fact, within its framework of relations, Hebraic law prescribes exactly the opposite of a retaliation rule: *"Do not avenge, and bear no ill (...). Love your neighbour as yourself"* (Leviticus 19:18).

206. ATTALI 2002, p. 155.
207. ATTALI 2002, p. 160.

The Athenian Democracy: Establishing Political Equality

30. The advent of democracy in Athens marks the transition from a political organization founded on clans towards a state in which only citizens count[208]. The individual as member of a clan had no existence as regards the city. The city distributed the burdens and benefits to the clans which they in turn distributed, according to a pyramidal order, to their basic components, the families[209]. The city was thus a great confederation of families, the aim of which was the management of the complicated relations between clans. The collapse of the system occurred when, following the introduction of industry, trade and currency, the inequalities among clans and within clans became so great that the individuals who suffered from them preferred to revolt rather than to be held dependent by their ancestral duties[210]. Draco tried by the enactment of overly severe penalties, to put an end to the bloodshed caused by the clannish wars[211].

Progress was slow. Peasants who became indebted and insolvent fell into slavery[212]. Solon, a new legislator, intervenes to save Athens from disorder. He prohibited constraint for debts in all its forms and releases debtors from their debts. To offer to the humble the possibilities of channelling their protests through the political institutions, he officialises the *ecclesia*, the people's great assembly[213]. He removes the barriers that kept the aristocrats away from other classes and limits parental authority in favour of the individual. Solon divided the population according to the capacity of individuals to participate in the financing of common tasks

208. MEULEAU 1971, p. 191.
209. GLOTZ 1968, p. 48.
210. GLOTZ 1968, pp. 77, 83.
211. GLOTZ 1968, pp. 116, 131.
212. GLOTZ 1968, p.131.
213. MEULEAU 1971, p. 188.

and decreed a participation in honours proportional to this capacity[214]. Distinction of birth counted for nothing: obligations and rights were fixed proportionally according to the ability of each to pay tax. The less wealthy of the Athenians became entitled to sit in the Assembly and tribunals, but serve in the military as rowers and have no access to magistracies[215]. The low middle-class had to arm themselves as hoplites and were eligible for some subordinate functions[216]. The citizens of the two higher classes must come to the army with their horses and were constrained to make contributions, called liturgies, but the law reserved the principal public offices for them. Solon said, proud of his construction: *"I gave the people such power as it is sufficient for them to have"*[217].

The people however remained impoverished and the aristocrats strong. No party was satisfied; all were still ready to fight. Pisistratus, the tyrant, gained the upper hand, championing the small farmers of the mountains. He managed once and for all to resolve the agrarian question by distributing confiscated or uncultivated land to the people[218]. But his governance was perceived by the Athenians to be despotic. His successors were killed and his regime overthrown[219]. Cleisthenes gave to the democratic constitution of Athens its final form by depriving the nobility of any opportunity to influence the working of the institutions[220]. Citizens were grouped into units based on criteria deliberately designed to discourage social or territorial alliances: social alliances were avoided by grouping the citizens inside the demes, districts classifying citizens according to a criterion drawn from their residence; and territorial alliances were avoided by joining together demes from

214. GLOTZ 1968, p. 132.
215. GLOTZ 1968, p. 132.
216. GLOTZ 1968 p. 133.
217. GLOTZ 1968, p. 88.
218. GLOTZ 1968, p. 134.
219. MEULEAU 1971, p. 190.
220. GLOTZ 1968, pp. 134-135.

different regions of Attica[221]. Emanating from the demes, the *Boule* consisted of five hundred Athenians. Its main function was to serve as the secretariat general to the *ecclesia*[222]. With regard to the state there were only individuals, deprived of any support that clan ties could give them.

31. The world of Greek morality revolved around an axis composed of two key ideas: *arete* and *hubris*, ideas that could be conventionally expressed respectively by the words *virtue* and *injury*. *Arete* is undoubtedly virtue, but in a functional sense, a man of *arete* is a man who adjusts his behaviour and performance to what is required by the social role he assumes[223]. Virtue is the quality of the man who, without doing too much or too little, discharges his duties and, within an organized society, assumes as it is expected from him his various roles, especially that of defending his country. *Hubris* expresses a negative idea, a transgression[224]. In the ordered universe where there is harmony imposed by Gods against the forces of chaos, every human being has his own place and must contribute by rightfully assuming his role in enforcing the order imposed on the universe by the Gods. To transgress this fundamental obligation is, in regard to the human being, an act of *hubris*, an insult against the cosmos, which Nemesis, the divine justice, will punish so that the disturbed order finds its balance[225].

Democratic ethics take up the ideas of *arete* and *hubris* to adapt them in the context of a society of equals. Thus, *arete* becomes the virtue of the citizen who, within the city, must take part

221. GLOTZ 1968, p. 135.
222. MEULEAU 1971, p. 191.
223. MACINTTYRE 1966, pp. 7-8.
224. L. FERRY 2008, p. 111: "*the biggest fault that can be committed in the eyes of Greeks and of which mythology continuously speaks to us, is precisely this famous hubris, the pride that pushes beings, mortals, immortals, to excess not knowing how to remain in their place within the universe*".
225. L. FERRY 2008, p. 112; MACINTTYRE 1966, p. 10.

honestly and effectively in the democratic process[226]. Virtue is in other words the positive quality of the citizen who adjusts his behaviour to the major objective of maintaining the proper functioning of democracy. The standards of behaviour of a virtuous man serve as the means of achieving this goal. *Hubris*, without losing its sacred basis, acquires a secular aspect[221]. In a society of equals, *hubris* is the equivalent of claiming a dignity which the democratic regime could not confer on each one of its subjects. The political equilibrium in Athens was maintained by the radical political equality granted to all citizens. *Hubris* resulted from the behaviour of the citizen whose words or actions take him outside the framework of equality. His disruptive behaviour disturbed the political order of equals which required appropriate measures to restore justice[228].

The Athenian citizen could be prosecuted for sacrilege when he offended the divine, for treason when he harmed the interests of his country, for physical damage to the property of others, and for *hubris* when he adopted a disrespectful behaviour towards fellow-citizens[229]. The right of action belonged in principle to any citizen, even when the case brought to trial did not directly affect the rights of the person who seized the court[230]. Demagogues animated popular passion against those regarded as class enemies[231]. Ostracism struck the aristocrats, who could, by their wealth or their influence, threaten the stability of the democratic regime[232]. A popular justice guaranteed the democratic order[233].

32. In the Athenian institutions a golden rule between command and obedience is founded on the principle that *"no one is held*

226. MACINTTYRE 1966, p. 94.
227. GLOTZ 1968, p. 269.
228. DE ROMILLY 1992, p. 102.
229. GLOTZ 1968, p. 269.
230. GLOTZ 1968, p. 242.
231. MEULEAU 1971, p. 219.
232. GLOTZ 1968, pp. 181-185.
233. GLOTZ 1968, pp. 181-185.

to obedience if he cannot in his turn command"[234]. By a series of reforms and new practices every state institution was accessible to every citizen[235]. Only functions which required a characterized competence (strategists, treasurers, architects) were elective. Citizens had the same speaking time at the assemblies[236] and were compensated for days off work to take part in the civic functions[237]. Civic distinctions, which were only exceptional, applied either by drawing a lot, or by election, or, concerning membership of the *Areopagus*[238], by virtue of the status of a former dignitary[239]. These distinctions were conceived as burdens, their holders being supposed to exercise a specific function under the constant control of the people[240]. However, women, slaves, immigrants and children had practically no rights of their own[241]. The city conducted a deliberate public policy of full employment[242] that allowed the Athenians at all levels of society to live properly[243]. The poor received public assistance[244]. Public officials were obliged to swear: *"I will be neither for an abolition of the debts nor for sharing the land and houses of Athenians"*[245]. Holders of great wealth were however taxed, but their imposition consisted in assigning to them liability to assume expenditure for specific tasks[246], whereas public finances were primarily constituted by indirect taxes or by contributions paid by the allies[247].

234. GLOTZ 1968, p. 217.
235. GLOTZ 1968, p. 139.
236. GLOTZ 1968, p. 141.
237. GLOTZ 1968, p. 138.
238. GLOTZ 1968, p. 224.
239. GLOTZ 1968, pp. 224-225.
240. GLOTZ 1968, p. 140.
241. MEULEAU 1971, pp. 213 *et seq.*
242. GLOTZ 1968, p. 138.
243. GLOTZ 1968, p. 143.
244. GLOTZ 1968, p. 143.
245. GLOTZ 1968, p. 248.
246. GLOTZ 1968, p. 133.
247. MEULEAU 1971, p. 220; GLOTZ 1968, p. 133.

The Roman Republic: The Calculus of Political Concessions

33. Roman political evolution is marked by confrontation between two classes, the patricians, on the one hand, jealous of their privileges, and the plebeians, on the other, resigned to their status of social inferiority[248]. The patrician class was organized into 73 families, each of which was headed by a paterfamilias, who represented the family in the Senate, the assembly of the heads of patrician families[249]. The plebeians lived in another city, which, together with the particular city of the patricians, comprised the administrative conglomeration of Rome. They had to incur indebtedness in order to survive[250]. Their arithmetical importance afforded them an unquestionable role to play in defending the country in the event of external crisis, which they exploited by brandishing the threat of secession[251]. The plebeians managed to secure the enactment of the law of the XII tables, and, then, acceptance of their representation in political life[252]. The councils of the plebs, assemblies of the people, elected the heads of the plebeians, the tribunes, and, in this way, the people weighed in the interplay of institutions[253]. By the mid-sixth century, the fusion of patricians and plebeians is at least legally achieved[254]. Under the law, there are only Roman citizens. But the institutions were still dependent on their origins as representative of different social classes[255]. The policy of territorial expansion accommodated both the patricians, who got rid of a cumbersome mob, and the plebeians, who found vast areas to cultivate freely[256]. Dur-

248. MEULEAU 1971, p. 340.
249. MEULEAU 1971, p. 339.
250. MEULEAU 1971, p. 334.
251. PETIT I 1925, p. 94; HOMO 1970, pp. 53-55.
252. HOMO 1970, pp. 59-62.
253. HOMO 1970, p. 57.
254. HOMO 1970, p. 64.
255. HOMO 1970, p. 65.
256. MEULEAU 1971, p. 357.

ing the third century, Rome underwent radical social change. The wars enriched the members of an ascending class, the equestrians, who were able to extract the maximum profit from their participation in the wars[257]. A new leading class appeared, the *nobilitas*, made up of the patricians and those of the plebeian class who knew how to benefit from the Roman economic evolution[258]. The idea of conquering neighbouring countries to settle the poor gave way to the idea of market domination. From the work of slaves held in Italy there emerged a class of alienated citizens, gathered in Rome where they survived from the philanthropy of the rich as well as the subsidies distributed by the state[259]. Conditions changed during the first century before our era. Two new formations were constituted: the conservatives, defenders of the privileges of *nobilitas*, and the progressive advocates of land reform[260]. Rough violence became the means of government. The generals, when they felt betrayed in their ambition, used their army to eliminate their opponents. Members of the Senate were often assassinated and promptly replaced by docile new recruits[261].

The establishment of the imperial regime began with the principacy of Octavian[262]. The emperor accumulated the functions of the tribunes, consuls, and questors. He was the great conciliator between noble and humble, rich and poor; the living law, the supreme judge of the empire[263]. Governing in a philosophical environment imbued by Stoic thought, the emperor was gradually seen as the governor of a single people united under the Roman peace. The *Constitutio Antonina* of 212, as enacted by Caracalla, granted to every man living in the empire, except the descendants

257. MEULEAU 1971, p. 367.
258. MEULEAU 1971, p. 358.
259. MEULEAU 1971, p. 366.
260. MEULEAU 1971, pp. 378-381.
261. MEULEAU 1971, pp. 398 *et seq.*, 402 *et seq.*
262. LÉVÊQUE 1998, pp. 754 *et seq.*
263. ROUCHE 1998, p. 915.

of peoples who had fought Rome, Roman citizenship[264]. The principacy was transformed, in the third century[265]. The will of the emperor, the foundation of the salvation of the people threatened by the barbarians, became sacred[266].

34. In Rome, the struggle for political power was only a reflection of the struggle for possession of material goods. The patrician families initially possessed all fertile grounds, had exclusive rights to pasture on the collective grounds, and the right to adjudicate in property cases[267]. The city artisans and small farmers had to struggle to survive. Usurious rates charged by lenders, almost all of them patricians, made them potential slaves[268]. However, plebeian violence and threats gradually bore fruit. Laws became accessible and foreseeable, debts were reduced on several occasions, and servitude for debts prohibited[269]. Cooperating in the conquests, they were assigned part of the *ager publicus* that the rapid conquest of Italy removed from the vanquished. Food was distributed to the town-dwelling plebeians who offered the patricians their political support, thus becoming their political clients. In that way, all found their place until the equestrians, big bankers and merchants of modest social origin, arrived on the scene[270]. Greedy for wealth, they fought to obtain concessions of public services and government contracts, and thus were working against the privileges and the monopolies from which the patricians profited[271]. But anxious to preserve their fortunes, they aligned with the conservative forces when they felt popular claims became threatening to them. As a result of imports, prices of foodstuffs produced in Italy col-

264. HOMO 1970, p. 380; MEULEAU 1971, p. 481.
265. HOMO 1970, pp. 271 *et seq.*
266. MEULEAU 1971, p. 494.
267. VAN EFFENTERRE 1998, pp. 592 *et seq.*
268. MEULEAU 1971, p. 339.
269. MEULEAU 1971, p 345.
270. MEULEAU 1971, p. 367.
271. MEULEAU 1971, p. 393

lapsed and servile work marginalized free labour. The rich got richer and the poor got into debt, sold their land and migrated to Rome. As the assemblies of the people were manipulated by the big families, the Senate operated virtually with unlimited power[272]. To remedy this state of affairs a generous land reform, distributing viable allotments to small people, was deemed necessary. The Gracchi brothers, who initiated these reforms, ultimately failed[273]. The balance of power had meanwhile been reversed[274]. A professional army was led by men who turned to their personal advantage the power that the army command gave to them. The soldiers required remuneration and the veterans demanded land[275]. Thus, the people lost the power to exert pressure which the threat of rebellion had given it. The generals with their armies entered the political game and the political parties had to learn how to manipulate them into submission[276]. The equilibrium of the old institutions had been disrupted[277]. Slaves and desperate Italians also had the capacity to exert pressure by organizing rebellions. The crushing of their attempts by the army further increased the prestige of generals covered with glory which they intended to transform into the people's ligitimating allegiance[278]. To maintain this allegiance the providential chiefs followed policies in favour of the people: reduction of the debts by a devaluation of the currency, prohibition of civil imprisonment, proclamation of a moratorium for debt repayment, writing-off of interest due, vast redistribution of lands to the Roman families, and agrarian colonization in favour in particular of the veterans[279]. These measures however brought only

272. MEULEAU 1971, pp. 375-376.
273. MEULEAU 1971, p. 371.
274. MEULEAU 1971, pp. 371-373.
275. MEULEAU 1971, p. 374.
276. HOMO 1970, pp. 126 *et seq.*; MEULEAU 1971, pp. 387-402.
277. MEULEAU 1971, p. 360; HOMO 1970, p. 128.
278. MEULEAU 1971, p. 387.
279. MEULEAU 1971, pp. 400-401.

brief appeasement. Too many vested interests competed with one another. Republican institutions were not inclusive enough to function within the framework of a vast empire. An arbitrator was needed, a conciliator who would have the capacity to subject the army to the service of social peace[280].

35. Rome could survive only by a constant search for a balance between the interests that competed in it. The patricians and plebeians, at the beginning, the noble and humble, later, with separate interests were obliged to live together. The former were not sufficiently numerous to cultivate their farms and to be defended against external enemies. The latter were too divided to use their numerical superiority to defeat the former. Both were condemned to cooperate and to do so they had developed a subtle dialectic of compromise in perpetual motion that never ceased to create new institutions. The patricians, masters of political power and wealth, were able to play to perfection the game of granting necessary concessions to avoid losing their essential constituent power. The plebeians, with only the threats of revolt and secession at their disposal, knew when to stop in pressing for satisfaction of their claims, namely at that particular moment when a certain fraction of them had had their claims met.

In Rome, all was so arranged that real political power was held by a minority. The very notion underpinning the institutions was the maintenance of that minority power with the minimum of concessions to the majority. The elegant structure of the republican institutions, which seemed to combine in perfect balance the monarchical element, with the government officials endowed by the imperium, the aristocratic element, with the Senate and its purely advisory capacity, and the democratic element, with the popular assemblies, was in reality only the concealment of a game played by the wealthy. Roman officials were not remunerated. Posts

280. MEULEAU, p. 407.

were therefore reserved for the rich[281]. The two tribunes of the people could together veto decisions taken by the Roman authorities, but the oligarchy could override them either by playing one off against the other or by nominating a dictator[282]. In addition, it fully domesticated the institution by integrating the tribune in the *curriculum honorum* and giving to tribunes the official rank of senators[283]. Within the *comitia tributa* citizens voted assembled in 35 tribes. However, 31 of the tribes were rustic, made up of the peasants closely monitored by the patricians; the four urban tribes, gathering the most radical elements, could not alter the outcome. Furthermore, the *comitia centuriata* were divided into 193 centuries of which the richest Romans held 98, therefore the majority[284]. Bills were introduced at the initiative of a magistrate. At least three weeks before the vote, the magistrate communicated the proposed bill to the people which met in assembly to deliberate on its adoption. Based on these discussions the initiating magistrate could make changes to the text or withdraw a bill. But on the day of the vote, the Assembly proceeded to vote without any discussion[285]. By a law of 339 BC, the Senate's *ex post* authorization was replaced by *ex ante* authorization[286].When it was decided that one of the consuls would be selected from members of the plebeian class, the ruling class demanded, in 367 BC, that the judicial functions be performed by a special magistrate, the praetor[287]. At the time of the

281. MEULEAU 1971, p. 349.
282. MEULEAU 1971, p. 340.
283. HOMO 1970, p. 160.
284. HOMO 1970, p. 81; MEULEAU 1971, pp. 348-349.
285. HOMO 1970, p. 154; MEULEAU 1971, p. 349.
286. PETIT I 1925, p. 94
287. PETIT I 1925, pp. 93-94, 128. The chief justice was in Rome initially the king, then the consul. According to the law of the XII tables the death penalty against a citizen could be decided only by the popular assemblies. A citizen sentenced in Rome to corporal punishment or death could appeal to the people. His case was then reviewed by the popular assemblies; see HOMO 1970, p. 84.

late republic, there were eight praetors who, like all Roman magistrates, were elected for one year, received no remuneration for their duties and were almost all of the ruling patrician class, at first, then of the nobles[288]. The praetors judged according to the written legislation. But they had the power to supplement and correct the law[289].

Islam: The Divine and the Practical Equilibriums

36. Mohammed, born in 570, began his preaching in 610[290]. Forced to flee Mecca, he moved with his community of the faithful to Medina where, on July 16, 622, he proclaimed the new era[291]. The message of the Prophet took up the generally widespread idea of a single god, creator of the universe and all-powerful[292]. For a clan-based backward society, living in the era of nomadism and driven by internal quarrels, this god represented a breath of modernity that could overcome the distinctions of family, free people from their totemic beliefs and cement a dynamic, all-inclusive unity[293]. The expansion of Islam was vertiginous. Most of Saudi Arabia was already Muslim on the death of Muhammad in 633. One hundred years later, Islam was at the heart of France, stopped at the gates of Constantinople, on the steppes of Asia. It occupied part of the Indian subcontinent; it was deeply advanced in North Africa[294].

Islam incorporated what was already in various forms dispersed in the religious and cultural environment of the time[295].

288. PETIT I 1925, p. 98.
289. PETIT I 1925, p. 129.
290. ARMSTRONG 2003, pp. 3 *et seq.*; PIETRI 1971, p. 589.
291. PIETRI 1971, p. 591.
292. PIETRI 1971, p. 590.
293. PIETRI 1971, pp. 593 *et seq.*
294. ARMSTRONG 2003, pp. 20 *et seq.*; PIETRI 1971, pp. 598 *et seq.*
295. CORBIN 1969, p. 1054.

From the ancient religions of Arabia, Islam kept the sacred places which are venerated even today; the sacred history of the Jews was taken in broad outline; the Christians found in the Koran the Virgin Mary, Jesus sent by God who went back to heaven at the end of his preaching on earth; the Manicheans could find in the new religion the radical distinction they professed between good and evil[296]. In addition, Islamic theology draws on Greek philosophical thought, in particular Neoplatonism[297].

Mohammed left behind as his lieutenant Ali, a member of his family. Ali, too young, did not immediately succeed the Prophet. Three caliphs ruled before him. In 661, Ali finally reached the caliphate, but was assassinated shortly thereafter[298]. A schism then occurred. Two different conceptions of faith appeared. The Sunnis, on the one hand, the people of the *Sunnah*, have the sacred tradition as a guide. Wise men and scholars interpret the meaning of the scriptures. Legal methods and colleges of lawyers help to implement the prescriptions of the Koran in new situations[299]. The Shiites, on the other hand, are clergy-based. For them, the gift of interpreting the scriptures was given by the prophet to his parental line. The descendants of the Prophet have the authority to release the holy Koran's meaning in order to solve specific problems occurring[300].

Islam's transition to the Abbasid era marks a turning point. Islam ceases to be the business of Arabs and the idea of a single Islamic state is crumbling[301]. In Spain, a branch of the Umayyad

296. PIETRI 1971, p. 595.
297. CORBIN 1969, p. 1089. The two major Muslim philosophers, Avicenna and Averroes, represent schools of Greek philosophy, the first, Plato's Academy; CORBIN 1969, p. 1082; and the second, Aristotle's Peripatos; CORBIN 1969, pp.1146, 1148, 1187.
298. ARMSTRONG 2003, p. 35.
299. PIETRI 1971, pp. 602-603.
300. CORBIN 1969, p. 1063.
301. ARMSTRONG 2003, p. 45.

founds an emirate, and later the caliphate[302]. The caliphate of Baghdad loses its strength and its caliphs become hostages in the hands of the Turks[303]. They are governed by a family that considers itself[304] the depositary of the caliphate[305]. The throne belongs to the son of the sultan who, at the end of a fratricidal war, restores order[306]. The *muftis* are assigned to inform the sultan and his advisers on what is prescribed by *sharia*, the divine law. The *qadis* are responsible for enforcing the law in deciding the cases[307]. Criminal offences, real estate cases and taxation, left to the sultan, confer a certain margin of discretion on him[308]. The non-Muslim subjects of the sultan are subject to their own law[309].

37. Islamic justice is entirely dictated by God who kept for himself the art of distinguishing good and evil[310]. Divine law should be the law of the state[311]. Little space is left for it to create its own rules of law alongside the divine law. It is the responsibility of the state to punish those who violate the laws of the Lord that the *Sunnah*, the Prophet's life as it was transcribed in the holy narratives, elucidates and completes[312]. The follower of the new religion can find in the Koran and *Sunnah*, all he needs to distinguish between right and wrong and know what he is to do and not to do. The faithful must assess their actions according to

302. PIETRI 1971, p. 625.
303. ARMSTRONG 2003, pp. 69 *et seq.*; PIETRI 1971, p. 627.
304. IMBER 2002, pp. 4 *et seq.*
305. IMBER 2002, pp. 115 *et seq.*
306. IMBER 2002, pp. 87 *et seq.*
307. IMBER 2002, pp. 225 *et seq.*
308. IMBER 2002, p. 244.
309. IMBER 2002, pp. 216-217.
310. PIETRI 1971, p. 594.
311. CALDER 2003, pp. 979 *et seq.*
312. PIETRI 1971, p. 597.

a five-step gradation that the law of God imposes[313]: there are acts that are mandatory, such as the confession of one God, others, such as charity, which are highly recommended; other acts are morally indifferent and others, without constituting mortal sins, are not recommended, such as the liberal interpretation of the Koran; finally, there are acts prohibited by law and punished by God without appeal. Material pleasures, apart from the consumption of alcohol and certain foods, are not prohibited. Wealth is not discredited and trade is considered a noble activity[314].

On the great *Day of Judgment*, every man will appear before God to account for his actions. Everyone will line up behind his prophet, the Jews behind Moses, Christians behind Jesus, and Muslims behind Muhammad. God will ask each to present his *balance sheet*, and each must explain his actions in respect to other men and his prophet[315]. God will weigh in his scales the acts of each one and reward the just man, who has developed with others and his prophet links of creative harmony[316]. The fair man will pass to paradise and will find there the spiritual and material reward for his terrestrial discipline in obedience to the divine will[317]. The Koran keeps repeating that God is forgiving and merciful, that men should have pity on other men, and that they must be tolerant and fair. The supreme judge of the end of time will weigh everything with the sense of relevance that belongs to his wisdom[318].

38. The maxim attributed to the Prophet *"the middle of things is the best"* was a commonplace among Muslim intellectuals during the middle Ages[319]. It is the medium that binds the separated and

313. PIETRI 1971, pp. 595-596.
314. PIETRI 1971, p. 597.
315. ROSEN 2000, p. 157.
316. SMIRNOV 1996, § 6.
317. CORBIN 1969, pp. 1108-1109.
318. CORBIN 1969, p. 1126.
319. SMIRNOV 1996, § 11.

opposite things to produce a creative unit. In Islamic thought, justice, when delivered by humans to humans, is not a deontological ideal to be attained by an exceptional effort; it is an ontological function of the reality of things, the normal structure of social relations[320]. There are three actors in the network of social relations[321]: the individual, who is guided by reason and the word of God in pursuing his interest; the community of believers, which asks its due of the individual and which, thus, makes the individual aware of his social duties; and the state, which controls individual and collective relations to preserve social peace. Within this network, each one finds his place when the links which are established are links of reciprocity[322]. Civil contracts, social awards, justice itself, operate to establish correct reciprocal links or to restore disturbed relationships of reciprocity. Every person is constituted by a chain of rights and duties he has imposed on himself, or society or God have imposed on him. Justice is achieved when the person performs his duties properly, and duly receives what the others should perform towards him[323].

Equity in relations of reciprocity is a process and a result[324]: it is a process because it is necessary to establish the *metrics* for calculating equivalences between different entities and then be able to balance them[325]; it is a result, because the metrics used must be reflected in a *decision* so that equity is achieved[326]. In Islamic thought, the search for justice is precisely the search for the point of equilibrium between separated and apparently opposed entities. The quality of the right man is his ingeniousness in producing solutions which harmonize the opposites in a creative point of

320. SMIRNOV 1996, § 10.
321. ROSEN 2000, p. 156.
322. ROSEN 2000, pp. 162 *et seq.*
323. SMIRNOV 1996, § 9.
324. ROSEN 2000, p. 155.
325. See *infra* § 163.
326. See *infra* § 164.

social order[327]. Human justice in Islam is empirical and contextual[328]. The man who does justice should not replace God by seeking the absolute. His task is human and the objective of human justice is social. Consequently, the man of justice must, in accordance with the Word of God, find the solution that links what is separated and opposed, harmonizes the rights and duties of each with the common good, stabilizes reciprocal links in a fair social order[329]. Human justice emerges when people of God feel they have had the treatment they deserve.

China and India: Quest for Universal Harmony

39. China consists of vast plains watered by large rivers. Periods of royal dynasties unifying the country were interrupted by warring periods[330]. Centrifugal forces were constant. But there was also a constant trend towards unity, perceived as a cosmic principle. Ancestral religion consisted in the worship of a vital force which manifested itself through the generations[331]. People still worshipped the deified forces of nature, and expected the emperor to intercede ensuring consistency and harmony in the world[332]. The emperor was the delegate of Heaven which at any time could withdraw its grace from him[333]. When land was needed, it was up to the government to plan and carry out new clearings[334]. When food was lacking, the benevolence and forethought of the sovereign filled the

327. ROSEN 2000, pp. 166-167.
328. ROSEN 2000, p. 171.
329. ROSEN 2000, pp. 171, 172.
330. MEULEAU 1971, pp. 295-298
331. CHENG 1997, pp. 51 *et seq.*; MEULEAU 1971, p. 300.
332. CHENG 1997, pp. 54 *et seq.*
333. MEULEAU 1971, p. 300.
334. MEULEAU 1971, p. 295.

gaps of fortune[335]. However, uprisings broke out, even real revolutions, organized by secret societies[336].

Chinese society was organized according to the hierarchical principle. At its head, the emperor, agent of Heaven, surrounded by the nobility whose ancestral deities were subject to the emperor's God[337]. The local nobility were subject to the central government, thanks to an effective imperial bureaucracy[338]. The peasants had to share a community lot and return their production to the community. Those among them who became indebted often lost their freedom or voluntarily constituted themselves as slaves[339].

In China, there was no such thing as law, a common rule for all, and equal for all. There were the rituals and the etiquette[340]. Each one was governed according to status and his relationship to the person with whom he was dealing. The penalties and rewards depended on the rank of the person concerned[341]. Men could not determine their behaviour based on what was objectively permitted or prohibited. Their whole life was subject to a role they had to interpret correctly all the time[342]. However, social mobility was possible. Government officials were selected following a national competition on the basis of merit. The rich merchants could buy titles of nobility and thus change social status[343]. Gifted children though of obscure origin could study and be prepared for a career as a civil servant[344].

40. Taoism, the popular religion of China, sought, in the reconciliation of *yin* and *yang*, the equilibrium which governs the

335. MEULEAU 1971, pp. 312-314.
336. MEULEAU 1971, p. 314.
337. MEULEAU 1971, p. 300.
338. VAN EFFENTERRE 1998, p. 646.
339. VAN EFFENTERRE 1998, p. 645.
340. GRANET 1988, pp. 318 *et seq.*
341. GRANET 1988, p. 336.
342. GRANET 1988, pp. 319 *et seq.*
343. VAN EFFENTERRE 1998, p. 646.
344. VAN EFFENTERRE 1998, p. 647.

universe in its entirety[345]. Although opposite, *yin* and *yang* are not a couple of conflicting forces, forever irreconcilable such as are pure and impure, good and evil, God and devil. The *yin* and *yang* are antithetical, but not contradictory; they are dedicated to living together, joining in a couple which generates the world's order. They are thus the right and the left, the female and the male, the valley and the mountains, the winter and the summer. They exist as independent entities, but are conceived only compared with one another[346]. The world order and the order of the human soul emerge by their reconciliation[347]. Tao is the force that reconciles opposites, coherently uniting competing forces. It is the path that leads to the establishment of universe's order. It is neither a god, nor a force of nature, a principle, or an idea of the human spirit. Tao is the *Logos*[348]. From chaos to order it is the Tao that makes the difference[349]. Civilization created the world order and the sovereign, supreme incarnation of civilization, gives meaning to space and time by the order it guarantees. The sovereign is the Tao in society[350], assigning to human beings their rightful places[351].

41. Confucianism, a widespread ethical philosophy in China, professed a morality designed to educate men to avoid excesses[352]. Morality, social ethics and law were all governed by the idea of

345. GRANET 1988, pp. 248 *et seq.*
346. GRANET 1988, p. 123.
347. GRANET 1988, p. 107.
348. See *infra* § 121.
349. GRANET 1988, pp. 252-254.
350. GRANET 1988, p. 275.
351. SCHENG 1997, p. 181, a text called Zhongyong attributed to the youngest son of Confucius: *"The Middle is the great foundation of the universe, Harmony is the universal Dao".*
352. GRANET 1988, p. 319: *"The aim was to form the scholars to serve the government, establishing in their soul a fair balance which would contribute, when they perform the fair balance exercise within the real world, to maintain balance in society, and finally equilibrium within the whole universe".*

total harmony, ruling over society as well as the human soul[353]. Equity dominates in the solution of any conflict between opposing forces and wills: *"Why can men form a society? They can live in society because they understand the importance of distributions. But how do they conduct these distributions? How do they do it? They do it by applying equity. When equity governs distributions, there is concord"*. The *ji*, the *li* and the *jen* operate, all together, to allow harmony's reign[354]. The *ji* is the quality of fairness: fair people issue symmetric judgements[355]. Symmetry is the golden rule of morality, prescribing *"you do not want them to do unto you what you do not do to others"*[356]. This high sense of reciprocity has two aspects: respect for others, and respect for oneself. Symmetry, as the basis of equity, must nevertheless be accompanied by another quality, the consistency of the solution in respect to the totality of its context. The *li* is the adjustment of all parties to ensure consistency[357]. However, men, because of their imperfection, are unable to reach perfect equitable solutions. Therefore, they need *jen,* the quality of charity and altruism that inspires tolerance and sacrifice.

42. India, as opposed to China, has never known political unity. There were always recalcitrant territories, populations which revolted, and small resisting kingdoms[358]. In the valleys of the Indus and Ganges the populace of India saw Greeks, Scythians,

353. ROBERTS 1995, p. 435; GRANET 1988, pp. 394 *et seq.*; VANDIER-NOCOLAS 1969, pp. 274 *et seq.*

354. VANDIER-NOCOLAS 1969, p. 280.

355. VANDIER-NOCOLAS 1969, p. 280.

356. The principle of the application of the spirit level, formulated by the Confucians, is to measure the respect due to others *"to the respect I owe to myself, and to improve constantly myself in order to raise steadily the standard of respect for the others"*, VANDIER-NOCOLAS 1969, p. 279.

357. VANDIER-NOCOLAS 1969, p. 280.

358. MEULEAU, PIETRI 1971, pp. 289-291.

Arabs, Parthians, Turks, and Mongols succeed one another. Whole empires were formed and then disappeared[359].

From the beginning of the Aryan era the population was divided into classes[360]. First was the class of priests, the Brahmins, whose task was to maintain order in the universe by the vows and rites they delivered. Then, there was the class of warriors and governors whose task was to maintain civil peace and good order internally and externally. A third class was composed of traders, artisans and farmers. Members of the fourth class, probably made up of conquered indigenous peoples, served the members of the first three classes. Those who did not fit into the classes were considered impure, untouchables. Within each class, several castes in hierarchical order were distinguished and within each caste, large families were gathered under a paterfamilias, the oldest male in direct line[361]. Mixed marriages were not tolerated. Class membership depended on blood ties, so that ascent to a higher class was almost impossible. On the contrary, descent was possible, if the member of a higher class was not respectful of the obligations deriving from his status. Children, students, fathers, hermits and anchorites were subject to different obligations. Women were sub--servient to men for marriage and procreation[362].

Each Indian, as part of this system of classification, drew a number of advantages. Unfailing solidarity was in fact developed among the members of the same family, same caste, and the same class[363]. The personality of their members was largely determined by that. A sacred law defined the rights and obligations of each one[364]. Transgression caused social disapproval, and exclusion.

359. MEULEAU 1971, p. 292; BASHAM 1988, pp. 37 *et seq.*

360. BASHAM 1988, pp. 122 *et seq.*

361. BASHAM 1988, pp. 132 *et seq.*, 139 *et seq.*

362. BASHAM 1988, pp. 130 *et seq.*

363. BASHAM 1988, pp. 1305 *et seq.*

364. MEULEAU 1971, 293.

However, for all humans aspiring to harmonize themselves with something common to all, the world soul, there was a background of common obligations to meet: respect for mankind, and the life and property of others. The condemnation of lying and respect for nature and living beings were also part of a background of duties common to all irrespective of class or status[365].

43. The unifying element of the Indian world, the Brahmin religion, initially naturalist and vitalist, subsequently evolved into a kind of metaphysical thinking. A caste of priests, the Brahmins, dominated it. They carried out the rites, as experts of *Veda*, the sacred literature of their religion[366]. In a finer version of Hinduism[367], God creates the universe according to a cyclical rhythm and equips it with his soul. The world is doomed to destruction at the end of a series of billions of years. But, from the original substance that composes the chaos, another world will be created and a new life cycle will start. Humans on earth are just pieces scattered on the ground coming from a divine substance, the soul of the world. They must *re-join* this soul, restoring the disrupted equilibrium. Every human being has the *atman*, individual soul, part of the universal soul or *brahman*. *Karma*, a kind of obstacle, prevents *atman* from unifying with the *brahman*. *Karma* is the result of acts done in the past. Each new birth is determined by the result of a weighing in the balance of good and bad *karma* from previous existences[368]. To release themselves from the *karma*, and thus be able to reach the universal soul, individual souls are subjected to a series of reincarnations. In this respect, human beings do their duty when they follow the law of the world, a sort of moral code, observance of which makes possible the purification

365. BASHAM 1988, pp. 240, 243, 273-275.
366. MEULEAU, PIETRI 1971, p. 292; BASHAM 1988, p. 84
367. BASHAM 1988, pp. 184 *et seq.*; MORINEAU 1998, p. 704.
368. MEULEAU, PIETRI 1971, p. 293.

of the soul[369]. The class in which they were born is the reward or punishment for the actions of their previous life. They must bear with patience their present position to wash away their sins committed during their previous life. To revolt against one's current state is to disobey the divine will. Justice thus consists in not revolting against the unequal system of the castes and, in spite of adversities, persisting in doing good[370].

44. Siddhartha Gautama, known as Buddha, an Indian prince, founded a religion which professes the removal of conditions that create conflict among humans. Once they are removed, there will be no need for justice[371]. Full satisfaction of our five senses is, according to Buddha, changeable and perishable[372]. Viewed in this light, it can only sadden us because while we possess it we already know that it will disappear[373]. Buddha, professes an attitude of withdrawal in respect of the satisfaction afforded to us by the senses. When viewing the objects of our senses, we must always have in contemplation, their changeability, and their disappearance[374]. So, Buddha perceives *awakening* as a state of being in which humans are freed from concerns related to self-interest[375]. He preaches a middle way, a life balanced between two extremes, both of which are equally reprehensible: *"There are two extremes, o monks, from which it is necessary to remain remote: a life of pleasures, it is low, ignoble, against the spirit, despicable and vain. And a life of asceticism, it is sad, annoying and vain. From these two extremes, O monks, the Perfect one was kept away,*

369. MEULEAU 1971, p. 293.
370. BASHAM 1988, pp. 258, 189, 232.
371. WIJAYARATNA 2001, p. 217.
372. WIJAYARATNA 2001, pp. 42, 52, 53.
373. WIJAYARATNA 2001, pp. 61, 68.
374. WIJAYARATNA 2001, p. 171.
375. BELLINGER 2000, pp. 79 *et seq.*

and he discovered the way which passes through the mean, and leads to rest, and with knowledge and with illumination, to Nirvana"[376].

376. MEULEAU, PIETRI 1971, p. 294

3

Justice within Human Rights

45. Medieval Christianity is governed by a Platonic order of law, inaccessible to the secular power. A message of love for his enemy, combined with the emergence of sects which claim their freedom from established churches, promoted the idea of tolerance. Personal interests and social classes are manifested. Equality before God, turns into equality before the law. Freedom of religious beliefs becomes freedom of political opinion. Parliamentary governance opens the way for empirical solutions. Legislative rules are dependent on the balance of power, which is constantly shifting. A consensus is, however, reached concerning fundamental rules which take the form of the Constitution and the declaration of basic rights. Political parties incorporate conceptions of justice widely shared by citizens. Impartial justice, as an institution of the state, is confirmed. The Western world is not thereby transformed into a terrestrial paradise. Capitalism recreates a class society and tolerates extreme poverty, pushing states to imperialism, with colonialism as a by-product. Unable to effectively defend itself, democracy falls prey to totalitarianism. Hitler and his regime organize and commit the Genocide. Democratic forces emerging victorious from World War II, later winning the Cold War, claim the right to act so that such attacks on justice can *"never again"* be repeated. Protection of human rights becomes a universal program of justice. Order in society is henceforth sought in the equilibrium that emerges from the equitable respect of each human being's unalterable dignity, unabridged political freedom and right to pursue happiness.

Christianity and the New Requirements of Justice

46. In the first century of the era which bears his name, Jesus, a Jew, preached a new alliance between the people of Israel and God. Paul, a contemporary of Jesus, took his word and turned it into a universal message[377]. Christianity professes a radical equality of human beings: *"There is neither Jew nor Greek, there is neither slave nor free man, there is no longer man and wife, for all of you are one in Christ Jesus"* (Galatians 3. 23 28). It praises a simple and at the same time radical system of equalization of means: *"since you have plenty at this time, it is only fair that you should help those who are in need. Then when you are in need and they have plenty, they will help you. In this way both are treated equally"* (Corinthians II, 8. 13-14). It advocates an unconditional respect to all: *"You have heard that it was said, an eye for an eye and a tooth for a tooth. But now I tell you: do not take revenge on someone who wrongs you. On the contrary, if someone strikes you on the right cheek, turn to him the other also"* (Matthew 5. 38, 39, 42). It introduces the idea of disinterested service in power relationships: *"The kings of the Nations act with them as lords and those who rule over them are called benefactors. But this is not the way it is with you; rather, the greatest one among you should take the place of the youngest, and the leader must be like the servant"* (Luke 22. 25 to 27)[378].

Christianity offers to the Roman empire the ideology which allows it to flourish in the East for over a thousand years[379]. The

377. MEULEAU, PIETRI 1971, p. 491.

378. MARITAIN 2005, pp. 53 *et seq.*

379. PIETRI 1971, p. 558.

Greek emperor considered himself the vicar of God and the way of righteousness on earth[380]. The empire is a sacred entity[381]. In the administration of justice, Roman equity is transformed into Christian humanism[382]. The liberation of slaves is seen as an act of Christian charity[383]. Cruel punishments are performed only exceptionally[384]. The coronation of Charlemagne as emperor of the Romans, on 25 December 800, constituted a major event for the West[385]. The Carolingian king, no longer a mere upholder of the Roman Law[386], assumes a duty inspired by Christian charity to protect orphans, widows, the poor, foreigners, and the needy. After the Scandinavian invasion[387], the insecurity which reigns again over Europe gives rise to chivalry[388]. The nobles, for their own security, attiliated themselves with the knights, providing them with fiefs and, thus, a comfortable life[389]. The pledging of the oath is enhanced by the idea of a contract founding a relationship of reciprocal rights[390]. As the noble and the humble of the kingdom are committed to supporting the king, so the king agrees to respect the rights and privileges of any subject of his kingdom[391]. Society spon-

380. BREHIER 1949, pp. 49 *et seq.*

381. J. PICQ 2009, p. 76.

382. BREHIER 1949, p. 58 who quotes the patriarch Nicolas the Mystique: *"If the basileus, inspired by the devil, gives an order against the divine law, nobody has to obey him".*

383. GIBBON 1983, pp. 220-232; PIETRI 1971, p. 571.

384. BREHIER 1949, pp. 195 *et seq.*

385. MEULEAU, PIETRI 1971, p. 639; SAINT-BONNET SASSIER 2004, pp. 63 *et seq.*

386. MEULEAU, PIETRI 1971, p. 525; SAINT-BONNET SASSIER 2004, pp. 56 *et seq.*

387. MEULEAU, PIETRI 1971, pp. 669 *et seq.*

388. MEULEAU, PIETRI 1971, pp. 712 *et seq.*

389. MEULEAU, PIETRI 1971, pp. 727, 731-732; SAINT-BONNET SASSIER 2004, p. 108.

390. MEULEAU, PIETRI 1971, pp. 655 *et seq.*; SAINT-BONNET SASSIER 2004, pp. 77, 88.

391. SAINT-BONNET SASSIER 2004, p. 113. A vast network of reciprocities is set up supported by the rights and privileges of class; SAINT-BONNET SASSIER 2004, pp. 110, 126. The jurisdictional prerogative is a component of the power of any lord; SAINT-BONNET SASSIER 2004, pp. 85 *et seq.*

taneously creates law which becomes customary and claims legitimacy by means of a tacit agreement through consensus of the interested parties[392]. Sometimes the judges of the kingdom, and the Church, rebel against bad customs which challenge the moral foundations of law[393]. The King intervenes to restore consistency in the order of justice by eliminating what is unacceptable in the law of his kingdom[394]. During this period, Saint Thomas Aquinas teaches that rules revealed by reason elucidate the natural law, embodying the justice of God[395].

47. The end of the Middle Ages starts in 1204 with the fall of Constantinople to the Crusaders[396]. The Eastern trade thus becomes entirely dominated by the Italian cities[397]. Contracts of association facilitate the sharing of navigation risks. New forms of payment are invented, banks are created[398], and contractual relationships enable holders of capital to enter trade without taking excessive risks[399]. A movement of the rural population towards the industrial towns is observed. Urban areas seek to establish their autonomy, big tradesmen affirm their influence on the government of their city, and the kings increase their power through the taxation of wealth[400]. The growth of taxation decreases the chances of profit, while farmers are starting to borrow money to pay taxes[401]. Meanwhile, autonomous universities are organized in which teachers and students enjoy a certain degree of independence[402].

392. SAINT-BONNET SASSIER 2004, p. 106.
393. SAINT-BONNET SASSIER 2004, p. 138.
394. SAINT-BONNET SASSIER 2004, pp. 126, 146, 148.
395. PIETRI, VENARD 1971, p. 92
396. MEULEAU, PIETRI 1971, p. 874.
397. PIETRI, VENARD 1971, p. 8.
398. PIETRI, VENARD 1971, p. 3.
399. PIETRI, VENARD 1971, p. 3.
400. PIETRI, VENARD 1971, pp. 16 *et seq.*
401. PIETRI, VENARD 1971, pp. 21 *et seq.*
402. PIETRI, VENARD 1971, pp. 85-88.

Uprisings of the masses become common and take a decidedly social revolutionary turn, alongside cases of rebellion against taxation. The poor demand better living conditions, and express their hatred of the nobility. Italian cities are in a state of constant rebellion against the empire[403]. The Lords are forced to offer political freedom to the cities. In these cities, many classes are formed. Big merchants are part of the patrician class which runs the city and legislate in favour of its class interests. The urban workforce, reinforced by peasant immigration, starts a series of social conflicts in order to improve its living conditions[404]. The social revolt of 1378 in Florence, led initially by a coalition of small industrialists and workers, who demanded their participation in government, was finally crushed when the small industrialists realized that popular unrest was also directed against them[405].

48. In England, the *common law* began to be developed under the impulse of Henry II[406]. It is based on two principles: its statement by a judge who reveals the law, and the force of precedent. However, although the judge reveals the common law and does not create it, he does not seek it in a world of immutable principles. The law that the common law judge reveals, emerges as the solution which is both the most acceptable in light of the facts of the case and the most coherent in light of previous judgements in similar cases[407].

On 15 June 1215, faced with the joint revolt of the nobility and the middle-class men of London, King John of England, signed the *Magna Carta*[408]. By signing this document, the king binds himself with promises of limitation of his power to all the *"archbishops,*

403. GUILLEMAIN 1998, pp. 443 *et seq.*

404. PIETRI, VENARD 1971, pp. 166-167.

405. PIETRI, VENARD 1971, p. 168.

406. PICQ 2009, pp. 139-141.

407. PICQ 2009, p.134.

408. PIETRI, VENARD 1971, p. 47.

bishops, abbots, earls, barons, justices, foresters, sheriffs, stewards, servants and to all his officials and loyal servants" (preamble). The principles of consent to taxation and free administration of the Commons are enshrined[409].The principle of respect of individual liberty is proclaimed with a guarantee of access to the courts[410], as well as the principles of proportionality and reasonableness of charges and penalties[411]. Unfulfilled promises cause a new crisis. This is settled by the *Provisions of Oxford*, which give rise to the Parliament[412]. From 1295, the king recognizes that royal taxation cannot be levied without parliamentary approval[413].

---

409. *"No scutage not aid shall be imposed on our kingdom, unless by common counsel of our kingdom, except for ransoming our person, for making our eldest son a knight, and for once marrying our eldest daughter; and for these there shall not be levied more than a reasonable aid"* (Article 12). *"(...)And the city of London shall have all it ancient liberties and free customs, as well by land as by water; furthermore, we decree and grant that all other cities, boroughs, towns, and ports shall have all their liberties and free customs"* (Article 13).

410. *"No freemen shall be taken or imprisoned or disseised or exiled or in any way destroyed, nor will we go upon him nor send upon him, except by the lawful judgment of his peers or by the law of the land"* (Article 39). *"To no one will we sell, to no one will we refuse or delay, right or justice"* (Article 40).

411. *"A freeman shall not be amerced for a slight offense, except in accordance with the degree of the offense; and for a grave offense he shall be amerced in accordance with the gravity of the offense, yet saving always his "contentment; and a merchant in the same way, saving his "merchandise"; and a villein shall be amerced in the same way, saving his "wainage" if they have fallen into our mercy: and none of the aforesaid amercements shall be imposed except by the oath of honest men of the neighbourhood"* (Article 20). *"Neither we nor our bailiffs will seize any land or rent for any debt, as long as the chattels of the debtor are sufficient to repay the debt; nor shall the sureties of the debtor be distrained so long as the principal debtor is able to satisfy the debt"* (Article 9). *"We will not for the future grant to anyone license to take an aid from his own free tenants, except to ransom his person, to make his eldest son a knight, and once to marry his eldest daughter; and on each of these occasions there shall be levied only a reasonable aid"* (Article 15).

412. PIETRI, VENARD 1971, p. 51.

413. PIETRI, VENARD 1971, p. 52.

49. In France, the end of the independent Burgundy state, a state within the state, marks the beginning of a strong central power and a France united under a national dynasty[414]. The strengthening of royal power, however, produced an increase in the tax burden. In August 1314, the *États Généraux* were convened and solicited to help the king[415]. King Louis the Saint, by his desire to do justice, cultivates the idea of the king as moral leader. Justice is dispensed by the king at the expense of the ecclesiastical courts. The king is henceforth presented as the guarantor of justice, and any justice dispensed in his kingdom is deemed to be based on delegation. He punishes not only the judges who refuse to do justice, but also those who make unfair judgments[416]. From the fourteenth century, appeal to the royal jurisdiction is allowed and any violation of a royal decree imposing a prohibition is brought before the royal courts for adjudication[417]. Moreover, parliaments are established in the regions of France with the function of adjudicating on appeals. They judge according to a rational evidence-based procedure[418].

Dynamic versus Immutable Equilibrium

50. During the sixteenth century, humanists teach the power of education and revive the old ideas of democracy and control of power by the citizens[419]. The theological explanation of the world is contested[420]. Erasmus in *"Praise of Folly"* condemns superstitions and medieval theology[421]. He interprets the Bible, rejecting

414. FAVIER 1998, pp. 562 *et seq.*; PIETRI, VENARD 1971, p. 34.
415. PIETRI, VENARD 1971, p. 46; SAINT-BONNET SASSIER 2004, p. 211.
416. PIETRI, VENARD 1971, p. 43.
417. SAINT-BONNET SASSIER 2004, p. 198.
418. SAINT-BONNET SASSIER 2004, p. 206.
419. PIETRI 1971, pp. 322-323.
420. VENARD 1971, p. 733.
421. VENARD 1971, pp. 401 *et seq.*

the authority of dogma. Paracelsus teaches that any knowledge apart that coming from observation should be rejected[422]. Cyrano de Bergerac castigates the forced confessions of witches to carrying out supernatural acts[423]. Friedrich Spee, a German inquisitor, denounced the procedural flaws that led to repression[424]. Bartolommeo de Las Casas rose against exploitation of natives in America[425] pushing Charles V to abolish, in 1542, the *encomienda*, under which private owners assumed unlimited power over the natives.

In 1517, Luther professed salvation by faith without the intervention of the Church[426]. He proclaimed freedom of conscience[427], teaching that each man may seek truth without barriers raised by civil and religious authorities[428]. Protestantism spreads: Luther in Germany, Calvin in France and Geneva, and Zwingli in Zurich. Princes and kings have to take a stance on the new phenomenon of religious differentiation of their subjects[429]. In England, the schism is state's policy[430]. It is not the same on the continent. Some princes, tiring of a policy of repression, are resigned to accepting reality and begin to tolerate Protestantism. In France, the rivalry between the opposing factions led quickly to fanatical armed confrontations. The night of Saint Bartholomew, with the massacre of some 4000 Protestant nobles worsens the problem[431]. The environment around the king begins to become aware of the king's interest to be detached from the opposing parties. In this context, Jean Bodin conceives the

422. VENARD 1971, p. 413.
423. VENARD 1971, p. 549.
424. VENARD 1971, p. 551.
425. VENARD 1971, p. 359.
426. SAINT-BONNET SASSIER 2004, p. 240; VENARD 1971, p. 429.
427. VENARD 1971, p. 435; J. PICQ, pp. 213 *et seq.*
428. VENARD 1971, p. 435.
429. VENARD 1971, pp. 442, 445, 447.
430. VENARD 1971, p. 449.
431. VENARD 1971, pp. 578-580.

idea of a kingdom bound by natural laws[432]. The Edict of Nantes, of April 13, 1598, is an important step in the process of establishing religious freedom[433]. Disputes between the two religions are resolved through a process of arbitration[434]. In Germany, the religious war takes an international turn because of the political structure of the country. The Thirty Years War, concluded in 1648 by the Treaty of Westphalia, led the belligerents to accept the rule of freedom of conscience and of worship[435].

51. The Treaty of Westphalia marks the disappearance of the two competing universalisms, the universalism of the emperor, on the one hand, and that of the Pope, on the other[436]. Henceforth, states are positioning themselves in history as autonomous actors capable of preserving their freedom against the dominance of the strongest. The order resulting from the Treaty of Westphalia establishes the European balance of power[437]. The weaker states form a coalition against the stronger. England, France, Austria and Spain watch over each other in order to prevent one from taking the lead over the other[438]. Defensive alliances allow states to counterbalance any established preponderance. European diplomacy works for the objective of maintaining balance[439].

Newton, Descartes, and Leibniz reduce the universe to a system of forces capable of equilibrium[440]. The balance of power in

432. VENARD 1971, p. 587.
433. VENARD 1971, p. 632.
434. VENARD 1971, p. 633.
435. VENARD 1971, p. 625.
436. J. PICQ 2009, p. 331.
437. J. PICQ 2009, p. 320.
438. J. PICQ 2009, pp. 324-326.
439. J. PICQ 2009, p. 324.
440. VENARD 1971, p. 741 (Descartes), p. 947 (Leibniz), p. 932 (Newton); J. PICQ 2009, pp. 322-323. However, on June 22, 1633, Galileo is sentenced by a court composed of cardinals because of the publication of his discoveries on the sun's position and movement of the earth; VENARD 1971, pp. 734-737.

Europe appears thus as a political and military fulcrum by which antagonistic forces are stabilized on a point, securing to all nations the best possible treatment of their interests. The idea of equilibrium also pervades the economy. Thanks to the *"invisible hand"*, as Adam Smith named the natural tendency towards equilibrium, freedom of prices and competition can eliminate dominant positions and allow moderate prices to be attained, together with reasonable wages and profit[441]. Montesquieu sees in the British political regime the realization of a balance between the opposing political forces, the Crown, the House of Lords, and the House of Commons, where each one, for its own interest, must cooperate with the others, as the tendency of each to dominate the others is neutralized by checks and balances exerted on it by the others[442].

Natural law, based on reason and opposed to the law enacted by the prince, becomes a central idea in this period. Philosophical thought begins to seek the rules by which society is governed. David Hume views justice as the convergence of different interests to the mutual benefit of all[443]. Jean-Jacques Rousseau sees the foundation of justice in the democratic process[444]. Immanuel Kant founded justice on equal respect for the autonomy of all persons[445].

52. In England, two political forces are in confrontation: the traditionalists, connected to the king, and the merchants, *nouveaux riches*, attached to the Parliament[446]. The location of the conflict is sited in the British Parliament, which holds the power to vote new taxes and change the *common law*. The conflict

441. BERGERON 1972, p. 63.
442. MONTESQUIEU 1979, I, pp. 294 *et seq.*
443. See *infra* § 136.
444. See *infra* § 140.
445. See *infra* § 131.
446. J. PICQ 2009, pp. 288, 291.

erupted when the royalty identified its policy with the traditionalists and Parliament took position in favour of the others[447]. The new parliamentarian elections led to civil war after the execution of the king[448]. Following the restoration of the monarchy, a new dynasty was elected by Parliament[449]. William and Mary were crowned only after having solemnly accepted the *Bill of Rights*, on February 13th, 1689[450].

English society of the early eighteenth century is marked by a great social movement[451]. The rational exploitation of land contributes to a significant increase in the yield and the peasant masses, deprived of work, crowded into the cities[452]. Parties, vehicles of class interests, are engaged in an institutionally organized struggle, and conquer power in order to assume the defence of the interests they represent. Two parties, the Tories and the Whigs, show clear differences[453]. The first sees in the king the representative of God on earth. The other refuses to recognise such a quality in the king, being in favour of limiting the royal prerogative. The Tories defend land ownership; they are for peace and against taxes.

447. VENARD 1971, p. 661.

448. VENARD 1971, pp. 664-665.

449. J. PICQ 2009, p. 298.

450. The *Bill of Rights* reaffirms the rights of Parliament: *"That the pretended power of suspending the laws or the execution of laws by regal authority without consent of Parliament is illegal"* (Article 2). *"That levying money for or to the use of the Crown by pretence of prerogative, without grant of Parliament, for longer time, or in other manner than the same is or shall be granted, is illegal"* (Article 4). A series of provisions against arbitrariness, the condemnation of the special courts, the prohibition on the king's intervening in proceedings of the courts of justice (Articles 3, 11 and 12) are laid down. Rights of subjects to present petitions to the king (Article 5), to bear arms (Article 7) and to be protected from unreasonable interferences with property or individual freedom (Article 10) are recognised; J. PICQ 2009, p. 299.

451. PILLORGET 1998, pp. 981 *et seq.*

452. BERGERON 1972, p. 19; VENARD, p. 869.

453. TREVELYAN 1987, pp. 329-332, 342-352; VENARD, p. 865.

The Whigs support an expansionist trade policy and conquest, be it through war, of new markets. The Tories defend the Anglican hierarchy, the Whigs are in favour of tolerance[454].

53. Until the 1789 revolution, the king of France is still the chief justice of his kingdom. But his judgments are respected only when they are perceived to be in conformity with the norms of justice. For that reason, he is under an obligation to decide on nothing without receiving relevant advice[455]. Whatever its content, the king's decision did not come from the will of an individual known as the king, but was the logical expression of the immutable order of justice, whose requirements were expressed by the king's voice[456]. The three *states*, nobility, clergy and the others, were separated by legal barriers; every human being was vested, according to his status, with a dignity that determined his duties and rights. The order of justice guaranteed to all this honour, and any attack on it, manifested by injuries to the person or property, was perceived by the person who suffered it as a rejection of his dignity[457].

In a society imbued with such a social ideology, the king had little room for manoeuvre in introducing reforms. He had to protect the order that had brought him to power, guaranteeing to all their honour[458]. The *Curia Regis* initially assumes the function of providing advice to the king. But, during the centuries preceding the 1789 revolution, the *Curia Regis* is divided into specialised sections and regional formations, the Parliaments[459]. These Parliaments lay claim to the legitimacy embodied in the person of the king[460]. Instead of being his assistants, subject to his will, they claim to be the emanation of the same order of justice which assigns to them the task of

454. VENARD 1971, pp. 889 *et seq.*
455. SAINT-BONNET SASSIER 2004, pp. 210, 280 *et seq.*, 320 *et seq.*, 366, 370, 371.
456. SAINT-BONNET SASSIER 2004, p. 356.
457. SAINT-BONNET SASSIER 2004, pp. 274 *et seq.*
458. SAINT-BONNET SASSIER 2004, p. 566.
459. SAINT-BONNET SASSIER 2004, p. 323.
460. SAINT-BONNET SASSIER 2004, pp. 277, 281.

contributing to the formation of the king's opinion by the advice they are required to provide him with, and which the king must in turn receive[461]. Within this world, the law was frozen forever[462]. When the kings legislate to introduce measures of government needed to restore order and peace[463], the resistance of Parliaments becomes fierce[464]. Nobilities of blood and function, attached to their privileges, band together to defend their privileges against the policy of the king[465]. Malherbe, Turgot, Necker introduce reforms, including those relating to the finances of the kingdom, provoking the fury of the nobility and their revolt[466]. The king, exhausted by the continued resistance of the nobility as well as by the endemic disobedience of the people, convenes in 1789 the *États Généraux*[467].

The Struggles against Inequalities

54. A dispute concerning the taxation of goods was elevated by the American Revolution of 1776 into a noble struggle for the equality of human beings and found its solution in the establishment of a new state order based on the principles of equality and freedom[468]. In the preamble to their Declaration of Independence from the British Crown the rebels declared their ontology of human beings: *"all men are created equal, (...) their Creator has endowed them with certain inalienable rights, among these are life, liberty and the pursuit of happiness"*. They also stated in the same document a *social contract* conception of power: *"to secure these rights, men establish among themselves the government whose just powers derive from the consent of the governed"*. They

461. SAINT-BONNET SASSIER 2004, p. 276.
462. SAINT-BONNET SASSIER 2004, pp. 274, 255.
463. VENARD 1971, pp. 637 *et seq.*
464. VENARD 1971, p. 460.
465. PICQ, p. 374; VENARD 1971, pp. 647, 651, 861.
466. BERGERON 1972, p. 31, 137.
467. BERGERON 1972, pp. 68-73.
468. BERGERON 1972, pp. 129 *et seq.*

further appealed to utilitarian principles to justify reaction against those who ignore the essence of man: *"If a government, of whatever form ignores this, the people has the right (...) to institute a new government (...) with the powers which it may deem best calculated to ensure their safety and happiness".*

The United States' Constitution of 1787, is built rationally on the idea of a balance of power[469]; each of the three powers, executive, legislature and judiciary, is provided with sufficient means to prevent the other two from dominating the government[470]. A Supreme Court, ensuring federated States' rights and separation of powers, censures laws contrary to the Constitution, guarantees the independence of justice and protects the fundamental rights of citizens[471]. Two major parties appear on the scene[472]. The Republicans stress the importance of federal government and business success. In contrast, the Democrats defend States' rights and rally the discontented. Based on the idea of equality, the new republic however contradicts itself by tolerating slavery[473].

55. In France, the educated middle class, enriched and imbued with the ideas of the Enlightenment, could no longer tolerate its

469. LE POURHIET 2008, pp. 175 *et seq.*; J. PICQ 2009, p. 398. See also KELLY, HARBISON, BELZ 1991, vol. I, p. 71 : *"In repudiating English authority Americans also repudiated the organizing principle of English constitutionalism, the theory of mixed government. In its place they substituted the theory of separation of powers. Because both of these doctrines aimed at achieving balance in government, they are often seen similar, if not interchangeable. In fact they differed profoundly. Mixed government (...) recognized and gave a place in the structure of government to the several orders of society. In the hierarchical, feudal society in which it developed it expressed the assumption that social and political authority were identical, that government and society were organically linked and overlapping. The separation of powers, by contrast, rested on recognition of distinct and clearly differentiated functions of government. It held that government powers, not social classes, must be kept in balance in order to preserve liberty."*

470. J. PICQ 2009, pp. 402 *et seq.*

471. J. PICQ 2009, p. 407.

472. J. PICQ 2009, p. 407.

473. J. PICQ 2009, p. 407.

legal inferiority compared to the nobility[474]. In 1789, a revolution shook the country and forced the *États Généraux*, self declared as the National Assembly, to vote for the abolition of the old regime[475]. The revolution eliminates distinctions based on birth[476]. Men are freed from mortmain and drudgeries[477]. Class justice is abolished[478]. Freedom of trade, profession, art and craft is proclaimed[479]. On August 10, 1792, the Republic was proclaimed and new elections were held on the basis of universal suffrage[480]. The governing *Gironde* proclaims the universal principles of freedom of the people and leads an international war inspired by the ideal of political freedom of the nations[481]. The *Mountain*, which succeeds, outlines a social democracy[482]. The leftist opposition is crystallized in the personality of Babeuf, a revolutionary communist[483]. Bonaparte[484] re-establishes order and, among other reforms, enacts the Civil Code, which consolidates the revolutionary ideas of equality of men, respect of property, and contractual freedom[485].

The spiritual foundations of the new regime, equality, property and political freedoms, are contained in the Universal Declaration of Human Rights and the Citizen[486]. Adopted by the Assembly on August 26, 1789, the Declaration reflects the same basic conception of justice as the Declaration of Independence of the United States[487]. It proclaims an essentialist conception of human rights, as *"natural,*

474. J. PICQ 2009, pp. 410 *et seq.*
475. BERGERON 1972, p. 147.
476. BERGERON 1972, p. 152.
477. BERGERON 1972, p. 152.
478. BERGERON 1972, p. 150.
479. BERGERON 1972, p. 152.
480. BERGERON 1972, p. 164.
481. BERGERON 1972, p. 167 *et seq.*
482. BERGERON 1972, p. 174 *et seq.*
483. BERGERON 1972, p. 204.
484. BERGERON 1972, pp. 210-214.
485. BERGERON 1972, p. 217.
486. WORMS 1993, pp. 73 *et seq.*
487. See *supra* § 54.

undeniable and sacred" (Preamble), being *"liberty, property, security and resistance to oppression"* (Article 2). It is imbued with social contract ideas, as law, which sets the limits in the exercise of natural rights (Article 4), is formed by citizens or their representatives (Article 6), while every citizen *"is entitled by himself or by his representatives, to see the need for public taxation, to consent to it freely, to monitor the use and to determine the amount, basis, collection and duration"* (Article 14). There is a utilitarian conception as to the objectives of the actions of public authority: *"Social distinctions may be based on the common good"* (Article 1); *"The law has the right to prohibit actions harmful to society"* (Article 5). Law enforcement is established *"for the benefit of all and not for the benefit of those to whom it is entrusted"* (Article 12). The social system, to which the Declaration aspires, requires citizens constantly to question accepted solutions in order to ensure that the legal order, and its specific application, is such that each person is benefiting from the best possible treatment in terms of his natural rights[488]. The Declaration allots, in its preamble, *"to all members of society"* the active role of comparing the acts of the legislature and those of the executive with the goal of any political organization, to preserve human rights. In such a society, where every citizen is a responsible actor, the rights conferred on each person become a question of optimal maximization: *"the exercise of the natural rights of each man is limited only by the need to secure to the other members of society the enjoyment of the same rights"* (article 4).

56. Nations awakened during the nineteenth century to claim their right to independence. The Greek national revolution, then that of the inhabitants of Brussels, caused deep emotion in Europe[489]. In Italy and Germany, romanticism led to national union[490]. In 1848, a

488. BERGERON 1972, p. 150.

489. J. PICQ 2009, pp. 431 *et seq.*; BERGERON 1972, p. 334.

490. BERGERON 1972, pp. 335-336.

French revolt gave rise in Europe to political movements demanding freedom and social justice[491]. In India, local elites, imbued by Western culture, but at the same time aware of their identity, exalt the Hindu civilization[492]. The movement gives rise to the foundation of the Congress party, which brings together modernist and nationalist forces[493]. China since 1851 has been living to the rhythm of revolution and counter-revolution. The Taiping revolution advocates collectivization of labour and labour for all, but its failure marks a return to absolutism and foreign domination[494]. The Boxers, a xenophobic movement, killed nearly 30.000 Chinese Christians, seeing in Christianism a symbol of foreign domination[495]. In Latin America, the end of the Spanish and Portuguese domination marks the birth of a new rule over the Indians by the white elites[496].

By the late nineteenth century struggles for recognition are intensified and put at the centre of the movement of history. A sense of justice dominates this movement, the deep equality of all human beings. Privileges based on status, race, gender, and economic conditions are questioned and their legitimacy as distinguishing criterion disputed. Slavery, abolished in France in 1794, is also abolished in the United Kingdom in 1833, and in 1865 in the United States after a civil war[497]. In the Western world, universal suffrage is granted to men in the early twentieth century, while women had to wait a few more decades[498]. The collapse of the Austro-Hungarian and Ottoman empires after the First World War opened the way for the creation of nation states[499]. The liberation

491. PICQ 1985, pp. 439-443; BERGERON 1972, p. 337.
492. ROBERTS 1995, p. 942.
493. ROBERTS 1995, p. 943.
494. BERGERON 1972, pp. 446 *et seq.*
495. BERGERON 1972, p. 451.
496. BERGERON 1972, pp. 423 *et seq.*
497. ROBERTS 1995, pp. 762, 746 *et seq.*
498. BERGERON 1972, pp. 407, 478-480.
499. RONCAYOLO 1972, p. 546.

movements of colonized peoples follow the same trend. The individual, defined by his membership of a cultural community, asserts the expression of his collective identity by struggling for the right of his people to self-determination[500]. Asia rejects Western domination, based on the idea of the equal dignity of peoples[501]. In China, a nationalist democratic and socialist revolution, led to the fall of the empire and the establishment of a republican system[502].

57. In the industrialized world, the introduction of machinery and electricity radically changes the conditions and nature of work: the working masses are concentrated in the great urban areas with elementary sanitary arrangements, the automatic nature of the work is dehumanizing, wages are barely sufficient for survival, and the prospects for an improvement of the workers' life are poor[503]. Under the inspiration of socialist thinkers, workers go beyond demanding specific improvements in their working conditions and begin to fight for the conquest of political power[504]. Saint-Simonism, socialism, and then Communism, constitute intellectual stages in the search for an appropriate response[505]. A materialist conception of justice is reborn through Marxism. It professes action by class struggle, revolution and the dictatorship of the proletariat[506]. A worldwide organization of the workers with the objective of a proletarian revolution is created[507]. In England, the workers are organized within trade-unions and initiate action days to protest about their bad conditions. Strikes and demonstrations are the first means of action[508]. The middle-class men

500. BERGERON 1972, pp. 436-437.

501. RONCAYOLO 1972, p. 555.

502. ROBERTS 1995, pp. 945 *et seq.*; BERGERON 1972, p. 453.

503. BERGERON 1972, p. 304-306.

504. BERGERON 1972, p. 305.

505. BERGERON 1972, pp. 297, 298.

506. See *infra* § 131.

507. BERGERON 1972, p. 305.

who put themselves at the head of the workers' struggle note that trade unionism is not enough; it is necessary to organize a workers' party making possible change using the parliamentary process[509]. The liberal party of Lloyd George, coerced by the labour movement, grants the eight-hour working day to miners and a system of compulsory insurance against sickness and unemployment[510]. In 1909, a progressive tax on income is imposed[511]. In France, where workers' association, strikes and demonstrations are prohibited, the workers' action is radicalized and comes close to being a revolution movement[512]. In 1884, a law recognizes the lawfulness of professional associations, but the working class does not manage to constitute a true workers' party, trade-unions remaining separated from left-wing parties[513]. In Germany, socialists participate in government[514]. The country has since 1890 a system of social insurance against the risks of sickness, accident and old age[515].

Confirmation of the Democratic Solution

58. After the First World War, the United States, France and the United Kingdom struggle to face economic and social challenges without renouncing their democratic traditions. In the United States, mass consumption becomes a principle of social organization[516], capitalism appears to triumph and President Wilson, a visionary person, sets himself the objective of organizing a

508. BERGERON 1972, p. 306.
509. LE POURHIET 2008, pp. 196 *et seq.*
510. BERGERON 1972, p. 357.
511. ATKINSON 2004, p. 125.
512. BERGERON, pp. 295, 303; BERGERON 1972, p. 304.
513. BERGERON 1972, p. 306.
514. BERGERON 1972, pp. 306-307.
515. BERGERON 1972, p. 364.
516. RONCAYOLO 1972, p. 583.

new world order founded on the principles of justice[517]. In 1929, an unprecedented financial crisis discredits the American model[518]. To pull the economy out of the crisis, the federal government tends toward dirigisme. The *New Deal* of President Roosevelt constitutes an audacious reaction to the crisis[519]. The unemployed are absorbed by government agencies which perform public works[520]. In France, the process of state control of the economy accelerates during the First World War: coordination of economic activities, control over stocks, various requisitions, and comprehensive planning[521]. Women, who had to replace the men gone to war, maintain, after the end of the hostilities, their new social status acquired during the War[522]. During the thirties, social insurance is organized[523]. In 1936, the workers obtain from employers the election of workers' delegates in the company, collective agreements for setting wages and better working conditions, two weeks of paid leave per year, and a forty-hour week[524]. In the United Kingdom, the government had recognized, at the end of the War, the principle compensation for unemployment[525]. Strikes broke out in 1926, which, because of their size, generated an atmosphere of insurrection. In May 1929, the Labour Party obtained a relative majority in the House of Commons and formed a coalition government with the Liberals[526]. Welfare state policies are pursued during the thirties at the behest of the powerful trade-unions[527].

517. RONCAYOLO 1972, p. 543.
518. RONCAYOLO 1972, pp. 669-670.
519. RONCAYOLO 1972, pp. 708 *et seq.*
520. RONCAYOLO 1972, pp. 669-671.
521. RONCAYOLO 1972, pp. 512-514.
522. THIBAULT 1998, p. 547.
523. RONCAYOLO 1972, p. 603.
524. THIBAULT 1998, p. 586.
525. RONCAYOLO 1972, p. 589.
526. RONCAYOLO 1972, p. 591.
527. THOMSON 1981, pp.100-101, 207-208, 264-265; RONCAYOLO 1972, p. 726.

59. In Russia, the Republicans, who come to power in March 1917, are not affiliated with the exhausted and demoralized people[528]. The revolutionary forces seize the opportunity offered to them by the chaotic nature of the situation[529]. In October 1917, the Communists occupy Petrograd[530]. They suspend the opposition newspapers and prohibit strikes, which are henceforth considered crimes against the people. The Constituent Assembly is dissolved[531]. In 1929, Stalin imposes forced economic planning, collectivization and industrialization[532]. The Kulaks were driven out, replaced by the kolkhozes, collective farms organized as cooperatives[533]. In a weak Italy, the fascists came to power, in October 1922, as the dominant classes felt threatened by the Communists and saw in Mussolini, the chief of the fascists, the solution for re-establishing order and peace[534]. The parliamentary regime is abolished, freedoms of press and of assembly are removed, members of the opposition imprisoned or deported. In 1928, the corporatist ideology is officially adopted. A strict discipline is imposed on producers by the state, whereas workers are dispossessed of their trade union rights[535]. In the thirties, economic activity is distributed[536] amongst twenty-five corporations whose presidents and vice-presidents are appointed by the fascists[537]. In Germany, people are torn between inflation and unemployment, and tormented by a sense of injustice suffered by the conditions of peace[538]. Hitler wins in 1932 a relative majority

528. RONCAYOLO 1972, p. 532.
529. BERGERON 1972, pp. 86, 323; RONCAYOLO 1972, pp. 524 *et seq.*
530. RONCAYOLO 1972, p. 533.
531. RONCAYOLO 1972, p. 538.
532. RONCAYOLO 1972, p. 759.
533. RONCAYOLO 1972, p. 761.
534. RONCAYOLO 1972, pp. 617 *et seq.*
535. RONCAYOLO 1972, pp. 620-621.
536. RONCAYOLO 1972, p. 622.
537. RONCAYOLO 1972, pp. 696-697.
538. RONCAYOLO 1972, pp. 676-677.

of seats in Parliament[539] and on January 30th, 1933[540], forms a coalition government[541]. He quickly organized new elections in a climate of terror. Within weeks, the opposition forces were dismantled, newspapers seized, the political leaders jailed or forced into exile. Political parties were dissolved or absorbed by the Nazi party[542]. Hitler established his personal power, becoming the Führer[543]. Strikes, free negotiation of wages, and collective agreements were prohibited. Trade-unions disappeared. Women were assigned to the home[544]. The regime professed eugenics and racism[545]. It organized and committed the Holocaust[546].

60. Nazism exalts collective effort and condemns individualism by a racist ideology: Germanic people are the chosen people through the process of natural selection, the people which embodies to the highest degree the qualities of humans. Germans must keep themselves pure by removing the elements that threaten them and, at the same time, fulfil their destiny to dominate the world. For this purpose, any internal or external opposition should be eliminated. The state should service the German people to ensure their racial purity and their expansive domination over the peoples of lower race. A Führer, emanation of the Germanic soul, expresses in a mystical way the people's will. Terror, eugenics, war and genocide were the natural fruits of that ideology which suppressed opposition and took away the dignity of the individual[547]. The same applies to fascism: Mussolini, exploiting post-war frustrations in

539. RONCAYOLO 1972, p. 681.
540. J. PICQ 2009, pp. 489-490.
541. RONCAYOLO 1972, p. 684.
542. RONCAYOLO 1972, pp. 684-686.
543. RONCAYOLO 1972, p. 686.
544. RONCAYOLO 1972, pp. 688-692.
545. RONCAYOLO 1972, pp. 34-37; PICQ, p. 493.
546. RONCAYOLO 1972, p. 687.
547. J. PICQ 2009, p. 495.

Italian society, imposes himself as dictator in the way proper to fascism, by a combination of physical violence, deception and terror. Although head of government, he continues to employ the same means. The endeavours exhorted are sublimated in an expansive nationalism that seeks to restore the Roman empire. The economic crisis of 1929 enables him to condemn capitalism and replace it by a kind of corporatism where the oppositions and the conflicts between economic actors are resolved under the direction of an authorian state. The price to be paid is heavy[548]. Any advantage that collective effort can produce is offset by the loss of freedoms and, finally, the national disaster that came with the fall of fascism. Communist regimes have, for their part, also failed to ensure the optimal result expected from the collective effort. In spite of early successes, the mandatory five-year plans implemented in the Soviet Union did not generate the hoped-for wealth, while the capitalist world, going from crisis to crisis but in constant progression, acquired a level of economic power that the Communist countries could not equal. Moreover, the lack of transparency that prevailed within the regimes favoured the development of hidden privileges from which Communist leaders benefited, spreading rumours within society as to the way in which the socialized wealth was being distributed.

Nazism, Fascism and Communism, the latter only in its historical version, have in common that they exalt the collective effort led by a strong central government seeking the optimal outcome for the community. The collapse of totalitarianism in all its described versions strengthens the idea that when the collective effort goes hand in hand with the suppression of the democratic process, there is too high a price to be paid[549].

548. RONCAYOLO 1972, pp. 696-697.

549. FUKUYAMA 2011, pp. 422 *et seq*; BUCHANAN, TULLOCK 2004, p. 95: "*One method of eliminating bargaining costs is to delegate decision-making authority to a single individual and agree to abide by the choices that he makes for the*

The Era of Human Rights

61. On 10th December 1948, the United Nations General Assembly adopted the Universal Declaration of Human Rights[550]. The document reflects a historical development dating back to the *Magna Carta*, through the wars of religion and the conviction of Galilee, the American and French revolutions, the social spirit of the 19th century, culminating in a condemnation of Nazism and fascism, leading to respect for the universal dignity of the human being, as the epicentre of any political system[551]. The Declaration contains, finally, the condemnation of the Holocaust, which, by its size alone, expresses the evil against which humanity must constantly fight[552].

States, which are the traditional subjects of public international law, are not a closed universe, subject to their own ethics, but are part of a building whose foundation is in the recognition of human dignity and equal rights for all: *"the recognition of the inherent dignity and of their equal and inalienable rights, of all members of the human family is the foundation of freedom, justice and peace in the world"* (Preamble). The rights that human dignity generates are not a catalogue of legal entities, but an organic whole in profound interdependence. The Declaration, pro-

whole group. If we look only at the costs of decisions-making is that of dictatorship. This provides the element of truth in the idea that dictatorial governments are more 'efficient' that democratically organized governments. However, just as the rule of unanimity must normally be tempered by a recognition of decision-making costs, so must the dictatorship rule be tempered by the recognition that external costs may be imposed on the individual by collective decisions. If the individual feels that he might possibly disagree with the decisions of the dictator, that such decisions might cause him harm, he will never rationally support the delegation of important decision-making authority to a single unit".

550. J. PICQ 2009, pp. 483 *et seq.*

551. J. PICQ 2009, p. 507.

552. DELSOL 2004, pp. 37 *et seq.*; DELMAS-MARTY 2004, pp. 76-77.

claims *"the advent of a world in which human beings shall enjoy freedom of speech and belief and freedom from fear and want"* (Preamble). The advent of this world presupposes that everyone is subject *"in the exercise of his rights and the enjoyment of his freedom"* to *"the limitations established by law solely for the purpose of securing due recognition and respect for human rights and freedoms of others and of meeting the just requirements of morality, public order and general welfare in a democratic society"* (Article 29.2). The *"democratic society"* is thus the unique framework within which human rights cease to be theoretical statements for an abstract man, to become practical and effective legal powers, suitable for securing to all human beings in their interaction with others, the enjoyment of their equal and inalienable rights.

62. Throughout the first decade of their operation, the United Nations were dominated by the Western countries. In the sixties, however, an anti-Western alliance is developped between the non-aligned and the socialist countries[553]. It appears in the condemnation of apartheid and all forms of racial inequality and in the setting aside of statements of Western-style human rights. India, independent since 1947, gradually establishes itself as a pole of the non-aligned movement. China joins the movement after the rupture of its relations with the Soviet empire[554]. In Arab countries, anti-Western progressive movements take power[555]. In the seventies, the ideological dominance of the Third World seems total. A *structuralist* conception of justice marginalizes individual freedoms of the conventional type[556]. Injustice is the product of an overall organization of international society, reflected in national societies. The distributions of global wealth, very unfavourable to

553. CASSESE 1995, pp. 23 *et seq.*
554. MILZA 1998, pp. 905-916.
555. RONCAYOLO 1972, pp. 632-645.
556. CASSESE 1995, p. 37.

Third World countries, and the markedly unequal distribution of national wealth, breed justified violence by the underprivileged. In this state of things, the Western policy of human rights seems a disguised attempt by the old colonizing countries to maintain their influence over the internal affairs of the decolonized countries. The dogma of non-interference and respect for national sovereignty undermines any effort to promote a global policy of protection of human rights. Latin America is overwhelmed by a wind of red revolution[557]. The West retaliates with repression. Military dictatorships are justified all around the world[558]. Apartheid is tolerated in South Africa, an anti-communist bastion. In addition, America falters, humiliated by its military failure in Vietnam, its political system discredited by the Watergate crisis[559]. In the eighties, a change begins to appear. Third World countries are suspicious of the Soviets, who seem to pursue, as clearly indicated in the case of Afghanistan, a policy of establishing communist regimes. The socialist economy is no longer able to allow the Soviet government to offer substantial assistance to poor countries. A victorious right-wing ideology, animated by the works of Milton Friedman[560], economist, and of Friedrich von Hayek[561], economist and philosopher, brings conservatives into government[562].

63. During the Cold War, two views of human rights confronted one another: the Western concept and that of the socialist regimes[563]. The first emerged from the historical evolution of Judeo-Christian civilization in nations whose institutions dated

557. MOLZA 1998, pp. 1219 *et seq.*
558. MOLZA 1998, pp. 897 *et seq.*
559. CASSESE 1995, p. 41.
560. CASSIDY 2009, pp. 72 *et seq.*
561. CASSIDY 2009, pp. 37 *et seq.*
562. SORMAN 1983, pp. 9-18, 195-223.
563. RONCAYOLO 1985, pp. 105 *et seq.*

back to old traditions, and reflected the foresight of spirits which proceeded without a route map[564]. Their law allowed for and tolerated different and even opposing political ideas. Their unity was constituted by the common endeavour to hold the balance in such a variegated system. Conversely, the Socialist bloc was based on clear, egalitarian ideas of justice[565]: the means of production should belong to the community so that the substantial inequality of men should cease to be perpetuated; without collectivization of wealth, the exploitation of man by man, and therefore the negation of the inherent dignity of man, would not cease. It was consequently necessary to destroy the Western system of production by a proletarian revolution and to replace it with a socialist system to carry out the progressive phasing-in of Communism. To do this, a rigorous regime of socialist policing or a dictatorship of the proletariat was needed. Bourgeois liberties would be respected in a socialist society but they would not become a weapon in the hands of reactionaries to overthrow the power of the people.

Viewed from the perspective of the confrontation between the two blocks, the rightful causes of the Socialist block appeared to the Western block basically unjust and vice-versa. Revolts in Eastern Europe were discredited as an attempt to destabilize socialism, the foundation of all justice. Military dictatorships and repressive regimes in the West were in turn justified as an appropriate means of saving these countries from Communist dictatorship, the negation of freedom's order. The misery caused by civil wars, military interventions and the arms race, hardly counted. A strategy justified all means: for the West, preventing the Soviets from achieving world domination; for the Socialist block, bringing about the victory of the oppressed over the oppressors[566].

564. CASSESE 1995, p. 23 *et seq.*

565. See *infra* § 131.

566. RONCAYOLO 1985, p. 102.

64. The fall of the Berlin Wall, in 1989, marked a dramatic turning point for mankind in its quest for justice. The Western world is now united by a common understanding of human rights and considers that democracy, as it was formed in the liberal tradition, constitutes the only system of government that legitimizes the exercise of power.

Some fundamental features characterize the idea of justice thus generated. Justice is of this world, it does not proceed from a remote world of ideas. Even if human rights, notwithstanding their historic origins, can be considered inalienable and sacred legal principles, and, even if they stem from the inalienable nature of the human being or overriding requirements of reason, they are nevertheless standards of behaviour laid down in human documents which have nothing transcendental and which, as part of the empirical reality, are subject to a world governed by evolution and change[567]. There are contradictions and conflicts as to the scope of protection of human rights in relation to each other, as to the appropriate means to employ to protect them and the sacrifices necessitated to ensure their respect. Democracy provides the natural framework within which these contradictions are raised and conflicts are regulated and resolved. The democratic regime sets up an institutional system to neutralize abuse of power, and seek solutions best able to satisfy those whose interests are affected by the action of power. The best solution for the protection of human rights is not provided in a deterministic manner by standards of rationality. It is rather a subject of constant conflict. Neither politicians, nor judges are expected to find a solution that by definition will be approved unanimously. Even if the principles expressed by human rights are universal and eternal, their actual materialization in reality can vary considerably according to the sensibilities of the persons called on to decide on specific cases.

567. KATSIMANIS 1976, p. 96.

Governed by the laws of experience, subject to the rules of democratic debate, the overall objective of the contemporary search for justice may be seen as attaining the most acceptable equilibrium between concurring fundamental rights within a democratic society.

CONCLUDING REMARKS

The Indicator of Justice

65. Mankind has established organizational systems of power built in accordance with various ideas of justice. In Pharaoh's Egypt, society served Ma'at, the goddess enhancing any other divinity and maintaining the world's equilibrium by her beneficial action[568]. The balance of cosmic forces, generator of good order, was maintained by the action of Egyptian society, led by the Pharaoh. Order in society and order in nature became intertwined in the minds of the inhabitants so that the social order became part of the physical order. This pattern of man as an instrument at the service of the cosmic order reached its zenith in the Aztec culture[569]. Aztec ontology requires the sacrifice of humans to keep the divinity constantly nourished with blood, for it is the divinity which holds this world in a state of order. Without conquering new lands for enslaving and sacrificing human beings, the world's equilibrium would fall apart. What in our view is the most heinous crime, namely the killing of innocent persons, is the supreme justice in the eyes of a people which considers itself to be the servant of the cosmic order. Other civilizations and cultures perceive there to be an interconnection between the natural world and the social world without making humans into essential workers for the maintenance of the cosmic order. In Mesopotamia, the existence of gods and the maintenance of cosmic order are not dependent on the actions of humans[570]. However, in order to live in prosperity, humans

568. See *supra* § 15.

569. See *supra* § 23.

570. See *supra* §§ 18, 19.

had to ensure that the rules desired by gods prevailed in their imperfect world. The king and his administration were the agents of the divine will which, by its beneficial action, imposed on earth the requirements of divine justice. In the Inca empire, the emperor is also an agent of divine forces[571]. But his beneficial action goes beyond the role of a guardian in the service of the forces of good. He is identified with providence. His corrective action is not limited to the punishment of criminals, he acts to feed the hungry, restore peace, and prevent any social disorder. In China, the respect of Tao, the essence of being, is a moral obligation in so far as it contributes to maintaining social order, part of the cosmic order[572]. The emperor, supreme agent of Tao, traces by his action the way of harmonious social life. The Hebrew God, Almighty, Master of the physical world, independent of humans, gives his law to his people and concludes with them an alliance that establishes an objective order of justice[573]. Moslems owe total obedience to God[574]. Their theocratic empire on earth supervises the action of the subjects whose main concern should be to save their souls in contemplation of a reward after death. Christianity is the agent of good offering through society an appropriate framework for eradicating evil and preparing humans for paradise. Terrestrial legislation should respect divine prescriptions[575].

66. The Athenian democracy departs from the practice of seeking a good that transcends the world[576]. In Athens, personal morality is certainly determined by reference to *hubris*, the arrogance by which man exceeds his limits, calling down on him divine punishment. But public life in Athens was not directed

571. See *supra* § 25.
572. See *supra* § 40.
573. See *supra* §§ 28, 29.
574. See *supra* § 37.
575. See *supra* §§ 45, 46.
576. See *supra* §§ 30-32.

towards attainment of a transcendent good. The public good was conceived and measured in terms of the prosperity of the city and its citizens. The Greeks did not expect the divine to prescribe to them the rules of their public life. The public domain thus remained apart from the religious sphere. Laws reflected practical concerns. Rome, which underwent a similar evolution, established a system of government with the major concern of securing within it a balance between the political and social forces, with the aim of maintaining order while preserving the privileges of the patrician class[577]. Ancient Rome and Athens were pious societies which, fearing the wrath of the gods, punished those who offended against religious beliefs and displeased the gods. But their leaders were not seen as agents of a divine power, implementing divine prescriptions on earth. They did not care about the salvation of souls and did not define their action in terms of a cosmic principle providing the measure of their success. Their program was the defence of their homeland, social peace, prosperity, and the means they employed to achieve this, besides ritual sacrifices or common prayers, were publicly debated and rationally chosen, leading to the adoption of a policy which was conducted with practical responsibility and realism.

67. The ideas of justice, order and equilibrium structure all the models we have seen. Justice can prevail only within order and order cannot be built without equilibrium as one of its components. What changes in the models presented is the *underlying ontology* which each time causes them to adopt a different view as to the configuration of equilibrium and justice[578]. In societies which considered justice to reflect physical forces, the world order was unique and the conditions of equilibrium were unique as well. In

577. See *supra* §§ 33-35.

578. WITTGENSTEIN 1961, p. 210, and 2001, p. 75, § 241; GRAYLING 1988, p. 84; GIBBARD 1996, pp. 246 *et seq.*; GLOCK 2003, pp. 250 *et seq.*; see *infra* §163.

theocratic societies aspiring to the reward after death, equilibrium was established after death by a *Last Judgement* rewarding good and punishing evil done in this world. Finally, according to the democratic and republican models, order is generated by balancing the power of all citizens, who, more or less satisfied, engaged in the interplay of forces in society in such a way as to make a reasonable profit. In cosmological models the forces of nature, gods and humans are all in the same arena, the order is global and the equilibrium is composed of all aspects of the world, material or not. In the theocratic models the actor in chief is God himself, justice is mainly his affair, order is established by securing observance of his will, and equilibrium is achieved when divine justice restores order in the *Last Judgment*. The role of humans is to collaborate humbly in the plan of God, to reflect his order in their societies, to carry out his justice. In the democratic and republican models, finally, the actors are the citizens of the city, the order in question is social and political, and justice only applies to conflicts between the actors. Gods are respected, but they do not themselves govern the city.

68. Depending on the approach adopted in relation to reality, the meaning of life changes and with it the idea of justice. In Pharaoh's Egypt it was necessary to devote significant working time to feeding the gods[579]. In the Judeo-Christian universe, an entity distinct from the body, the soul, obtains priority in the satisfaction of its needs[580]. In Athenian democracy, arbitrariness is discerned as the desire to be regarded as superior compared to other citizens[581]. The arrival of modern times in the West is marked by the scientific explanation of the world, the self-sufficiency of reason in elucidating the idea of good, the conception of the human

579. See *supra* § 15.
580. See *supra* §§ 28, 29, 45, 46.
581. See *supra* § 31.

being as an autonomous subject, whose interests are the basis for any conception of justice[582]. The central idea that emerges from all models of justice, however, is similar: it is in the interest of men and women governed under these models to submit themselves to their domination not only to avoid punishment, but also to draw benefit from them. Order emerging from a general equilibrium is by definition good and the models presented claim, each for its part, to establish and maintain the best equilibrium possible. Men and women subject to it were convinced that it was in their interest to be governed in that way. But when food was scarce, when violence thrived, and arbitrariness became the rule, people rose against the explanations of the world they had been living under and asked for another kind of justice[583]. All models claim to be effective in meeting the basic needs of their subjects in their ceaseless struggle against arbitrariness, and to be a bulwark against the forces of disorder that threaten society. All models advance an ideology giving meaning to the life of their subjects, and obtain in return their allegiance to the project of cooperative action that they implement.

582. See *supra* §§ 54, 55, 61.

583. See *supra* §§ 16, 19.

PART II

Case-Studies on Justice and Equilibriums

INTRODUCTION

69. Three observations, related to the origins, the holders and the domain of human rights, indicate that the idea of justice cannot be entirely identified with them. Between the French and the United Nations Declaration of human rights, several new rights appeared under the generic denomination of human rights, emerging as a reaction to the excesses of capitalism or to totalitarian rule. They were not generated as a logical extension of existing rights, but rather as a fitting response to new social conditions[584]. Furthermore, from John Locke and Jean-Jacques Rousseau to John Rawls and Jürgen Habermas, political philosophy relating to human rights has focused on the idea that these rights are specific to human beings[585]. To add to human rights, as advocated by a strand of contemporary thought, the rights of animals, life or nature would obviously mean that human rights cannot be considered the only foundation of justice[586]. Finally, human rights have been designed to address specific abuses of state power, and as such they reflect obligations of the state. Human rights are not about right and wrong in every kind of human relation, as they do not cover all relations between individuals where state power is not involved. These three observations suggest that there must be something that transcends human rights explaining the process of their proliferation, something which should be more profound, more inclusive and more extended than they are.

In the second part of this work, we propose to scrutinize features of justice with a view to better understanding both the

584. See *supra* §§ 57, 60, 61.

585. See *supra* §§ 132, 139, 140, 141.

586. See *supra* § 129.

history set out in the first part of this book and the social arrangements which surround us in our daily life. As we have seen in the previous pages, equality, liberty and the pursuit of happiness, the imperatives on which human rights are focussed, are in permanent search of a right balance. A delicate equilibrium, that is always being called in question, has to be constantly established among them. We will thus focus on the close relations between equilibrium and justice which invite us to deepen our study.

70. The second part of this book consists of three chapters. In the first, *Judges' Balancing Exercise,* we will study a number of judgments in respect of the conditions for striking a fair balance between conflicting interests. All the judgments were delivered in matters concerning the protection of human rights. Human rights are flexible principles, stated generally in a vague way; their application to concrete cases is not automatic. Courts of justice in democratic countries deal daily with problems of reconciling conflicting human rights. In doing so, the judges indicate the components of the balancing exercise, as will be presented in the first chapter. In a second chapter, *The Calculus of Social Harmonization,* we will study social situations where justice emerges as a product of factors allowing the right choice to be made. What we propose to study here is how justice emerges as a result of a process of confrontation and conciliation between interacting interests and values. We will note in this context the reasons why men decide to abandon their dispute, being satisfied with the solution given. Finally, in the third chapter, *Equilibrating the Forces of Attraction and Repulsion,* we will seek an approach that will enable us to judge how far our concrete findings can be validated on the basis of generally applicable principles. The problem that concerns us is in fact the search for a solution where two or more autonomous entities interact, developing their own power of attraction and repulsion. Modern science deals with such situations in various areas, and the conclusions drawn from the researches made, centred around the idea of equilibrium, may be used as an adequate basis for drawing further conclusions.

4

Jusdges' Balancing Exercise

71. The present chapter deals with judgments delivered by the European Court of Human Rights and the Supreme Court of the United States over controversies on the protection of human rights. These Courts enjoy great authority as their jurisdiction extends over more than one billion people and their judgments enjoy broad notoriety thanks to the publicity which is given to them. In addition, the legal reasoning underlying their decisions is, by settled tradition, sufficiently explicit to allow their readers to have access to the reasoning followed by judges in their rulings. We will thus present ten judgments grouped in five sub-units (relevance, weighing, proportionality, coherence and equilibrium), each one corresponding to a specific component of the balancing exercise. These five components are not independent of one another; they correspond to aggregate requirements of the search for justice and should, in principle, all be met for a legal decision to be really correct. The cases presented illustrate, for their part, a particular aspect of each of these requirements. The objective of the chapter is to show that, in the cases studied, the judges employ techniques which indicate the existence of an *underlying structure*, which guides their thinking as they discover the right solution.

Selecting what Matters

72. In its ruling of June 26, 1997 (*Washington, et al.* versus *Harold Gluckberg*[587]), the Supreme Court of the United States decided on *"the right to commit suicide which includes in itself the right to be assisted to commit suicide"*. The plaintiffs argued that recognition of such a right would be the logical consequence of the principles already upheld by the Court, on the one hand, in the case of cessation of medical treatment at the request of the parents of a patient in a chronic vegetative state and, on the other hand, in the case of non-therapeutic abortion. These arguments based on the respect of human dignity and personal autonomy were countered by the State of Washington relying on its interest in preserving human life, by prohibiting assisted suicide which could degenerate into uncontrollable abuses.

The majority opinion of the Court examined first whether the interests of the State of Washington in protecting life in the way it did was reasonably linked to the promotion and protection of a legitimate objective of government and it found, in this respect, that the State had indeed *"an interest in protecting vulnerable groups - including the poor, the elderly and disabled persons - from abuse, neglect and mistakes"*. It then observed that, according to the statistics, 95% of individuals who commit suicide were suffering from a serious mental illness at the time of death, or bodily pain that was an uncontrolled risk factor for their decision to commit suicide and that many patients had withdrawn their request for euthanasia when their pain had faded. In addition, the opinion referred to a series of data drawn from a report issued by the Government of the Netherlands, a country where euthanasia is legal. There were 2300 cases of euthanasia in 1990, 400 cases of assisted suicide and more than 1000 cases of euthanasia on explicit request. In addition to these 1000 cases, 4941 cases were recorded in which a lethal dose of

587. 521 U.S. 702; see AMAR 2012, pp.123-124; NOWAK, ROTUNDA 2007, pp. 518-519.

morphine had been administered without the prior permission of the patient. The judges were thus able to perceive an important risk: *"If physician-assisted suicide were permitted, many might resort to it to spare their families the substantial financial burden of end of life health care costs"*. According to the majority opinion, the litigant State may have a legitimate fear that permission to assisted suicide will open the way to involuntary euthanasia. In other words, the *risk of abusing* assisted suicide by turning it into involuntary euthanasia is the element which justifies, in the eyes of the majority of the Court, the impugned prohibition.

73. In its decision of May 17, 1954 (*Brown* versus *Board of Education*[588]), the Supreme Court of the United States condemned the education system of segregation between blacks and whites, applied by certain States of the Union. The text to be interpreted was a provision of the 14th amendment to the Constitution of the United States, which provides that the States shall not deny to any person within their jurisdiction the equal protection of laws. According to the arguments of the applicants, schools which segregate blacks and whites operate in violation of the principle of equal protection by the law. The argument of their opponents, who drew support from the doctrine *"separate but equal"*, consisted in making the point that insofar as the schools for blacks are equal to the schools for whites in respect of tangible elements of evaluation (qualifications and experience of the teachers, course of studies, pupils per class, means of transport, buildings, equipment), the question of equality before the law did not arise.

In the statement of reasons for its decision, the Court observes that education has become the most important function within the remits of States and local authorities, and notes that it is doubtful if a child to whom the opportunity of education is de-

588. 347 U.S. 483; see AMAR 2012, pp. 143-151, 211-216.

nied may reasonably be expected to succeed in life. Such an opportunity, when a State decides to offer it, constitutes, says the Court, a right which, as such, must be available to all on the basis of equality. The Court states that, if one separates black children from primary and secondary education solely on the basis of the colour of their skin, one engenders in them a sense of inferiority as to their status in the community which can affect their minds and spirits in a manner which is difficult to recover from. The education system resulting from the principle *"separate but equal"*, by *engendering in black children, because of their race, this sense of inferiority* is incompatible with the principle of non discrimination before the law. The Court holds consequently that separate educational facilities are basically unequal and thus contrary to the Constitution.

74. During the process of adjudicating in a case, it is initially necessary to make a distinction between the elements which come into play and those which must be excluded[589]. A judge seized of a case, after having resolved the admissibility issues[590], must identify which rules, among the whole set of rules that govern the legal order, are relevant to the case before her[591]. She must then make a choice, from among the judgments of courts called on to interpret them, to find the judgments that are most relevant[592]. Moreover, several facts are adduced by the parties[593], which according to them, play a determining role in the application of the rules governing the case[594]. There, too, the judge has to make choices. She will find that some facts relied on by the parties are not related to

589. U.S.A. Supr. Court, 12 Juin, 2008, *Boumediene* v. *Bush*, III.
590. U.S.A. Supr. Court, 24 July 1974, *U.S.* v. *Nixon*, I, II.
591. ECHR, 30 Jan. 1998, *Unified Communist Party of Turkey* v. *Turkey*, §§ 24, 25.
592. ECHR, 23 Febr. 2012, *Creangă* v. *Romania*, §§ 23.
593. ECHR, 17 Febr. 2004, *Maestri* v. *Italy*, §§ 28.
594. ECHR, 15 Febr. 2002, *Iwanczuk* v. *Poland*, §§ 57.

the case[595], that others are connected in a secondary way[596], and that some of them play indeed a significant role[597]. Any operation of delivering justice is necessarily made up of such elements[598]. The judge, in order to provide a proper statement of reasons for her decision, has to present the elements informing her thinking and entitling her to reach the conclusion she has adopted.

As regards case-law specific to human rights, where the judges enjoy a wide margin of discretion, the detailed reasoning in the Courts' judgments help us better to realise the importance of relevance in the decision-making process. Relevance refers to all the elements, normative or factual, which weigh in a case. However, it often happens that a limited number of them, sometimes even one of them[599], may *make the difference* in the reasoning of the judge.

595. U.S.A. Supr. Court, 13 June 2013, *Association for Molecular Pathology* v. *Myriad Genetics*, III: "*It is important to note what is not implicated by this decision. First, there are no method claims before this Court. Had Myriad created an innovative method of manipulating genes while searching for the BRCA1 and BRCA2 genes, it could possibly have sought a method patent. But the processes used by Myriad to isolate DNA were well understood by geneticists at the time of Myriad's patents "were well understood, widely used, and fairly uniform insofar as any scientist engaged in the search for a gene would likely have utilized a similar approach,"* and are not at issue in this case. Similarly, this case does not involve patents on new applications of knowledge about the BRCA1 and BRCA2 genes. Judge Bryson aptly noted that, *"[a]s the first party with knowledge of the [BRCA1 and BRCA2] sequences, Myriad was in an excellent position to claim applications of that knowledge. Many of its unchallenged claims are limited to such applications." Nor do we consider the patentability of DNA in which the order of the naturally occurring nucleotides has been altered. Scientific alteration of the genetic code presents a different inquiry, and we express no opinion about the application of §101 to such endeavors. We merely hold that genes and the information they encode are not patent eligible under §101 simply because they have been isolated from the surrounding genetic material."*

596. U.S.A. Supr. Court, 23 May 2011, *Brown* v. *Plata*, II, B, 3.

597. ECHR, 17 Dec. 2004, *Cumpănă* v. *Romania*, § 100.

598. SCALIA, GARNER 2012, pp. 1-3.

599. U.S.A. Supr. Court, 13 June 2013, *Association for Molecular Pathology* v. *Myriad Genetics*, III, B: *"In Chakrabarty, scientists added four plasmids to a bac-*

What determined the decision of the Court in the *Brown* case, as we have just seen, was the detection of a *psychological element*, the sense of inferiority engendered in the minds and spirits of black children attending *"separated but equal"* schools[600]. It described a state of reality incompatible with the requirements which flow from the principle of equality of all before the law. In the case of euthanasia, the judges noted, in view of the evidence before them, that assistance to suicide could be transformed into forced suicide[601]. They thus held that this *risk factor*, which was impossible to circumvent, constituted the element providing sufficient justification for their decision.

---

terium, which enabled it to break down various components of crude oil. The Court held that the modified bacterium was patentable. It explained that the patent claim was "not to a hitherto unknown natural phenomenon, but to a non-naturally occurring manufacture or composition of matter—a product of human ingenuity 'having a distinctive name, character [and] use.'" (...) The Chakrabarty bacterium was new "with markedly different characteristics from any found in nature," 447 U.S., at 310, due to the additional plasmids and resultant "capacity for degrading oil." In this case, by contrast, Myriad did not create anything. To be sure, it found an important and useful gene, but separating that gene from its surrounding genetic material is not an act of invention."

600. U.S.A. Supr. Court, 17 May 1954, *Brown* v. *Board of Education*: *"We come then to the question presented: Does segregation of children in public schools solely on the basis of race, even though the physical facilities and other "tangible" factors may be equal, deprive the children of the minority group of equal educational opportunities? We believe that it does. (...) To separate them from others of similar age and qualifications solely because of their race generates a feeling of inferiority as to their status in the community that may affect their hearts and minds in a way unlikely ever to be undone".*

601. U.S.A. Supr. Court, 26 June 1997, *Washington* v. *Gluckberg*, II: *"The State's interest here goes beyond protecting the vulnerable from coercion; it extends to protecting disabled and terminally ill people from prejudice, negative and inaccurate stereotypes, and societal indifference. The State's assisted suicide ban reflects and reinforces its policy that the lives of terminally ill, disabled, and elderly people must be no less valued than the lives of the young and healthy, and that a seriously disabled person's suicidal impulses should be interpreted and treated the same way as anyone else's. Finally, the State may fear that permitting assisted suicide will start it down the path to voluntary and perhaps even involuntary euthanasia".*

Weighting the Relevant Elements

75. The case of *EB* versus *France* (judgment of the European Court of Human Rights, January 22, 2008)[602], concerned the refusal of an application to adopt a child. The request for approval was rejected by the administration on the basis of the lack of paternal reference in the life of the applicant, a lady living in a stable relationship with a person of the same sex, and the refusal of the latter to get involved in the project. The national authorities did not base themselves on the sexual orientation of the applicant in order to reject her application; they however took into account her *"life conditions"* in their decision to refuse her request.

The European Court of Human Rights conducted a detailed analysis of the component elements of the case. There were elements in favour of the applicant: first, French legislation allowed the adoption of a child even by an unmarried person, thus accepting implicitely the adoption of a child by a homosexual; and second, as to the human and educational qualities of the applicant, she herself was a kindergarten teacher. There were essentially two elements against her: first, the lack of paternal reference in her environment, considered by the authorities as an essential criterium for adoption; and, second, the ambiguity of the commitment, or the indifference, of the person with whom the interested party lived, to the proposed adoption. The Court lessened, initially, the weight given by the French authorities to the first reason for the refusal based on the lack of paternal reference. The Court noted that French law allows the adoption of children by unmarried persons, and thus also by women living alone, and that requiring a paternal reference for women applying for approval, would indirectly deny them a right which the law grants them[603]. Moreover, regarding the re-

602. ECHR, no 43546/02.

603. ECHR, 22 Jan. 2008, *E.B.* v. *France*, §§ 94, 95: *"The Court points out that French law allows single persons to adopt a child (...), thereby opening up the*

quirement of a male presence in the life of the child to be adopted, the Court finds that this position is not supported by studies demonstrating its merits, making its relevance doubtful. The Court then considered that the second reason for refusal, based on the lack of a clear commitment by the applicant's partner to her proposal to adopt a child, was an important factor that weighs against the grant of approval. However, the Court observed that in the decision taken by the authorities this reason was not stated as being determinant in itself to justifying the refusal. It was taken into account as one of the overall elements weighed to the detriment of the applicant.

This allowed the Court to re-evaluate the elements selected by the French authorities to support their refusal. The Court invalidated the argument based on the lack of a paternal reference, by adducing legal and scientific data. As for the lack of commitment by the partner, it finds that this argument, which is advanced in combination with the others and not as determinant by itself, is tainted by the discriminatory attitude against homosexuals, which is clearly apparent from the file. The *value allocated* by the authorities to the elements selected to support their decision was incorrect. The Court consequently upheld the applicant's claim.

76. *Nilsen and Johnsen* versus *Norway* (judgement of the European Court of Human Rights, November 25, 1999[604]) was a libel

possibility of adoption by a single homosexual, which is not disputed. Against the background of the domestic legal provisions, it considers that the reasons put forward by the Government cannot be regarded as particularly convincing and weighty such as to justify refusing to grant the applicant authorisation. The Court notes, lastly, that the relevant provisions of the Civil Code are silent as to the necessity of a referent of the other sex, which would not, in any event, be dependent on the sexual orientation of the adoptive single parent. In this case, moreover, the applicant presented, in the terms of the judgment of the Conseil d'État, undoubted personal qualities and an aptitude for bringing up children, which were assuredly in the child's best interests, a key notion in the relevant international instruments (...)".

604. ECHR, no. 23118/93.

case in the context of a wider case on police brutality. There was first a study into police brutality in Bergen by a student, a summary of which was published in 1981. The emotion aroused by this publication led the Minister of Justice to form a commission of inquiry, composed of a law professor, Mr. B and a lawyer in the Supreme Court. In their report published in 1982 the investigators concluded that, according to the most careful estimates, the extent of police brutality in Bergen was alarming. In 1986 Mr B published a book on police brutality. His thesis was related primarily to the idea of *"false honesty"* of the police officers who, although witnesses to cases of excessive and illegal use of force, covered officials responsible for abuses by delivering false testimony. In spring 1987, Mr. B published a new book in which he repeated his thesis on the false honesty of the police officers of Bergen. Two statements of the first applicant, then president of the Association of Norwegian police, were respectively disclosed in the press about the publications made by Mr. B: *"In my opinion, these private investigations are a form of chicanery". "The Association of the Norwegian police officers will not accept (...) private investigations carried out on a large scale by dilettantes in order to manufacture allegations of police brutality which are then made public".* The second applicant, in his capacity as president of the Bergen Police Association, was interviewed by a newspaper. He described the report on police brutality in Bergen as *"pure misinformation"*, while declaring on the intentions of the professor: *"there must have been ulterior motives. It seems that the purpose (...) was to undermine confidence in the police".* In 1988, the Police Association and the Norwegian section of Bergen brought against Mr B defamation proceedings, while in May 1989 Mr B, for his part, brought a libel action against the applicants for their statements cited above. In 1992, the police officers desisted from their action, but Mr B refused to desist. The Norwegian court upheld the action for defamation against the two officers.

This judgment was brought before the European Court of Human Rights. In its decision on the case, the Court weighed a series of elements that it considered relevant. First, the incriminating statements, which had a factual basis[605], were delivered orally by the applicants and subsequently reported by the press. The Court notes in this respect that the applicants did not have the time necessary to reflect on them and possibly to correct them. The Court finds that the contested statements were all expressed by the applicants as representatives of the trade-union interests and their declarations at issue were formulated in answer to allegations discrediting the practices and integrity of the profession. The Court combines this element with the general context of the case: a constant and impassioned debate having raised great public interest and the nub of the debate, police brutality, which constitutes a subject of general interest. Moreover, another element attracted the attention of the Court. The remarks made by the applicants were in

605. ECHR, 25 Nov. 1999, *Nilsen* v. *Norway*, § 51: *"(...) In so far as the said statements implied that Mr B had misinformed about police violence and fabricated allegations of such misconduct, there existed at the material time certain objective factors supporting the applicants' questioning of Mr B's investigations. The libel action brought by Mr No and Mr V in respect of allegations of lies in certain newspaper articles had been unsuccessful and the Prosecutor General's criminal investigations of the Bergen police had reached the overall conclusion that the various allegations of police brutality were unfounded (...). In the ensuing "boomerang cases" a number of informers had been convicted of false accusations against the police. It is true that the manner of conduct of those proceedings gave rise to criticism, notably by Mr B himself. The Court is also mindful of the differences as to focus, approach and evidentiary standards between these investigations and those conducted by Mr B. The Court is further aware that in the libel case against the applicants the City Court observed that the occurrence of unlawful use of force by the Bergen police had been established during the hearings before it and that, although this concerned very few police officers, the extent of the misconduct was problematic (...). It remains, however, that at the time when the Norwegian courts adjudicated the applicants' case (...) there was some factual basis for their statements to the effect that false and fabricated allegations of police brutality had been made. This is not altered by the fact that the Supreme Court subsequently reopened the "boomerang cases" and acquitted the defendants".*

the nature of a response to the writings and statements of the plaintiff on the behaviour of the police officers. The complainant himself had accused the police officers of misinformation and he described the situation in the police station in Bergen as constituting false honesty by deliberately dissimulating reality. The Court considers that these elements in favour of the applicants were *not allocated the appropriate value* by the Norwegian court when judgment was given against the applicants. There was therefore an inaccuracy in the evaluation of the elements of the case which leads the Court to conclude that a fair balance was not struck in the solution arrived at.

77. We mentioned above[606] that a number of relevant normative and factual elements constitute the primary material of the reasoning on justice matters. Concerning relevant facts, the primary judicial operation is to evaluate their truth value. In this case, evaluation is deciding on the accuracy of fact statements in a binary way, by accepting or refusing their truth. Criminal proceedings are mainly focused on truth issues[607], but justice on facts is not all about their truth as the two cases presented above indicate. Once the truth value of facts is established, another evaluation takes place: judges should allocate to the facts *the value they deserve*[608]. In the universe of law, units of measurement are directly provided by legal provisions, which lay down rules of right conduct[609].

Weighing calls for a specific evaluation of all the relevant elements of a case[610] in order subsequently to balance each one of them in favour or to the detriment of the opposing parties in a case[611].

606. See *supra* § 74.
607. ECHR, 13 Dec. 2012, *El-Masri* v. *FYROM*, §§ 151-153.
608. ECHR, 3 Nov. 2011, *S.H.* v. *Austria*, §106.
609. See *infra* § 159.
610. ECHR, 16 Nov. 2010, *Perdigao* v. *Portugal*, §§ 68, 74, 75.
611. ECHR, 8 July 1999, *Polat* v. *Turkey*, §§ 46, 47, 48.

In a first stage, the relevant elements identified are evaluated to assess the weight to be attached to them individually[612] and, in a second stage, an assessment takes place that determines the relative value to be accorded to each of these elements compared to the others[613]. Justice arises in the form of a decision accurately weighing the various concurring and conflicting elements of a case[614].

Weighing operations appear in a comprehensive manner in court judgments delivered in respect of human rights[615]. As we can observe, in the two judgments presented above, judges differentiate the relevant elements of a case and then try to evaluate them by using the normative elements to hand. We have seen that in the adoption case, the judges invalidated the weighing conclusions reached by the national authorities, after reassessing themselves the value of the two elements playing against the applicant[616]. In

612. ECHR, 12 Apr. 2006, *Martinie* v. *France*, § 43.

613. ECHR, 22 Apr. 2003, *Animal Defenders International* v. *U.K.*, § 124.

614. See *infra* §§ 163, 164; see SCALIA, GARNER 2012, pp. 44-46 on how to evaluate the relevant normative elements when construing a legal text.

615. ECHR, 27 Apr. 2010, *Tanase* v. *Moldova*, §§ 171-179; see *infra* § 102 *in fine*.

616. ECHR, *E.B.* v. *France*, §§ 75-85: *"(...) In the Court's view, the second ground relied on by the domestic authorities, based on the attitude of the applicant's partner, calls for a different approach. Although she was the long-standing and declared partner of the applicant, Ms R. did not feel committed by her partner's application to adopt (...). Nonetheless, these two main grounds form part of an overall assessment of the applicant's situation. For this reason, the Court considers that they should not be considered alternatively, but concurrently. Consequently, the illegitimacy of one of the grounds has the effect of contaminating the entire decision. (...) The Court therefore notes that the administrative courts went to some lengths to rule that although regard had been had to the applicant's sexual orientation, it had not been the basis for the decision in question and had not been considered from a hostile position of principle. However, in the Court's opinion the fact that the applicant's homosexuality featured to such an extent in the reasoning of the domestic authorities is significant. Besides their considerations regarding the applicant's "lifestyle", they above all confirmed the decision of the president of the council for the département. The Court points out that*

the defamation case, we observed how the judges, by giving more value to some elements of the case than the national authorities did, arrived at the conclusion that the impugned decision could not be justified[617]. Judges didn't give arirthmetical values to their assessments. But there was clearly a negative or positive value attached to each one of their evaluations.

the latter reached his decision in the light of the opinion given by the adoption board whose various members had expressed themselves individually in writing, mainly recommending, with reasons in support of that recommendation, that the application be refused on the basis of the two grounds in question. It observes that the manner in which certain opinions were expressed was indeed revealing in that the applicant's homosexuality was a determining factor. In particular, the Court notes that in his opinion of 12 October 1998 the psychologist from the children's welfare service recommended that authorisation be refused, referring to, among other things, an "unusual attitude [on the part of the applicant] to men in that men are rejected".

617. ECHR, 25 Nov. 1999, *Nilsen* v. *Norway*, §§ 52-53: *"However, bearing in mind that the applicants were, in their capacity as elected representatives of professional associations, responding to criticism of the working methods and ethics within the profession, the Court considers that, in weighing the interests of free speech against those of protection of reputation under the necessity test in Article 10 § 2 of the Convention, greater weight should be attached to the plaintiff's own active involvement in a lively public discussion than was done by the national courts when applying national law (...). The statements at issue were directly concerned with the plaintiff's contribution to that discussion. In the Court's view, a degree of exaggeration should be tolerated in the context of such a heated and continuing public debate of affairs of general concern, where on both sides professional reputations were at stake. (...) At the heart of the long and heated public discussion was the question of the truth of allegations of police violence and there was factual support for the assumption that false allegations had been made by informers. The statements in question essentially addressed this issue and the admittedly harsh language in which they were expressed was not incommensurate with that used by the injured party who, since an early stage, had participated as a leading figure in the debate. Accordingly, the Court finds that the resultant interference with the applicants' exercise of their freedom of expression was not supported by sufficient reasons in terms of Article 10 and was disproportionate to the legitimate aim of protecting the reputation of Mr B. There has thus been a violation of Article 10 of the Convention".*

No Less, no More

78. The cases *Grutter* versus *Bollingers* and *Gratz versus Bollingers* (decisions of the Supreme Court of the United States of June 23, 2003[618]), concerned complaints by candidates for enrolment at University, whose applications were rejected as a result, according to the plaintiffs, of the policy of positive racial discrimination pursued by the university authorities. The selection systems challenged by the plaintiffs had in common that they were inspired by the desire to create a diverse student body, not only based on race, but also on other elements, such as the place of residence of candidates, the specific circumstances of their lives, their talents or their abilities. However, the two cases presented different features as to the articulation and the weighting of the selection criteria applied. According to the system challenged in the *Gratz* case (College of Literature, Science and Arts of the University of Michigan), the candidates belonging to an underrepresented racial or ethnic group (African Americans, Latinos, Native Americans) could get 20 points on the scale of 100 points required for admission. In the *Grutter* case (Faculty of Law of the University of Michigan), the disputed system provided that the African American, Latino and Native American candidates assessed individually could, because of their origin, obtain an advantage compared to other candidates, in the same way as a white candidate having artistic or leadership qualities or having overcome particular personal difficulties could also obtain an advantage. This system required, however, that individuals from underrepresented ethnic groups should constitute a *critical mass* to facilitate interracial understanding and eliminate stereotypical thinking that persons of different race and ethnic groups have fixed qualities and defects[619].

618. 539 U.S. 306 (*Grutter*), 539 U.S. 244 (*Gratz*); BREYER 2007, pp. 109 *et seq.*; NOWAK, ROTUNDA 2007, pp. 431-436.

619. SANDEL 2007, pp. 243 *et seq.*; NOWAK, ROTUNDA 2007, pp. 395 *et seq.* DIMITRAKOPOULOS 2007, pp. 906 *et seq.*, 910 *et seq.*

The Court accepted that the creation of a diverse student body, in which an element of diversity is the racial or ethnic diversity of students, is amongst the legitimate aims that university authorities can pursue in order to facilitate interracial understanding and combat stereotypes. It remained to be seen whether the disputed systems, while working towards a legitimate end, were at the same time well structured to reach it without producing unnecessary discrimination. In the *Gratz* case, the Court found that the principle of proportionality was not observed. Automatically allotting 20 points to the black, Latino or Amerindian candidates, where 100 points were necessary for their admission, was, the Court held, giving them a decisive advantage, while those 20 points could not be offset by the qualities that the other candidates could have. The Court underlined in this respect that a white candidate having the extraordinary artistic qualities of a Picasso could not obtain, as a result of the assessment of his talent, more than a maximum of 5 points, whereas an Afro-American candidate, without any other effort, would obtain, just because of skin colour, 20 points[620]. As for the disputed system in the *Grutter* case, the majority of the Court

620. U.S.A. Supr. Court, 23 June 2003, *Gratz* v. *Bollingers*, II B: *"Even if student C's "extraordinary artistic talent" rivalled that of Monet or Picasso, the applicant would receive, at most, five points under the LSA's system. At the same time, every single underrepresented minority applicant, including students A and B, would automatically receive 20 points for submitting an application. Clearly, the LSA's system does not offer applicants the individualized selection process described in Harvard's example. Instead of considering how the differing backgrounds, experiences, and characteristics of students A, B, and C might benefit the University, admissions counsellors reviewing LSA applications would simply award both A and B 20 points because their applications indicate that they are African-American, and student C would receive up to 5 points for his "extraordinary talent." (...) We conclude, therefore, that because the University's use of race in its current freshman admissions policy is not narrowly tailored to achieve respondents' asserted compelling interest in diversity, the admissions policy violates the Equal Protection Clause of the Fourteenth Amendment. (...) Accordingly, we reverse that portion of the District Court's decision granting respondents summary judgment with respect to liability and remand the case for proceedings consistent with this opinion."*

judged differently. Within this system, the majority considered, each candidate was assessed individually without quotas set in advance. Diversity was not limited to race or ethnicity; each candidate had to explain in an essay in what way he could contribute to diversity and each candidate was assessed by the selection board as to their potential to contribute to the diversity of the student body[621]. The majority of the Court also found that the critical mass requirement sufficiently served the aim in view, being well

621. U.S.A. Supr. Court, 23 June 2003, *Grutter* v. *Bollingers*, III B: *"Here, the Law School engages in a highly individualized, holistic review of each applicant's file, giving serious consideration to all the ways an applicant might contribute to a diverse educational environment. The Law School affords this individualized consideration to applicants of all races. There is no policy, either de jure or de facto, of automatic acceptance or rejection based on any single "soft" variable. Unlike the program at issue in Gratz v. Bollinger, ante, the Law School awards no mechanical, predetermined diversity "bonuses" based on race or ethnicity. (...) The Law School does not, however, limit in any way the broad range of qualities and experiences that may be considered valuable contributions to student body diversity. To the contrary, the 1992 policy makes clear "[t]here are many possible bases for diversity admissions," and provides examples of admittees who have lived or travelled widely abroad, are fluent in several languages, have overcome personal adversity and family hardship, have exceptional records of extensive community service, and have had successful careers in other fields. The Law School seriously considers each "applicant's promise of making a notable contribution to the class by way of a particular strength, attainment, or characteristic - e.g., an unusual intellectual achievement, employment experience, non-academic performance, or personal background." All applicants have the opportunity to highlight their own potential diversity contributions through the submission of a personal statement, letters of recommendation, and an essay describing the ways in which the applicant will contribute to the life and diversity of the Law School. What is more, the Law School actually gives substantial weight to diversity factors besides race. The Law School frequently accepts nonminority applicants with grades and test scores lower than underrepresented minority applicants (and other nonminority applicants) who are rejected. This shows that the Law School seriously weighs many other diversity factors besides race that can make a real and dispositive difference for nonminority applicants as well. By this flexible approach, the Law School sufficiently takes into account, in practice as well as in theory, a wide variety of characteristics besides race and ethnicity that contribute to a diverse student body"*; see NOWAK, ROTUNDA 2007, pp. 414 *et seq.*

designed for this purpose, as by the enrolment of the adequate number of black, Latino or Amerindian students in the University, students of racial or ethnic communities could be expected by themselves to be diversified enough *to dismantle stereotypes* as to their qualities and defects.

79. *Refah Partisi and Others* versus *Turkey* (judgment of the European Court of Human Rights, February 18, 2003[622]) was about a decision of the Turkish Constitutional Court ordering the dissolution of a political party for activity contrary to the Constitution, the forfeiture of five members of this party as members of the parliament, and their banishment from any political activity for a period of five years.

Before the European Court of Human Rights, the case was discussed in terms of freedom of association. The essence of the debate focused on whether there were compelling reasons of general interest that justified the drastic measures taken by the Turkish authorities. The Court lengthily examined the objections which weighed against the dissolved party[623]. First, on the plurality of legal systems it professed, the Court held that the establishment of legal systems to which individuals would adhere according to their religion, would lead to a breakdown of society into several autonomous communities and to a breach of equality of individuals before the law as a result of their being subject to different systems of rights and freedoms according to their religious affiliation. The

622. ECHR, nos 41340/98, 41342/98, 41343/98 and 41344/98.

623. ECHR, 18 Febr. 2003, *Refah Partisi* v. *Turkey*, § 132: *"In making an overall assessment of the points it has just listed above in connection with its examination of the question whether there was a pressing social need for the interference in issue in the present case, the Court finds that the acts and speeches of Refah's members and leaders cited by the Constitutional Court were imputable to the whole of the party, that those acts and speeches revealed Refah's long-term policy of setting up a regime based on sharia within the framework of a plurality of legal systems and that Refah did not exclude recourse to force in order to implement its policy and keep the system it envisaged in place".*

Court condemned, secondly, the introduction of Islamic religious law, the *sharia*, as a normative system governing the lives of Muslims in Turkey. It considered that the *sharia* is contrary to the democratic principle according to which laws governing rights and freedoms of individuals are not the reflection of a dogmatic order, forever fixed, but emanate from the synthesis of a plurality of approaches operated within a society open to the discussion of ideas and to change. Finally, the Court considered incompatible with democracy, based on the peaceful confrontation of ideas, the recourse to force as a means of imposition of political will, as professed in statements made by several dignitaries of the party, never disapproved by the party's official authorities and even honoured by the attribution to them of responsible posts within the party.

The Court, after the above evaluations, assessed the proportionality of the measures taken in relation to the objective in view. The imposed sanctions, dissolution of a great governing party, forfeiture of five of its deputies, temporary banishment of these five people from public life, were serious. But what was at stake was also serious. It was about the very life of democracy as the foundation of human rights protection in Turkey. In this respect, there was a feature that made the case exceptional. The dissolved party was a party of government which opinion polls predicted would soon acquire an absolute majority in the parliament. There was an imminent danger that *democracy would be replaced by a theocratic regime* where democratic values of society would be suppressed, women would have a lower status compared to men, and opponents would be regarded as violating the word of God. The Court held, consequently, that the impugned measures, though radical, were not disproportionate compared to the imminent danger which threatened democracy, because of the activities of the party dissolved.

80. Proportionality is a rule of rational behaviour[624]; it requires the means for reaching the objective in view to be appro-

624 GILBOA 2010, pp. 5, 6; FAIGMAN 1994, pp. 753 *et seq.*; SWEET 2010, pp. 1 *et seq.*

priate[625]. They will be appropriate when they are *suitable* for reaching the objective in view[626]; *sufficient* for this purpose[627]; and well-tailored to *avoid unjustified burdens*[628]. Legislating or judging are conscious human actions which as such entail the requirement of rationality as to the appropriateness of the means to the objective pursued. If, for instance, the objective pursued is utility[629] or equality[630] or liberty[631], or any other political objective – protection of the environment[632], national security[633] or health protection[634] –, in all cases the means to achieve the objective in view should be selected and articulated using as the criterion their appropriateness for achieving the pursued objective. The quest for proportionality of the means to the objective pursued constitutes the *structuring idea* by which the relevant elements of a lawmaking or judicial operation are selected and articulated in an ordered manner.

This picture, so easy to understand and maybe so attractive, is however too simplistic when we apply it to reality. In terms of justice there are by definition many human interests which interact asking for fair treatment[635]. In the case of the applicants for university admission, the objective pursued by the university authorities was to create a diversified body of students, not for the benefit of specific racial or ethnic groups, but for the good of education as a whole. The objective was legitimate, the Court held, but this was not sufficient to determine the case. White applicants for admis-

625. See *infra* §§ 114, 118, 164; see CHRISTOFFERSEN 2009, pp. 69-75.

626. ECHR, 30 Jan. 1998, *Unified Communist Party of Turkey* v. *Turkey*, § 53, 54, see CHRISTOFFERSEN 2009, pp. 163-165.

627. ECHR, 7 Oct. 2008, *Barb* v. *Romania*, § 37

628. ECHR, 28 Sept. 2010, *Mangouras* v. *Spain*, § 88

629. ECHR, 22 June 2004, *Broniowski* v. *Poland*, §§ 148, 149.

630. ECHR, 26 June 2012, *Kuric* v. *Slovenia*, §§ 390-392.

631. ECHR, 7 June 2012, *CENTRO EUROPA* 7 v. *Italy*, §§134, 156.

632. ECHR, 28 Sept. 2010, *Mangouras* v. *Spain*, § 86.

633. ECHR, 15 March 2012, *Austin* v. *U.K.*, § 66.

634. ECHR, 3 Nov. 2011, *S.H.* v. *Austria*, § 90.

635. ECHR, 7 July 2011, *Stummer* v. *Austria*, §§ 89, 106-109.

sion were complaining that, because of the colour of their skin and although their educational credentials were superior, they were not selected. They therefore claimed that, in their case, the equality principle had been violated[636]. In the case of the Islamic party dissolution, severe measures had been taken against a political organization to protect democracy. There was no doubt that protecting democratic values and processes is a legitimate aim which may justify various sacrifices, but in the specific case, the question was about the excessive nature of the impugned measures[637]. Even if the

636. U.S.A. Supr. Court, 23 June 2003, *Grutter* v. *Bollingers*, III B: "*We acknowledge that there are serious problems of justice connected with the idea of preference itself. Narrow tailoring, therefore, requires that a race-conscious admissions program not unduly harm members of any racial group. Even remedial race-based governmental action generally remains subject to continuing oversight to assure that it will work the least harm possible to other innocent persons competing for the benefit. To be narrowly tailored, a race-conscious admissions program must not unduly burden individuals who are not members of the favored racial and ethnic groups. We are satisfied that the Law School's admissions program does not. Because the Law School considers all pertinent elements of diversity, it can (and does) select nonminority applicants who have greater potential to enhance student body diversity over underrepresented minority applicants*".

637. ECHR, 18 Febr. 2003, *Refah Partisi v. Turkey*, §§ 132-133: "*In view of the fact that these plans were incompatible with the concept of a "democratic society" and that the real opportunities Refah had to put them into practice made the danger to democracy more tangible and more immediate, the penalty imposed on the applicants by the Constitutional Court, even in the context of the restricted margin of appreciation left to Contracting States, may reasonably be considered to have met a "pressing social need". (...) The Court considers in that connection that the nature and severity of the interference are also factors to be taken into account when assessing its proportionality. The Court also notes that the pecuniary damage alleged by the applicants was made up largely of a loss of earnings and is speculative in nature. In view of the low value of Refah's assets, their transfer to the Treasury can have no bearing on the proportionality of the interference in issue. Moreover, the Court observes that the prohibition barring three of the applicants, (...), from engaging in certain types of political activity for a period of five years was temporary, and that, through their speeches and the stances they adopted in their capacity as the chairman and vice-chairmen of the party, they bear the main responsibility for Refah's dissolution. It follows that the interfer-*

dissolved party preached an Islamic ideology, it still was an association under the protection of a freedom guaranteed as a human right by the applicable international convention.

Proportionality requires the decision dealing with conflicting interests to combine in a harmonious whole the appropriateness of the means selected to achieve the objective. In order to be proportional a decision should, not only be adequate to achieve its objective; it should also avoid any burden from being imposed to others without legitimate reason. This second aspect of proportionality raises real difficulties. Which is the *right proportion of sacrifices* to impose to white candidates in order to promote University diversity? And, which is the *right proportion of sanctions* to impose to the members of a political movement in order to save democracy? There were no easy answers to these questions as we have seen above. Subjective assessments are unavoidable in such operations[638]. This is indeed the main reason why proportionality issues on human rights protection are so often decided by the Courts with narrow majorities[639].

Integrating within the Global Order

81. In its ruling of 26 June 2003 (*Lawrence* versus *Texas*[640]), the Supreme Court of the United States reversed its previous ruling of 1986[641] on the criminal treatment of homosexual practices between consenting adults acting in private. To justify the reversal, the

ence in issue in the present case cannot be regarded as disproportionate in relation to the aims pursued".

638. See *infra* §146.

639. ECHR, 13 July 2012, *Raëlien Movement* v. *Switzerland* (majority of one vote).

640. 539 U.S. 558; see NOWAK, ROTUNDA 2007, p. 242-243; DIMITRAKOPOULOS 2007, p. 339.

641. In its 1986 ruling in *Bowers* v. *Hardwick* (478 U.S.186, 1986) regarding the application of a law of the State of Georgia which made sodomy a crime, the U.S.A. Supr. Court said that the U.S. Constitution did not guarantee citizens the right to engage in homosexual practices.

majority opinion of the Court engaged in a major undertaking to place the data of homosexuality criminalization in a new context.

First, the judges reviewed the previous legislation and case-law as at 1986 justifying the solution arrived at that time. They made two observations. On the one hand, they noted that the moral and legal considerations of the nation did not so much condemn homosexuality as such, but rather sodomy as a non-procreative sexual practice, without regard to its character as heterosexual or homosexual. They observed, on the other hand, that laws prohibiting sodomy or homosexuality were applied in the different States of the Union in cases involving paedophile contact, abuse of status or use of violence. Application of these laws to consenting adults acting in private was very rare. Second, the judges examined developments that had occurred since 1986. They noted that within their own jurisdiction, the principle of respect for privacy had been confirmed in respect of cases concerning basic choices regarding privacy of sexual life, such as condom use or the option not to have a child[642]. They further observed that, in 1986, 25 United Union States criminalized sodomy while in 2003 the number was only nine and, even in the States where it is a criminal offence, its enforcement in cases of consenting adults acting in

642. U.S.A. Supr. Court, 26 June 2003, *Lawrence* v. *Texas*, II: "*The present case does not involve minors. It does not involve persons who might be injured or coerced or who are situated in relationships where consent might not easily be refused. It does not involve public conduct or prostitution. It does not involve whether the government must give formal recognition to any relationship that homosexual persons seek to enter. The case does involve two adults who, with full and mutual consent from each other, engaged in sexual practices common to a homosexual lifestyle. The petitioners are entitled to respect for their private lives. The State cannot demean their existence or control their destiny by making their private sexual conduct a crime. Their right to liberty under the Due Process Clause gives them the full right to engage in their conduct without intervention of the government. It is a promise of the Constitution that there is a realm of personal liberty which the government may not enter*".

private is virtually non-existent. They also observed that in the Member States of the Council of Europe homosexual practice was allowed as an aspect of an individual's private life. Finally, the judges faced the arguments which militate for or against the permissibility of the act in question. They considered that the applicants, consenting adults acting in private, harmed nobody. Their act was criminalized because a majority in the State of Texas condemned homosexuality on moral grounds. However, according to the majority opinion of the Court, a *people's majority cannot employ the coercive means of the State to enforce on all citizens its own conceptions of morality.*

82. In its ruling of 11 July 2002 (*Christine Goodwin* versus *United Kingdom*), the European Court of Human Rights reversed its case-law as regards the treatment of transsexuals[643]. X, born in 1937 and recorded in the register of births as a boy on the basis of his external features, rather quickly displayed symptoms of disturbance of his sexual identity. While being diagnosed as a transsexual in the mid Sixties, he married as a man and four children were born of the marriage. He dressed at work as a man and at home as a woman. In the middle of the Eighties, she started to live entirely as a woman, undertook hormonal therapy and a series of surgical operations which led her to change her gender in 1990. The authorities refused to recognize the sex change of X and to correct accordingly their registrations in order to allow her to be considered in her administrative contacts as a lady. Contesting this refusal, X brought the case before the European Court of Human Rights.

The Court in its judgment, first, describes the personal situation of the applicant. It notes the stress which emerges from the

643. In its ruling in a similar case, *Rees* v. *United Kingdom* (no 9532/81, 17 Oct. 1986), the Court, weighing the conflicting interests, ruled that it could not consider imposing on the Defendant State such important positive obligations as a radical change in its system of birth recording (§ 45).

contradiction between her position as a transsexual after being operated on and her status imposed by the legislation which refuses to recognize a sex change. The situation facing transsexuals in Britain is incomprehensible, the Court notes, as it is marked by deep contradictions. Indeed, British legislation, although refusing to recognize sex change, considers however trans-sexuality to be a disorder of the sexual identity and finances its treatment and even the surgical operations which aim at relieving the condition of transsexuals. Turning to the medical and scientific data concerning the issue, the Court notes two certainties: first, trans-sexuality is internationally recognized as a medical condition for which there is a treatment intended to relieve it; secondly, having regard to the suffering endured by persons undergoing a sex change, her decision to change sex cannot be considered to be arbitrary or capricious. As for the state of the European or international consensus on the legal treatment of trans-sexuality, the Court considers that it is necessary to attach less importance to the lack of such a consensus and more to the positive trend, not only towards social acceptance of transsexuals, but also towards legal recognition of the new sexual identity of transsexuals who have undergone surgical gender re-assignment[644]. The Court further measured the impact of any change in its case-law on the system of births registration operated in the United Kingdom. It first

644. ECHR, 11 July 2002, *Goodwin* v. *U.K.*, §§ 100, 101: *"There have been major social changes in the institution of marriage since the adoption of the Convention as well as dramatic changes brought about by developments in medicine and science in the field of trans-sexuality. The Court has found above, under Article 8 of the Convention, that a test of congruent biological factors can no longer be decisive in denying legal recognition to the change of gender of a post-operative transsexual. There are other important factors – the acceptance of the condition of gender identity disorder by the medical professions and health authorities within Contracting States, the provision of treatment including surgery to assimilate the individual as closely as possible to the gender in which they perceive that they properly belong and the assumption by the transsexual of the social role of the assigned gender. The Court would also note that Article 9 of*

notes that exceptions to the historical mode of registration have already been introduced in the case of legitimated and adopted children. It further considers that an exception to cover the 2000 to 5000 people estimated to have undergone the sex change operation in the United Kingdom, does not seem likely to overturn the whole system. After conducting this analysis, the Court finds that, in the 21th century, the right of transsexuals to personal development and to physical and moral security in a full sense, in the way these rights are conferred on others, cannot be seen as a question which requires from the Court more time in order to shed more light on the subject. The Court observes that all the problems raised (birth recording, access to the register, family law and law of inheritance, criminal law, employment, social security) are not insurmountable. It considers, in conclusion, that *society may reasonably be expected to tolerate certain inconveniences* in order *to enable individuals to live in dignity* in accordance with the sexual identity chosen by them at great personal cost[645].

---

the recently adopted Charter of Fundamental Rights of the European Union departs, no doubt deliberately, from the wording of Article 12 of the Convention in removing the reference to men and women (see paragraph 58 above). The right under Article 8 to respect for private life does not however subsume all the issues under Article 12, where conditions imposed by national laws are accorded a specific mention. The Court has therefore considered whether the allocation of sex in national law to that registered at birth is a limitation impairing the very essence of the right to marry in this case. In that regard, it finds that it is artificial to assert that post-operative transsexuals have not been deprived of the right to marry as, according to law, they remain able to marry a person of their former opposite sex. The applicant in this case lives as a woman, is in a relationship with a man and would only wish to marry a man. She has no possibility of doing so. In the Court's view, she may therefore claim that the very essence of her right to marry has been infringed".

645. ECHR, 11 July 2002, *Goodwin* v. *U.K.*, §§ 103: *"It may be noted from the materials submitted by Liberty that though there is widespread acceptance of the marriage of transsexuals, fewer countries permit the marriage of transsexuals in their assigned gender than recognise the change of gender itself. The Court is not persuaded however that this supports an argument for leaving the matter entirely*

83. Discerning the relevant elements of a case, weighing them according to values of justice, and then structuring the whole around the idea of proportionality are not operations isolated one from the other. Justice is a set of components interwoven so as to generate an order[646] allowing for the prediction both the behaviour of others toward us as well as the expectations that others have of us[647]. Thus, justice's solutions may be deemed to be integrated harmoniously in a broader picture, in which earlier solutions coexist with future ones[648]. In this sense, the search for justice is a quest for *coherence*[649]. It obliges the judges to integrate the isolated solution on an issue of justice into the order of justice in which this solution is intended to apply. When a court decides on an issue of justice, it should find the solution which is compatible with the overall framework of rules and principles proper to the legal order in which

to the Contracting States as being within their margin of appreciation. This would be tantamount to finding that the range of options open to a Contracting State included an effective bar on any exercise of the right to marry. The margin of appreciation cannot extend so far. While it is for the Contracting State to determine inter alia the conditions under which a person claiming legal recognition as a transsexual establishes that gender re-assignment has been properly effected or under which past marriages cease to be valid and the formalities applicable to future marriages (including, for example, the information to be furnished to intended spouses), the Court finds no justification for barring the transsexual from enjoying the right to marry under any circumstances".

646. See *infra* § 5.

647. See *infra* §§ 114, 174, 175.

648. DWORKIN 2012, p. 225: *"Law as integrity denies that statements of law are either the backward-looking factual reports of conventionalism or the forward-looking instrumental programs of legal pragmatism. It insists that legal claims are interpretive judgements and therefore combine backward- and forward-looking elements; they interpret contemporary legal practice seen as an unfolding political narrative. So law as integrity rejects as unhelpful the ancient question whether judges find or invent the law; we understand legal reasoning, it suggests, only by seeing the sense in which they do both and neither".*

649. ECHR, 20 Oct. 2011, *Nejdet Sahin* v. *Turkey*, §§ 80-87; ECHR, 12 Sept 2012, *Nada* v. *Switzerland*, § 170; ECHR, 7 July 2011, *Al-Jedda* v. *U.K.*, § 105; ECHR, 29 March 2006, *Achour* v. *France*, §§ 45-58.

the court operates[650]. Order is primarily coherence in the articulation of its elements. However, coherence is not only the lack of contradiction between the normative elements comprising the order, or the articulation of these elements within a hierarchy governed by a principle underpinning them. The coherence requirement aims to adopt or reconcile the standards of justice with the evolving reality of social life. This coherence seeks to *reconcile the perception of "is" in society with the "ought" in the legal texts*[651]. Ultimately, coherence is founded on the initial pact under which the individual participates in society for the mutual advantage of the parties[652].

The treatment of homosexuality and trans-sexuality in Western societies illustrates the ideas on coherence and their relation to justice set forth above. A few decades ago, it would have been unthinkable to speak about gay and lesbian marriage or adoption of children by same-sex couples[653]. Sodomy was a criminal offence and homosexuality was stigmatised as immoral behaviour or at best as a mental disturbance. But in recent decades, our moral universe and our scientific knowledge have evolved. Freedom of private life has provided a new perception of the role of state power in our private life (unconstitutionality of the prohibition of sodomy between consenting adults in private, since this act does not harm anybody[654]). The suffering of transsexuals, which was deemed tolerable or immaterial, is no longer so (reversal of

650. See *infra* §§ 111-113.

651. ECHR, 7 July 2011, *Byatyan* v. *Armenia*, § 102.

652. ECHR, 16 Dec. 2010, *A, B, C,* v. *Ireland*, § 241.

653. U.S.A. Supr. Court, 26 June 2013, *United States* v. *Windsor*; ECHR, 19 Febr. 2013, *X. and others* v. *Austria*, 7 Nov. 2013, *Vallianatos* v. *Greece*, § 92.

654. U.S.A. Supr. Court, 26 June 2003, *Lawrence* v. *Texas*, II: *"The doctrine of* stare decisis *is essential to the respect accorded to the judgments of the Court and to the stability of the law. It is not, however, an inexorable command (...). In Casey we noted that when a Court is asked to overrule a precedent recognizing a constitutional liberty interest, individual or societal reliance on the existence of that liberty cautions with particular strength against reversing course".*

case-law on the administrative treatment of trans-sexuality because social conditions have advanced in the meantime[655]). As a whole the ordering of fundamental principles and basic ideas on life has evolved so as to render intolerable and, thus, illegitimate the solutions on homosexuality and trans-sexuality adopted before that evolution.

No Better Solution Is Possible

84. In the case of *Roe* versus *Wade* (decided by the Supreme Court of the United States on January 22, 1972[656]), a pregnant unmarried woman, resident in the State of Texas, who wanted an abortion, argued the unconstitutionality of the law of the State of Texas prohibiting the voluntary interruption of pregnancy. In support of her application, she argued that her economic situation did not allow her to move to another State of the Union, where abortion was not prohibited[657]. The Supreme Court considered that the

655. ECHR, 11 July 2002, *Goodwin* v. *U.K.* (no 28957/95) § 74: "*While the Court is not formally bound to follow its previous judgments, it is in the interests of legal certainty, foreseeability and equality before the law that it should not depart, without good reason, from precedents laid down in previous cases (...). However, since the Convention is first and foremost a system for the protection of human rights, the Court must have regard to the changing conditions within the respondent State and within Contracting States generally and respond, for example, to any evolving convergence as to the standards to be achieved (...). It is of crucial importance that the Convention is interpreted and applied in a manner which renders its rights practical and effective, not theoretical and illusory. A failure by the Court to maintain a dynamic and evolutive approach would indeed risk rendering it a bar to reform or improvement (...). In the present context the Court has, on several occasions since 1986, signalled its consciousness of the serious problems facing transsexuals and stressed the importance of keeping the need for appropriate legal measures in this area under review*".

656. 410 U.S.113 (1973); DWORKIN 2005, pp. 44 *et seq.*; DIMITRAKOPOULOS 2007, pp. 351-352; NOWAK, ROTUNDA 2007, pp. 490 *et seq.*

657. DIMITRAKOPOULOS 2007, pp. 331 *et seq.*

fact that a State prohibits a pregnant woman from terminating her pregnancy constitutes interference in the freedom of an individual to determine her own life but it did not accept that the right of women to abortion is an absolute right because it relates to the body of an individual[658]. It pointed out that pregnancy leads to the birth of a human being and for this reason it could not be identified with situations relating purely to the private life of the pregnant person concerned. As for the question of when human life begins, it examined the various theories advanced (original conception, quickening in the womb, viability of the embryo in the event of termination of pregnancy, birth) to reach the conclusion that there is no scientific and ethical consensus in these matters.

The Court then faced the problem of balance between competing interests. First, against the freedom of the pregnant woman to terminate her pregnancy lies the interest of the State in protecting the life or health of that woman from the risks entailed by surgery. Are these risks so serious as to preclude the exercise of that freedom? The Court refers to statistics: for abortions carried out during the first quarter of pregnancy, the figures reveal a death rate lower than the death rate for normal deliveries. The Court found that for the first quarter the risk is minor and therefore recognizes

658. U.S.A. Supr. Court, 22 Jan. 1973, *Roe* v. *Wade*, VIII: *"On the basis of elements such as these, appellant and some amici argue that the woman's right is absolute and that she is entitled to terminate her pregnancy at whatever time, in whatever way, and for whatever reason she alone chooses. With this we do not agree. (...) The Court's decisions recognizing a right of privacy also acknowledge that some state regulation in areas protected by that right is appropriate. As noted above, a State may properly assert important interests in safeguarding health, in maintaining medical standards, and in protecting potential life. At some point in pregnancy, these respective interests become sufficiently compelling to sustain regulation of the factors that govern the abortion decision. The privacy right involved, therefore, cannot be said to be absolute. In fact, it is not clear to us that the claim asserted by some amici that one has an unlimited right to do with one's body as one pleases bears a close relationship to the right of privacy previously articulated in the Court's decisions".*

the freedom of the woman freely to terminate her pregnancy until the end of the first trimester of gestation. It recognizes the right of States to regulate abortion after that time on the basis of considerations pertaining to the protection of the health of the pregnant woman. Furthermore, against the freedom of pregnant women to abort stands as a legitimate interest of the State, the protection of prenatal life. In this regard, the Court finds that, after the termination of the pregnancy of its mother, a viable embryo deserves the protection of the State. Being viable outside the womb, its abortion could be considered as equivalent to killing a human being[659]. The Court concludes, therefore, that abortion may be prohibited if the embryo is viable outside the womb which is always the case after the seventh and sometimes after the sixth month of pregnancy. The Court was thus prompted to adapt the solution by applying as its criterion the intensity of competing interests in the matter. Solutions differentiated according to the month of pregnancy during which the abortion takes place, are better able, the Court held, to deal with the specific features of abortion[660]. The Court thus established an *equilibrium* between the *intensity of conflicting interests* and the *solution which harmonizes and reconciles* them. Until the end of the third month of gestation, it recognizes the freedom of pregnant women to abort. After the seventh month, the Court admits a prohibition on abortion, unless there

659. DIMITRAKOPOULOS 2007, p. 353; NOWAK, ROTUNDA 2007, pp. 508-509.

660. U.S.A. Supr. Court, 22 Jan. 1973, *Roe* v. *Wade*, VIII: *"In view of all this, we do not agree that, by adopting one theory of life, Texas may override the rights of the pregnant woman that are at stake. We repeat, however, that the State does have an important and legitimate interest in preserving and protecting the health of the pregnant woman, whether she be a resident of the State or a non-resident who seeks medical consultation and treatment there, and that it has still another important and legitimate interest in protecting the potentiality of human life. These interests are separate and distinct. Each grows in substantiality as the woman approaches term and, at a point during pregnancy, each becomes "compelling." With respect to the State's important and legitimate interest in the health of the mother, the "compelling" point, in the light of present medical knowledge,*

is a danger to the life of the pregnant woman. Between the third and seventh months, it considers that it is for States to regulate abortions, taking into account, first, the protection of the health of pregnant women and, secondly, the possibility of the birth of a viable child[661].

85. In the case of *Von Hannover* versus *Germany* (judgment of the European Court of Human Rights June 24, 2004[662]), the ap-

is at approximately the end of the first trimester. This is so because of the now-established medical fact (...), that until the end of the first trimester mortality in abortion may be less than mortality in normal childbirth. It follows that, from and after this point, a State may regulate the abortion procedure to the extent that the regulation reasonably relates to the preservation and protection of maternal health. Examples of permissible state regulation in this area are requirements as to the qualifications of the person who is to perform the abortion; as to the licensure of that person; as to the facility in which the procedure is to be performed, that is, whether it must be a hospital or may be a clinic or some other place of less-than-hospital status; as to the licensing of the facility; and the like. This means, on the other hand, that, for the period of pregnancy prior to this "compelling" point, the attending physician, in consultation with his patient, is free to determine, without regulation by the State, that, in his medical judgment, the patient's pregnancy should be terminated. If that decision is reached, the judgment may be effectuated by an abortion free of interference by the State. With respect to the State's important and legitimate interest in potential life, the "compelling" point is at viability. This is so because the foetus then presumably has the capability of meaningful life outside the mother's womb. State regulation protective of fetal life after viability thus has both logical and biological justifications. If the State is interested in protecting fetal life after viability, it may go so far as to proscribe abortion [410 U.S. 113, 164] during that period, except when it is necessary to preserve the life or health of the mother. Measured against these standards, Art. 1196 of the Texas Penal Code, in restricting legal abortions to those "procured or attempted by medical advice for the purpose of saving the life of the mother," sweeps too broadly. The statute makes no distinction between abortions performed early in pregnancy and those performed later, and it limits to a single reason, "saving" the mother's life, the legal justification for the procedure. The statute, therefore, cannot survive the constitutional attack made upon it here".

661. NOWAK, ROTUNDA 2007, pp. 492 *et seq.*

662. ECHR, no 59320/00.

plicant complained that the defendant had not provided the level of protection of privacy that Article 8 of the European Convention on Human Rights requires. The applicant, a member of a princely family, complained of constant harassment she was subjected to by some photographers, acting on behalf of the tabloid press, who followed her continuously during her public appearances[663]. The German Constitutional Court ruled that the applicant was regarded as a model of behaviour in the eyes of the general public and served to crystallize different points of view commanding adherence or rejection. According to this Court, the public had a legitimate interest in monitoring aspects of the private life of the princess, so as to enable an opinion to be formed on a person who has become a contemporary model of behaviour.

The European Court of Human Rights does not follow this reasoning. The Court distinguishes between the reporting of facts – even controversial – that may contribute to a debate in a democratic society relating to politicians in the exercise of their official duties, and reporting on details of the privacy of a person who does not occupy such a position. According to the Court, the press deserves increased protection when it plays its role of watchdog in a democratic society by helping in the communication of ideas and information on matters of public interest[664]. The Court observes

---

663. The photos published in dispute showed the princess alone when she was shopping, in a restaurant with a movie star, alone on a bicycle, with his bodyguard to the market, during a skiing holiday, alone leaving her home in Paris, playing tennis. Other pictures showed her in the territory belonging to a private club tripping over an obstacle and falling down (ECHR, 24 June 2004, *Von Hannover* v. *Germany*, § 49)

664. ECHR, 24 June 2004, *Von Hannover* v. *Germany*, §§ 63, 64: "*The Court considers that a fundamental distinction needs to be made between reporting facts – even controversial ones – capable of contributing to a debate in a democratic society relating to politicians in the exercise of their functions, for example, and reporting details of the private life of an individual who, moreover, as in this case, does not exercise official functions. While in the former case the press exercises its vital role of "watchdog" in a democracy by contributing to*

that publication of the photographs and the litigious articles, with the sole aim of satisfying the curiosity of a certain section of the public about the details of the private life of the applicant could not contribute to any discussion of general interest to society, in spite of the notoriety of the applicant. The Court weighs the competing interests on the basis of the principles it had enunciated. The applicant found herself in the situation described without her free assent: her family's origins and her status as a role model for life were imposed on her by a state of affairs or by the will of the authors. There is no ethical link between these facts and the treatment she suffered as a result of them, the German authorities having failed to protect her from such a treatment. Nor is any public interest served that would justify the treatment suffered by the princess. The analysis of the Court on this point is different from that of the German Constitutional Court. The latter cites the concepts of entertaining information, of personality as a role model for life, of crystallization of the opinions on the rejection or acceptance of a mode of behaviour. The Court of Human Rights, faced with an applicant *who is suffering undeservedly*, considers that it must find a stronger interest in order to be able to uphold the submissions of the respondent state authorities[665]. It considers that the

---

"impart[ing] information and ideas on matters of public interest (...), it does not do so in the latter case. Similarly, although the public has a right to be informed, which is an essential right in a democratic society that, in certain special circumstances, can even extend to aspects of the private life of public figures, particularly where politicians are concerned (...), this is not the case here. The situation here does not come within the sphere of any political or public debate because the published photos and accompanying commentaries relate exclusively to details of the applicant's private life. As in other similar cases it has examined, the Court considers that the publication of the photos and articles in question, the sole purpose of which was to satisfy the curiosity of a particular readership regarding the details of the applicant's private life, cannot be deemed to contribute to any debate of general interest to society despite the applicant being known to the public (...)".

665. ECHR, 24 June 2004, *Von Hannover* v. *Germany*, §§ 68-73: *"The Court finds*

publications at issue satisfy purely the curiosity of the public on the private life of a person who has no public office and whose acts have no impact on the general interest. The Court adjudges consequently that the point of equilibrium between the competing principles established in the case was not the appropriate one.

86. The relevant elements in a case are weighed in order to reach a decision. However, a decision made by judges, allotting to each party what is foreseen for them by law, means that each party must obtain the *right proportion of good or bad treatment* they legally deserve. Equilibrium, in such a perspective, appears to be

another point to be of importance: even though, strictly speaking, the present application concerns only the publication of the photos and articles by various German magazines, the context in which these photos were taken – without the applicant's knowledge or consent – and the harassment endured by many public figures in their daily lives cannot be fully disregarded (...). In the present case this point is illustrated in particularly striking fashion by the photos taken of the applicant at the Monte Carlo Beach Club tripping over an obstacle and falling down (...). It appears that these photos were taken secretly at a distance of several hundred metres, probably from a neighbouring house, whereas journalists' and photographers' access to the club was strictly regulated (...). The Court reiterates the fundamental importance of protecting private life from the point of view of the development of every human being's personality. That protection – as stated above – extends beyond the private family circle and also includes a social dimension. The Court considers that anyone, even if they are known to the general public, must be able to enjoy a "legitimate expectation" of protection of and respect for their private life (...). Furthermore, increased vigilance in protecting private life is necessary to contend with new communication technologies which make it possible to store and reproduce personal data (...). This also applies to the systematic taking of specific photos and their dissemination to a broad section of the public. (...). Lastly, the distinction drawn between figures of contemporary society "par excellence" and "relatively" public figures has to be clear and obvious so that, in a State governed by the rule of law, the individual has precise indications as to the behaviour he or she should adopt. Above all, they need to know exactly when and where they are in a protected sphere or, on the contrary, in a sphere in which they must expect interference from others, especially the tabloid press".

the ultimate goal of any justice operation. Without justice, there would either be chaos, as a result of perpetual conflicts[666], or extreme order, owing to the submission of the ones to the others[667]. In any operation of justice, the solution aimed at is one that is not considered to be arbitrary by those who feel its consequences[668]. Justice is thus not only an intention, an operation and an evaluation, but ultimately also a *decision*[667] fixing an *equilibrium point*, where conflicting interests or competing principles find their best possible treatment[670] within the framework of a global order. This *equilibrium point* is either of a general rule indicating what to do or to omit to do in analogous situations[671], or in the form of a specific ruling prescribing to specific individuals the behaviour to be followed[672] or that which had to be followed[673]. Conceived in this way, this final requirement of justice subsumes within itself all previous ones.

In the jurisdictional domain, in particular when it is about a case of concurring and competing fundamental rights, it is for the court to establish, by its decision, the best possible treatment of the interests in collision, by the best possible ordering of the values which come into play[674]. In her conscience the judge ought to feel that *she cannot do better* and, in the decision she is to write, she must be able to demonstrate, supported by adequate legal reasoning, that *no better ordering of the conflicting interests and values was to be considered*[675]. It is when this state of consciousness

666. See *infra* § 121.
667. See *infra* § 110.
668. See *infra* § 109.
669. See *infra* § 164.
670. SCHMIDT 2001, pp. 200-210.
671. See *infra* § 98.
672. See *infra* § 97.
673. See *infra* § 101.
674. ECHR, 18 January 2001, *Coster v. U.K.*, §§ 104-128.
675. See *infra* § 118.

of the judge is reflected in her decision, duly based on sound reasoning, that equilibrium occurs. Thus, the interests or the values in interaction must be accorded the best possible treatment with respect to what each one deserves having regard to the treatment given to the other (respect for freedom of pregnant women wishing to have abortion and for prenatal life, allowing abortion in the first months and banning of abortion during the last months of pregnancy[676]). However, establishing justice's equilibrium is not a mathematical operation with only one correct result. The opinions of the judges diverge[677] or may even be totally opposed[678] as to where this point of equilibrium may be reached (publications found not to violate the right to protection of private life by a constitutional court on the basis of considerations not accepted as correct by the reviewing international court[679]).

676. U.S.A. Supr. Court, 22 Jan. 1973, *Roe* v. *Wade*, XI.

677. ECHR, 6 July 2010, *Neulinger* v. *Switzerland, joint separate opinion of three judges.*

678. U.S.A. Supr. Court 12 June 2008, *Boumediene* v. *Bush*, dissenting opinion of J. Scalia.

679. ECHR, 24 June 2004, *Von Hannover* v. *Germany*, §§ 74, 75: "*The Court therefore considers that the criteria on which the domestic courts based their decisions were not sufficient to protect the applicant's private life effectively. As a figure of contemporary society "par excellence" she cannot – in the name of freedom of the press and the public interest – rely on protection of her private life unless she is in a secluded place out of the public eye and, moreover, succeeds in proving it (which can be difficult). Where that is not the case, she has to accept that she might be photographed at almost any time, systematically, and that the photos are then very widely disseminated even if, as was the case here, the photos and accompanying articles relate exclusively to details of her private life. In the Court's view, the criterion of spatial isolation, although apposite in theory, is in reality too vague and difficult for the person concerned to determine in advance. In the present case, merely classifying the applicant as a figure of contemporary society "par excellence" does not suffice to justify such an intrusion into her private life*".

5

The Calculus of Social Harmonization

87. In the previous chapter we studied court judgments in order to discover common features in the approach of judges when they operate a balancing exercise in human rights cases. In the pages which follow we will present social cases where justice's solutions emerge as a requirement of harmonization in social life disputes. Starting from these cases some identical constants may be observed as to the means and the process of harmonizing conflicting interests and values. The first case will invite us to delimit the area where we may select our weighing criteria. In pluralistic societies, traditional moral conceptions should be converted into secular ethical approaches in order to achieve large consensus. The second case to be studied will pose the question of limitation of freedom between individuals linked by a general obligation of mutual respect. Individuals have to coordinate their behaviour by making the necessary concessions in order to render social life possible. In the third case, we will see how two people may find a solution to a problem of cooperation. Equality between them is the starting point, but other considerations will also contribute to defining the way they will finally share the burdens and benefits of their cooperative undertaking. The fourth case will invite us to revisit the issue of discrimination against homosexuals[680]. We will see the kind of method legislatures will use to overcome conflicting demands by social and political groups on whether and how to institutionalize same-sex unions. The last case will bring us back to a problem already tackled[681]. Here, we will show how a judge proceeds, according to the most plausible scenario, to identify the criteria by which she will select among all possible solutions, the one which better does justice to the interests at stake.

Ethical Standards to Evaluate Social Cases

88. A student has a series of ethical issues to deal with in three stories given to him by his professor. The first two stories are the following: *"Denise is a passenger on an out-of-control trolley. The conductor has fainted and the trolley is headed toward five people walking on the track; the banks are so steep that they will not be able to get off the track in time. The track has a side track leading off to the left, and Denise can turn the trolley onto it. There is, however, one person on the left-hand track. Denise can turn the trolley, killing the one; or she can refrain from flipping the switch, letting the five die"*[682]. *"Frank is on a footbridge over the trolley tracks. He knows trolleys and can see that the one approaching the bridge is out of control, with its conductor passed out. On the track under the bridge there are five people; the banks are so steep that they will not be able to get off the track in time. Frank knows that the only way to stop an out-of-control trolley is to drop a very heavy weight into its path. But the only available, sufficiently heavy weight is a large person also watching the trolley from the footbridge. Frank can shove the large person onto the track in the*

680. See *infra* §§ 75, 81; see also § 82.

681. See *infra* § 72.

682. HAUSER 2006, p. 114.

path of the trolley, resulting in death; or he can refrain from doing this, letting the five die" [683].

The professor asks the student to explain how to treat the cases in terms of justice. He asks the student to present in the classroom, rather than an intuitive reaction of approval or disapproval, a moral reasoning supported by rational arguments[684]. What will be necessary for the student to find in these cases, is the criterion on the basis of which he will decide how, in terms of *distributive justice*[685], to distribute rights and obligations and, in terms of *corrective justice*[686], to consider the merits of the punishment of Denise and Frank accused of homicide[687].

89. In terms of *distributive justice*, the Kantian duty to act so that the person is always treated at the same time as an end and never as a mere means[688], seems to offer to the student an obvious solution at least to the second case. To push a man on to the rails without his consent, and for him to die only because he is of suitable stoutness to save five lives, is to act as if this man was nothing more than a means of serving a purpose which absorbs him totally. This is against respect to human dignity, a principle expressed as a rational requirement by the Kantian moral doctrine.

For the first case, the answer seems less clear. The man, who will be killed by the bifurcation of the train, is not used, strictly speaking, as merely a means. The loss of his life is collateral dam-

683. HAUSER 2006, p. 115; EDMONDS 2014, pp. 9, 37.

684. ELEFTHERIADIS 2008, pp. 58-59.

685. ANGELIS 1999, pp. 30-31, 425-438; FINNIS 1986, pp. 178, 179: *"(...) Thomas Aquinas, purporting to interpret Aristotle faithfully, silently shifted the meaning of Aristotle's second class of particular justice, and invented a new term for it: commutative justice. Many followers of Aquinas have understood* commutativa *as pertaining to exchanges".*

686. ANGELIS 1999, pp. 30-31, 428-470, 438-440.

687. ARISTOTLE 1920, 130 b, 131a, b 132 b; ANGELIS 1999, pp. 425-427.

688. See *infra* § 131.

age that occurs in the pursuit of the goal of saving lives. If the person inside the train was the pilot of one of the planes that crashed on September 11, 2001 into the World Trade Centre and had the opportunity to guide the airplane into an isolated house, what would he have done? He would probably have opted for a utilitarian solution[689]. Seeking a universally applicable and impersonal standard of behaviour for increasing the overall utility, the student restates the original question. Now he wonders about the merits of introducing a *rule*[690] enabling a person to save the life of a certain number of persons by diverting the object which threatens them, even if, by this diversion, other persons will lose their lives, provided that the first are more numerous than the second. Formulated in its new terms, the question opens up new perspectives. Certainly, a repeated application of such a rule seems likely to increase overall utility as society may expect more lives to be saved than lost. However, the student has, according to the utilitarian doctrine[691], to balance the advantages and disadvantages of the rule to be adopted. In this case, the disadvantages of this rule are obvious. To allot to any person the right to decide, in an emergency, whether it is necessary to cause the death of one in order to save the life of the other, is to assign a power of life or death to any person in such a situation. The student believes that the calculation of the social utility of such a solution would be strongly artificial because of a lack of objective data[692]. He then raises the question: if people present on the scene in the first case were unaware of their own identity, which society would they have chosen[693]; a society which gives the right to Denise to change the direction of the train or a society which refuses to grant such a right? The answer to this question

689. See *infra* §§ 135-138; GROSS 2010, pp. 733 *et seq.*

690. BINMORE 2005, p. 150.

691. KYMLICKA 1999, pp. 18 *et seq.*

692. GILBOA 2010, pp. 41-43.

693. BARRY 1989, pp. 330 *et seq.*

depends mainly on the terms, broad or otherwise, in which it is worded. If the question refers only to cases in which Denise has to decide to save five lives against one, the answer probably would be to recognize that Denise has such a right. But if the question arises in more general terms, taking the perspective of a person living in a society where all people around potentially have the capacity of sacrificing her in order to save others' lives, the answer to the question would probably be negative. It is not about a likely calculation of the balance of utilities, but a defensive reaction to a risk[694] which is due to the almost absolute power conferred on a person to decide in a manner not free from error, on the life or death of other people.

90. In terms of *corrective justice*, the student is applying a similar reasoning as above. Frank's victim was on the bridge not involved in any activity that could be seen as generating a risk of accident. Not to punish Frank for using as a mere tool an innocent person to save lives would be, in the eyes of Kantian morality[695], incompatible with respect for human dignity. Utilitarianism would be attentive to compensation to the family of the victim and would insist on the beneficiaries of Frank's act paying that compensation. Concerning the criminal sanction, utilitarians would not be ready to accept an excuse justifying the act or exempting its author from liability. They would think that it would be dangerous to pass the message to society that the authors of acts such as that perpetrated by Frank are automatically excused[696]. To decide the case in terms of the social contract doctrine, the student feels that it is necessary to try to harmonize the claims which the two protagonists could raise. Each for his part, the victim and Frank, have their own reasoning and for a third person who listens to them and who feels

694. GILBOA 2010, pp. 41-43; EDMONDS 2014, p. 79.

695. See *infra* § 131.

696. SANDEL 2007, pp. 3-7; BINMORE 2005, pp. 193, 196.

she could equally well be in the position of one or other, it is not easy to adjudicate. However, the student considers that most of the people, if they were in Frank's position, would not have the idea of killing a man in order to save the lives of five individuals. They would therefore have little sympathy for the killer, and his arguments would not affect them deeply. They would feel rather near to the victim, fearing that one day they too could share the same fate[697]. Hence, they would opt for an intermediate solution, which as a matter of principle would reject the idea of granting to Frank a complete excuse.

Denise's case is simpler. The Kantian argument against Frank does not apply to her because she did not use the victim as a means: the damage here was collateral. A utilitarian would not have reservations if an excuse granted to Denise were stated to be generally applicable in any analogous case, subject, however, to the condition of compensating the close relatives of the victim. In a social contract perspective, while most of the people who found themselves in the position of Frank may not have acted like him, this is not the same with the case of Denise. We understand her state of moral stress and we note the symmetrical situation of the victim in relation to the situation of the five people whose lives were saved. The student therefore finds that it is sustainable to apply to Denise an excuse enabling her to avoid a penal sanction. With regard to civic liability, he would prefer the beneficiaries of the act to be liable for payment of damages and, if they are impecunious, would give the courts the power to adjudicate equitably, according to the financial capacity of the parties.

91. The third story the student has to comment upon is the following: *"John is on the footbridge over the trolley tracks and can see the track, there are five chimpanzees, and the banks are so*

697. GAUTHIER 2006, pp. 284-287.

steep that they will not be able to get off the track in time. John knows that the only way to stop an out-of-control trolley is to drop a very heavy weight into its path. But the only available, sufficiently, heavy weight is a large chimpanzee, sitting on the footbridge. John can shove this chimpanzee on to the track in the path of the trolley, killing him; or he can refrain from doing this, letting the five chimpanzees die" [698].

Concerning this story, the student feels that the criteria of justice, employed by him earlier for humans will not be easy to apply to animals. Humanity was in its conception of the animal throughout history very contradictory in this regard[699]. Under the Christian approach, shared also by other monotheistic religions, between man and animals there is a radical ontological difference, the first being a special creation of God endowed with an eternal soul, while animals and the rest of creation are only the means made available by God to man for use in his fight to earn eternal life[700]. If the student uses such a conception of the animal as opposed to human, he will have no difficulty in applying a purely utilitarian reasoning to draw the conclusion that sacrificing one to save many is the proper standard to apply in the matter. However, he knows that if he dares to present such ideas, his agnostic and atheist class comrades will not follow his reasoning. It is thus necessary for him to revisit the secular doctrines on justice.

Kantian moral doctrine presupposes actors sufficiently rational to understand and apply to themselves and to others universal ethical maxims[701]. However, the student knows no animal other than man which is able by his own rationality to submit himself to these maxims. He thus arrives at the conclusion that Kantianism, as he understands it, cannot give to chimpanzees the

698. HAUSER 2006, p. 307.
699. MIDGLEY 2006, p. 28.
700. JEANGENE VILMER2008, p. 26.
701. See *infra* § 131.

status of humans and, consequently, this doctrine does not impose the same obstacles as with humans in using animals exclusively as means. For similar reasons, the social contract doctrine seems to him not applicable here. Whichever version of it is to apply[702], the players that will participate in the negotiation must be able to answer the question as to which society they prefer to live in, and whether a standard of behaviour to be adopted is compatible with this society. Animals would not form part, as real participants, of the negotiation, being unable to delegate their voice to anybody. What remains to be considered is the utilitarian doctrine[703]. This one advocates consideration of all beings capable of experiencing pleasure and suffering, and chooses the rule which, more than any other, maximizes the total amount of pleasure of all these beings[704]. We have seen that, with respect to humans, utilitarianism would not be so willing to accept that to save five lives there would be no problem in sacrificing one. The application of such a standard to humans does not maximize overall utility, but rather increases insecurity among them. However, one can be less rigorous in the application of such a conclusion in the case of chimpanzees. The student feels that by proposing a solution for chimpanzees based on numerical criteria, he would attract the objections of those who regard big apes as humans[705]. There is neither scientific consensus on their status, nor precise constitutional rules to regulate this matter. The student thinks that the status of big apes, at least at present, is a question to be treated by a majority vote reflecting the ideas and sentiments of society on matters submitted for public discussion[706].

702. See *infra* §§ 139, 140; EDMONDS 2014, p. 132.
703. NOZICK 1988, pp. 60 *et seq.*; EDMONDS 2014, p. 132.
704. JEANGENE VILMER 2008, pp. 71 *et seq.*
705. JEANGENE VILMER 2008, p. 63.
706. SICARD 2003, p. 484; HABERMAS 1997, pp. 306-310.

Reciprocal Empathy to Make Coordination of Behaviours Possible

92. Between the two extremes as regards social relations, namely, on the one hand, cooperation and, on the other, conflict, there is the vast space of interactions where each one, in his particular domain of freedoms and rights, interferes, without being animated by a specific intention to harm, with the freedoms and rights of others[707]. The most common case of such kind of interaction is the conflict between the residents of two apartments in the same building, which arises because of the noise generated by one of them[708]. The resident who generates the noise considers that she is making normal use of her apartment in causing this noise. She has no specific intention to harm. She considers that if she deprives herself of the activity which generates the noise, she will undergo an unjustified sacrifice. The second resident however finds that this noise constitutes an attack on the free enjoyment of her property. It does not matter to her that the tenant who produces the noise does not do it on purpose to embarrass her. It still bothers her, and sometimes it bothers her so much that she cannot use her residence in the most elementary way, such as, for example, to sleep in during the night.

To realize the importance of this apparently trivial interaction, we should take to their extremes the claims which both parties could raise against each other. The first could claim to be able to make as much noise as she wishes without regard to the hour of

707. BUCHANAN, TULLOCK 2004, p. 240: *"Much political discussion seems to have proceeded as follows: 'If the interests of two or more individuals conflict, unanimity is impossible. Some interests must prevail over others if action is not to be wholly stifled'. This line of reasoning seems quite plausible until one confronts ordinary economic exchange. Note that in such exchange the interests of the two contracting parties clearly conflict. Yet unanimity is reached. Contracts are made; bargains are struck without the introduction of explicit or implicit coercion. In this case, no interest prevails over the other; both interests are furthered".*

708. BRAITHWAITE 1955, pp. 6 *et seq.*

the day, and the second could require the first to abstain from producing any noise that is audible in the second's apartment, irrespective of the hour. Both, in other words, could *maximize* the extent of their freedoms and rights with the inevitable consequence that they enter into a situation of mutual conflict.

93. Both parties might consider resolving their conflict by the use of physical force, in order to obtain either the extermination or the subjugation of the other. However, as the use of violence entails multiple risks, it is reasonable to assume that in many cases individuals who are placed in one of the two states described above, would prefer, as rational beings able to conduct a risk assessment, to resolve their conflict through a series of mutual concessions in respect of their maximalist positions[709]. These trade-offs are conceived as mutual concessions by each of the parties to the requirements of the other, and may be made successively to the point where a certain stabilization is reached in what both parties can accept as tolerable. To achieve such a state, there is no need of a process of negotiation between the opponents that would lead them to an agreement[710]. Each of the parties, having the experience of what can be expected of an average neighbouring tenant, will prefer to limit herself in respect of her extreme requirements, while waiting for the other to do the same so that, by mutual limitations, an overall adjustment emerges, a kind of implicit agreement[711] between the opposing parties, which allows them to live in peace.

The exercise in question requires from both parties the empathetic capacity of being able *"to put oneself in the shoes of the other"* and predict her reactions even if she is unknown[712]. The

709. BARRY 1989, pp. 41, 65.
710. GAUTHIER 2006, p. 145; BARRY 1989, p. 55.
711. BARRY 1989, p. 55; BINMORE 2005, p. 158.
712. BINMORE 2005, p. 113.

change of shoes in which each of the parties will engage, will not necessarily be done out of sympathy to the other, to protect and defend her interests more than the interests of the individual who engages in this exercise. On the contrary, the change of shoes must be seen as necessary to predict the reactions of the other in order to see what one can reasonably claim for oneself[713]. Thereafter, a strict comparison of the sacrifices compared to the advantages, would be necessary, each party having to play the continuous game of changing shoes in order to decide up to which point she would be ready to suffer a disadvantage with its attendant hindrance of her freedom to act. Of course, each one for her part will in the end be inclined to exaggerate in order to protect her own position to the detriment of the other's[714].

94. The party wishing to enhance her position as much as possible would be led to introduce into her reflexion more rational elements of analysis such as, for example, a consideration of what it would be reasonable to expect individuals of common sense to require or to concede in a similar situation or, further, what may be presented as a generally applicable standard[715] in such cases of social relations. It will not always be a question of substituting one's own conception of what is right for the view held by the other person. It will be rather a question of providing a pattern of behaviour the two persons could respectively follow in order to reconcile their competing interests. Each individual, freed from her selfish approach in defending her interests, should position herself on the concessions reasonably to be made in order to defend her interests at stake[716]. Thus, the adjustment of behaviours initially required would not be based on concessions underpinned by the *balance of power* of the

713. BRAITHWAITE 1955, pp. 27 *et seq.*

714. BINMORE 2005, p. 17.

715. See *infra* § 159.

716. BARRY 1989, p. 79.

concrete conflicting individuals, but on standards of the *equitable reconciliation of interests*, such as the ones we have seen in the previous section, applicable to all similar cases that could emerge.

It may be argued that one should tolerate her genius neighbour who plays piano day and night in preparation for a monumental public performance[717], or that, in such situations, the question is not of establishing a rule of impersonal justice, but rather of determining the responsibility of the stronger towards the most vulnerable[718]. These objections do not call into question the basis of the approach taken up to now. Because, first, if a genius artist needs, for the good of humanity, to train his talent, he should not do it at the expense of his neighbour, who, by bad luck, is placed too close to the artist; the community, if it decides to promote arts, must assume the corresponding burdens. And, second, caring for the vulnerable is a matter of personal discretion; the fact that a rule determines the right behaviour when two competing interests are in conflict does not necessarily mean that the party who benefits from the arrangement is denied the opportunity to be generous by giving up her advantages.

Using Practical Equality to Resolve Issues Arising from Cooperation

95. Two men hunt together[719]. They are in an environment where only the hunting of deer is possible and, to capture it, it is necessary to cooperate. The two men are of similar physical strength, motivation and intelligence. With equal forces and with the need for cooperating, we may assume that they will decide to put themselves on an equal footing for sharing the benefits of their cooperation. Suppose now that it is possible for two other hunters

717. NIETZSCHE 1971, pp. 40 *et seq.*

718. GILLIGAN 2008, p. 121.

719. GILBOA 2010, p. 109; BINMORE 1994, pp. 120 *et seq.*

to hunt alone[720]. The more skilful of the two can capture in a day three small animals, the nutritional value of each amounting to 1000 calories. The less skilful hunter, may, as far as he is concerned, capture only two small animals in a day. If they cooperate, they can capture one big animal producing 6000 calories with less effort. Suppose the one is weak and lazy, his metabolism is fast and, in addition, he has an invalid father who is dependent on him. The contribution of the other hunter to the capture of the dear is greater, without however the contribution of the first being insignificant. Based on the size of his contribution, the second claims two-thirds of each captured deer. The first hunter responds by claiming the two-thirds share because of his fast metabolism and the fact that he has charge of a disabled person. The second hunter argues that the first deserves nothing more than that which is consonant with his merits and the first's reply is that he is doing his best and can do nothing more. If they cannot reach an agreement, they will have to hunt alone, and consume less meat than they could obtain if they had decided to cooperate[721].

96. Both hunters claiming for themselves two-thirds of the booty, they decide to assign to an arbitrator the task of making to them a proposal. If the arbitrator proposed a solution based on the principle *"to each according to his needs"*[722], this would certainly satisfy the needier hunter, but the more skilful hunter would reject it. If he proposed a solution on the basis of the principle *"to each*

720. BINMORE 2005, pp. 67, 175.

721. BUCHANAN, TULLOCK 2004, p. 188: *"At the outset of a hunt each of two hunters may consider that his expected utility will be maximized by agreeing on a predefined rule for sharing the day's catch. Each might realize that, only by agreeing to such a rule, could a 'fair' sharing be assured. Otherwise, without rules, the hunter securing the major share of the game would probably think that his good fortune was due to his exceptional skill, and he would be extremely reluctant to part voluntarily with a share of the size that he might otherwise have agreed to under predefined sharing rule".*

722. The Marxist solution, see RENAUT 2004, pp. 135, 136.

according to his ability"[723], it is likely that the less skilful hunter would reject it[724].

Suppose that the arbitrator assesses the chances of his proposal being accepted in light of the intensity of the interests at stake between the two concerned parties. In this regard, he finds that there are at least two interests that push the parties to reach an agreement: the interest in securing the booty, on the one hand, and the interest in valorising their efforts to secure it, on the other hand. If the arbitrator assigned values to the interest of both parties in obtaining a greater share of the booty, he would certainly give more points to the least skilled hunter, given his stated need to consume more calories, being in addition the less advantaged in the labour market. This state would thus push him to insist on obtaining more, unless an agreement was urgent to prevent his father from dying of hunger. In this case, his relative advantage would be transformed into a serious disadvantage and he would be ready to conclude an agreement in which the pressure which would weigh on him to obtain the booty as quickly as possible would count against him. On the other hand, the stronger hunter hardly finds it beneficial to him to obtain more of the booty, his interest in the negotiation at this stage being to get a fair price corresponding to the value of his effort, as perceived by himself.

97. The two hunters are placed now in the setting of a village whose chief is on the point of solving their disagreement. The chief of the village does not intend to act as an arbitrator. What he wishes to obtain by his intervention is a solution serving all who comprise the village's community[725]. And as chief of the village, he has the capacity and the means of imposing[726] his solution on the hunters, even if the parties are not satisfied.

723. The free market solution, see RENAUT 2004, pp. 137, 139.

724. RENAUT 2004, pp. 133, 135, 137, 136, 139.

725. BINMORE 1994, p. 109.

726. BINMORE 2005, p. 143.

Seeking such a solution, he starts first by accepting what is obvious: it is good for the community that the two hunters cooperate because, in that way, they will bring to the community 6000 calories, whereas working alone they will bring 5000 calories. For the chief of the village there are two requirements that must be satisfied: he must, on the one hand, ensure the effectiveness of food production, which leads him to ensure that cooperation between the hunters takes place; and, on the other hand, he must establish an equitable distribution of food which should take into account the percentage of calories available. He envisages, initially, imposing mandatory cooperation and equal distribution[727]. This solution appears at first glance to be effective and equitable at the same time. However, he examines the opposite solution by rewarding the merit and ability of the most skilful hunter. This will offer incentives[728] to skilful people to work and produce, but, as the neighbourhood ties are tight in his village, he fears that too much inequality may lead to quarrels. He thus wishes a rather egalitarian solution, which, however, guarantees at the same time to the most motivated and able persons the incentives which are necessary for them to work and produce. The chief of the village will seek, consequently, to harmonize two competing requirements: on the one hand, to produce wealth, and thus be efficient, by rewarding merit and effort[729], and, on the other, to satisfy the needs of the less privileged, ensuring stability to his village[730]. In other words, he has to achieve by his ruling this equilibrium point of dialectical harmonization in which all members involved, the talented and the needy, will have the feeling that their interests have received the best possible treatment[731].

727. BINMORE 2005, p. 180.

728. See *infra* §177.

729. See *infra* § 145.

730. See *infra* §161.

731. BINMORE 2005, p. 184; BUCHANAN, TULLOCK 2004, p. 46: *"The choice between voluntary action, individual or co-operative, and political action, which must be collective, rests on the relative costs of organizing decisions, on the rel-*

Sublimating Individual Interests into Defendable Social Values

98. In a democratic country a number of organizations have brought before the competent minister a request for the institutionalization of same-sex unions. The minister has to choose between several options: the loose union changing the succession law to provide some rights to the survivor of homosexual couples; a union identified with the traditional marriage ceremony before the mayor, using the words "marriage" and "spouse" and all legal rights provided to heterosexual marriages; a union with all legal rights of heterosexual couples, but not any kind of symbolism drawn from traditional marriage, such as the description of same-sex unions as "marriage". Let us suppose that the government, after all useful consultations, chooses the first solution, prepares a bill to this effect and asks Parliament to pass it. Having regard to the moderate contents of the reform, the minister will have in particular to face, during the parliamentary procedure: first, the homosexual organizations which, almost unanimously, will argue that their rightful claims have not been satisfied; secondly, the traditionalist organizations which will protest against the alleged attack on the institution of the family; third, the progressive parties of Parliament which will find the reform too timid; and, finally, the members of the governmental majority who, for reasons of principle, are opposed to the reform in its principle. Advocates of the bill on same-sex unions and their opponents could obviously mobilize pressure groups and associations that militate, according to their beliefs, in favour of or against the bill by using arguments in line with their interests or ideology. But,

ative costs of social interdependence. The costs of organizing voluntary contractual arrangements sufficient to remove an externality or to reduce the externality to reasonable proportions may be higher than the costs of organizing collective action sufficient to accomplish the same purpose. Or, both of these costs may be higher than the costs of bearing the externality, the spill-over costs that purely individual behaviour is expected to impose".

wishing to reach the general public and publicly justifying their choice, they have to look for arguments that transcend their particular groupings and touch the citizen as a member of the national community[732].

99. The opponents of the bill will be the first to burst into the public debate by putting forward arguments of a *consequentialist* character[733]. They will try to influence the public by saying that the bill would bring nothing new in fact, as all the purported benefits in favour of homosexuals already exist in the law, provided that it is correctly implemented, such as for example, succession rights which could be settled by an appropriate last will and statement. They will, moreover, argue that such a bill, whilst being in itself of no utility, will provoke discordance within the people just for the satisfaction of a handful of ideologues hostile to the moral foundations of society. Supporters of the bill will prefer to place their arguments on a *deontological* footing[734]. They will argue especially that it would be incompatible with the principles of dignity of the individual and of non-discrimination on the basis of sexual orientation for homosexuals to be denied access to a basic legal institution. Their argument will therefore go to the lack of coherence[735] of the legal order which, while prohibiting any discrimination against homosexuals, allows them to found unions on which no legal status comparable with heterosexual unions is conferred. A third group of arguments regarding the *acceptability* of the bill will also be used. The opinion polls and, possibly, public meetings will show the mood of the public towards the bill. Such elements used in the public debate are often inconclusive. But, it happens sometimes that the public shows, in

732. HABERMAS 1986, p. 86.
733. SEN 2010, pp. 23, 24, 210, 221; BINMORE 2005, pp. 93, 188.
734. SANDEL 2007, pp. 379 *et seq.*; SEN 2010, pp. 205-210, 169-173.
735. See *supra* § 83.

surveys or by its massive participation in meetings or demonstrations, a clear preference. The government, even in such a case, may insist on its bill and use its majority to have it passed by the Parliament, or, on the contrary, it may make concessions, such as moderating the scope of the reform. Whatever its decision is, it will have to justify it in the public debate that has opened[736], and for this reason it will have no other means than to focus on arguments based on shared common values and the risks which threaten them or on the necessary compromises to preserve them.

100. Women and men who put themselves in the political arena to gain political influence are driven by ideas, feelings or instincts that only they can really know. Gaining fame or wealth, satisfying personal hatreds, serving the country or a badly treated social class, are often the underlying motives that drive individuals into politics. However, in a system where convictions are displayed on the public stage, discussed and form the subject-matter of controversy, convictions held by public figures are expected to be defended before the general public. Around persons who have a vocation to become leaders, various individuals or groupings are united who consider that their interests are better defended if they are taken on board by persons who seem able to acquire power. These people or these groupings may also be animated by non-avowable feelings or instincts. But, whatever their motives, those in politics must be able to address the masses by putting forward ideas and projects that may be defended in public discussion[737]. Lobbies also may exert several kinds of pressure, ranging from a simple muscled discussion to a general strike or even to orchestrating the fall of the government. However, regardless of the nature of the interests they defend, lobbyists cannot expect to be effective if they are openly selfish, standing out against the public

736. See *infra* §§ 180-181.
737. See *infra* §§ 180-182.

interest. In a country governed under the control of public opinion, the government tries not to be presented as yielding to pressures exerted in the name of selfish interests[738]. The winning strategy of any pressure group is built on arguments acceptable to a large proportion of the population.

Thus, the non-avowable defence of egoistic interests or interests of a class should be dialectically synthesised and sublimated in ideas of justice which are conceived to be addressed to a great number of people and to be suitable for attracting them. Institutionalizing same-sex unions, as a matter of legislative discretion, is consequently a question of political synthesis. Two tests play a crucial role in this respect. They both respond to two questions whose answer reveals the character of the legislative proposal as going beyond the defence of selfish interests in order, thus, to obtain the *consent of the people*. The first is whether the proposal, once adopted, is compatible with the maintenance of a desirable *social order* with regard to the social values to which the society adheres[739]. And the second is whether this proposal, once enacted, furthers *collective interests* in a way that can be convincingly defended in public debate[740].

Applying Generalization Tests to Find the Most Acceptable Solution

101. A husband helped his wife, who was suffering from terminal cancer, to kill herself. He was prosecuted for murder. In court he pleaded not guilty, claiming that assistance to euthanasia is not criminally punishable. His legal argument could be presented as follows: *"The crime of assistance to suicide seems to cover the facts that constitute aid to euthanasia, as euthanasia is*

738. See *infra* § 172.
739. See *infra* §§ 163, 164.
740. BINMORE 1994, p. 109; see *infra* § 181.

committed by a person who knows she will die soon while suffering unbearable pains. However, under the right to protection of privacy, the individual in such a situation is entitled to enlist the help of a third party for the purpose of administering death to herself. It follows that the crime of assistance to suicide is not made out in this case because on the facts of the case there is a legitimate exercise of a right guaranteed by the Constitution". The judge-rapporteur to whom such arguments are advanced will see initially whether there is any case-law on the matter. Suppose that she finds two cases in point. In the first, it was decided that an aspect of the right to respect for private life is the right of a person to refuse to continue receiving medical care to keep her artificially alive[741]; and in the second, that the respect for the right to privacy forbids the state to feed by force a prisoner on a hunger strike to protest against her imprisonment[742]. The judge deepens her understanding of these two judgments and tries to identify the common principle that drives them. In this regard, there will be two ways open to her. The first would be to say that the idea which explains the judgments is only that the state should not keep individuals alive by administering to them medication or food against their will. The second interpretation would be to admit that the explanatory principle is the right of each person to choose the time of her death when she considers that her life becomes intolerable[743]. The judge finds that the outcome of this research is unclear and thus not conlcusive.

102. Let us now imagine the judges deciding this case entering the deliberations chamber. The judge-rapporteur is an enthusiastic believer. For her, human life is, in accordance with the teaching of

741. U.S.A. Supr. Court, 20 Febr. 1905, *Jacobson* v. *Massachusetts.*

742. U.S.A. Supr. Court, 18 May 1902, *Riggins* v. *Nevada*, 1992; 27 Febr. 1990, *Washington* v. *Harper.*

743. DWORKIN 1993, pp. 343-347.

the Church, sacred; no concession is allowed by her to euthanasia. There is, also an agnostic judge who is rather worried by the excessive costs, according to her assessment, of maintaining life in desperate cases; she thinks that, even if human life is sacred, it is necessary, for practical reasons, to recognize in some exceptional cases the impunity of assisted suicide. There is also a sentimental judge, who is deeply sorry for the suffering of the person concerned and who, invoking human dignity, is inclined to accept the argument of impunity, finding euthanasia to be the lesser of two evils. There are, finally, other judges, who on entering the deliberations chamber are undecided as to which option they will favour. Suppose that the believer, as the reporting judge, takes the floor first and sets out the arguments against impunity, on the basis of the teachings of the Church. Will her view be echoed by her colleagues? It would be highly unlikely. The message of the Gospel is addressed in principle only to believers and even if among the judges there are those sympathetic to Jesus' message, these judges would think it better for beliefs not to interfere with this case. The pragmatic judge then speaks to present an argument exclusively founded on the economic and social costs of the terminally ill elderly, concluding that, should euthanasia be authorized, considerable public funds would be freed to be spent more effectively. Would this judge's views be echoed more widely than the previous one's? It would be rather unlikely. Generally, any too narrowly based argument would be unlikely to find an echo within a court which is not united as to the convictions of its members. What will happen then?

When judges interpret legislation guaranteeing fundamental rights, the traditional techniques of interpretation become inoperative. Undoubtedly, the case-law which is built up gradually in this respect may provide certain pointers. But the dynamic nature of human rights[744] prevents judges from discharging their responsibilities by

744. See *supra* §§ 81, 82; see also STRAUSS 2010, pp. 51-98, RENQUIST 1976, pp. 693 *et seq.*

referring to the decisions of others. Each case has its specific features, and for each one a solution adapted to its specific features must be established.

103. The judges of the above case continue to question the legal order until they find a solution to the problem. It remains for them to assess and weigh a series of elements: they must take into account the suffering of the dying person, the good faith and prudence shown by the accused, the moral principles which govern the case, the possibility of obtaining equivalent results by more acceptable means, the risks that the generalization[745] of the incriminated behaviour could involve. In other words, they will conduct an assessment in respect of the values at stake, giving particular attention to the moral risks, and arbitrating, when possible, between legitimate values and interests which require their attention. To do so the judges will have to apply to the potential solutions a series of tests. Firstly, they will apply a *compatibility test* as to whether the behaviour in question could be generally upheld without involving normative consequences incompatible with the respect for the fundamental values to which their legal order is attached. Secondly, they will use a *utilitarian test* inquiring as to the practical consequences, the advantages and disadvantages of the potential solutions to the conflict. Finally, the judges will examine whether, as a result of the proposed solution to the dispute, the legal system is imposing a disproportionate sacrifice on one of the parties, which would not be reasonable to impose in a society founded on a social contract between equal individuals. This would be obviously a *contractarian test.*

In other words, judges will conduct their legal analysis, using arguments drawn from secular ethical values and standards, which will allow their differences to be harmonized or, at least, when they express separated opinions, the greatest possible number of their readers to be persuaded.

745. BINMORE 1994, p. 111.

6

Equilibrating the Forces of Attraction and Repulsion

104. We have already studied[746] a series of judgments delivered on human rights issues and we have identified, in these judgments, component features of the judges' balancing exercise. In the previous chapter, we have studied social situations where justice emerges through processes of confrontation and conciliation by the application of proper weighing criteria. In both categories of cases, we have seen that public utility must be reconciled with respect for the dignity of the individual which requires that burdens imposed are justified by sufficient reasons, or offset by adequate benefits. In both cases the idea of equilibrium is key. In the final chapter of the second part, we will present a number of scientific findings that enlarge the framework of our reflexion on justice and equilibrium. In all the cases to be studied there is a problem of reconciling forces of attraction and repulsion, of regulating and stabilising interactions in an equilibrium which appears to assign to each interactive force its proper place. Reciprocity among primates will thus form the subject-matter of our attention as an equilibrium-achieving behaviour founded on the mutual interest of the participants. We will also observe some broad features of regularization of behaviours in

746. See *supra* §§ 72-86.

animal societies. Without mutually destroying each other, without either merging into the other, the elements of life coordinate their forces and form cooperative communities that serve their fundamental interests. As we will see, common rules may be found behind the order emerging from interactions, whatever the elements that interact. Game theory provides a rational form of what has been described. It highlights individuals animated by the purpose to maximize their profits, alongside other individuals having the same purpose.

Reciprocity: How It Works among Primates

105. Common objectives, shared by members of the primates' group, urge them to adjust their behaviour. But egoistic interests, which each member continuously satisfies[747], constitute a permanent factor of discord within the group and a continuous threat to its integrity[748]. Great apes[749] are capable of negative reactions to anti-social behaviour by their partners, they punish it if necessary or, in any case, they ensure that a stop is put to what they conceive to be a deviation. They are able to make mental representations of what they expect from others toward themselves and, conversely, of what others should expect of themselves[750]. These representations create role models while the deviations from these models cause reactions of disapproval. When this reaction comes from the subordinate individuals it takes more specifically the form of a protest, whereas when emanating from dominant individuals it assumes the form of a sanction[751]. Females in the apes' communities have an innate tendency to avoid conflict, while males have the innate tendency towards reconciliation, after their quarrels,

747. DAWKINS 2003, p. 171; DE WAAL 1997, pp. 154 *et seq.*
748. DE WAAL 1997, p. 188
749. Chimpanzees, bonobos, gorillas; see DE WAAL 2006, p. 13.
750. DE WAAL 2006, p. 195.
751. DE WAAL 1997, pp. 192 *et seq.*

which females find less easy[752]. Isolation of the trouble-maker and scape goating are usual technics. This behaviour also produces closer ties among the members of the group, who cooperate in order to punish the disturbers under the common goal of eliminating the threat that any trouble-maker can represent[753].

106. With their high intelligence, a big memorising capacity and strong feelings of sympathy, great apes exhibit behaviours characteristic of their individuality. Reciprocity dominates their relationships. Within their groups, distribution of goods is based on an implied contract among members for the provision of mutual aid, as is the case with females raising their offspring together, or with hunters, working together with the common aim of sharing the prey[754]. The relationship which binds a male to a female is the exchange of access to the female sex for the offer of food security, participation in offspring care or even protection against predation[755]. Implied contracts such as *"scratch my back so I'll scratch yours later"* between females, or *"food against sex"* between males and females, or *"share my booty now and tomorrow we will share yours"* between hunters, are the common currency in relations between great apes, and ensure that a collective spirit develops among the members of the same group in spite of their sometimes conflicting or contradictory interests[756]. It is a reciprocity founded not on an immediate exchange, but on an implied promise, whose satisfaction is left for later.

Groups of great apes practice the exchange of a broad range of services: it includes grooming, protection against predation, sharing of food, rearing of offspring, access to sex and even protection of the weak. The animals involved in this exchange of services, expect of others reciprocal behaviour and are ready to continue

752. DE WAAL 1997, pp. 223 *et seq.*
753. DE WAAL 1997, p. 135.
754. DE WAAL 1997, pp. 195 *et seq.*
755. RIDLEY 2003, pp. 89, 91.
756. RIDLEY 1997, p. 81; DAWKINS 2003, pp. 228 *et seq.*

offering their services as long as the other members of society meet the expectations on them[757]. The hunters cooperate in the realization of random tasks, which however may yield the goods of most value to all[758]. They know that these tasks cannot be realized without a common contribution and thus they appreciate beforehand the individual contribution of each, even if this contribution does not turn out to be determinant in all cases[759].

Sharing and giving are features common to the practice of food distribution among great apes. Individuals with food supplies share them at the request of indigent companions[760]. The begging member can cause irresistible reactions of sympathy in his companions[761]. A disabled member can survive by getting the food it needs, despite its inability to contribute to the common good of the colony like a normal individual of its age and sex[762]. Cries of despair, calls for help, and expressions of suffering provoke tensions among individuals which produce behaviour leading to the provision of assistance for the relief of the suffering member of the group[763].

107. In chimpanzees' societies, the dominant male, the alpha, gives the impression of assuming a duty rather than of enjoying a privilege. He is tolerant, affectionate, protects the weak, shares his food, does not stifle competitors by precluding them from enjoyment[764]. Chimpanzees are egalitarians and their leader is a *primus inter pares*. His essential quality is his ability to intervene in emerging conflicts by providing appropriate solutions, reconciling adversaries or intimidating disturbers. The more impartial he is

757. DE WAAL 1997, p. 195.
758. DE WAAL 2010, p. 265.
759. RIDLEY 1997, p. 96.
760. DE WAAL 1997, p. 185.
761. DE WAAL 1997, pp. 101, 183.
762. DE WAAL 1997, p. 60.
763. DE WAAL 1997, pp. 70 *et seq.*
764. DE WAAL 1997, p. 160.

in appeasing disputes, the more he is appreciated and confirmed in his position. An alpha rarely owes his power solely to his own efforts. He has access to leadership, either by the support of his friends, a band within the group which unites to support him, or by a complicit tolerance among competitors who prefer to bide their time before claiming leadership for themselves. The power of the alpha is not maintained, moreover, by physical force and terror. Qualities of a political expert are sometimes required from him in order not to cause his subordinates to react too negatively[765]. The community requires the dominant male, under the threat of his replacement, to assume responsibilities of guide, peacemaker and protector[766]. Chimpanzees are able to form coalitions to overthrow a too dominating ruler[767]. There is a line which separates what an alpha can do against his subordinate males, and what he cannot if he is not willing to cause a rebellion leading to his overthrow[768]. He should not forget those to whom he owes his rise to power: their direct aid or their tolerance can easily be withdrawn and be offered to another male member of the group who would seem to respect and pursue their interests better[769].

Regulation: How Animals Use Social Roles, Priority and Property Rights

108. The size and composition of animal societies are determined, not only by the scarcity or abundance of natural resources, but also by the nature and degree of the threat posed by predatory animals, the conditions governing copulation, the gestation period and the need to rear the new born[770]. Ungulates, which are animals

765. DE WAAL 1997, pp. 162.
766. DE WAAL 1997, p. 164.
767. RIDLEY 1997, p. 159.
768. DE WAAL 2006, pp. 77-83.
769. RIDLEY 1997, p. 157.
770. WILSON 2012, pp. 183 *et seq.*

that find their food easily but who are weak vis-à-vis their predators, tend to congregate in large numbers, while the wolves, for which access to food is rare and accidental, are organized in small bands to ensure ease of movement and cooperation in the rearing of new born[771]. Altruism takes different forms depending on the needs of species to adjust to dangers that threaten them: crowding out predators, cooperating for the purpose of raising infants, sharing of food, amnestying enemies within the group or, in case of an internal fight, not insisting on the extermination of the defeated[772]. At the risk of their lives, some animals act as sentinels, warning their flocks of the presence of predators, while others take on the role of a guardian defending the flock, and others sacrifice themselves to defuse the attack[773]. In periods where animals are facing the danger of extinction because of external threats, heroic individuals acting at the risk of their lives, face the threats, trying to overcome them to the benefit of their community[774]. When the threat of extinction comes from within, because the community has become too crowded and has lost its inner balance, altruistic animals prefer to tolerate aggression, give up their reproductive effort to care for the children of others, or emigrate[775]. Solidarity is manifested in the sharing of food when food is rare and random[776]. Cooperative associations of sisters are composed in which collective treatment is provided to the young[777]. In birds, the mother who nurtures her offspring acts so that she can maintain adequate resources for all of them and for herself[778]. She rejects the well-nourished offspring mature enough to allow her to offer food to hungrier or younger

771. WILSON 2000, p. 341.
772. WILSON 2000, pp.121-129.
773. RIDLEY 1997, pp. 144-146.
774. WILSON 2000, p. 120
775. WILSON 2000, pp. 121-125.
776. DEWAAL 1997, p. 185.
777. WILSON 2000, p. 125
778. WILSON 2000, pp. 338-340.

offspring. In dolphins and whales, stress is accompanied by compassionate empathy based on the intellectual capacity of these animals, comparable to that of man, to sympathise with the sufferer and, showing solidarity, devise a plan to save the suffering animal[779].

109. Attacks between individuals of the same species are aimed at domination of the animal attacked, its eviction from a nutritional resource or the submission of a sexual partner[780]. Assault may lead to the elimination of one of the two parties, but this outcome is rarely seen. In almost all cases, the weaker party knows when to stop the fight by showing signs of submission, while the stronger party is satisfied with the acceptance of defeat by his opponent and does not seek to take absolute advantage of his victory[781].

In the case of the sharing of prey[782] or confrontation with predators[783], conflicts among individuals of the same species are managed by assigning to each a specific role. The regulation of behaviours within mammalian groups is operated mainly by the setting up of a hierarchical system to which members of the group have to adhere. The despotic domination of the strongest is a phenomenon, which, whilst not rare, is at least not as common as might be expected[784]. The oldest impose themselves on the young, the males on the females, the stronger on the weaker[785]. Hierarchical systems are observed where each member occupies a different place on a hierarchical scale which includes all, male and female and their children placed also hierarchically according to the order of their mother[786]. Reversals of hierarchy are the rule, depending on the

779. WILSON 2000, p. 475.
780. WILSON 2000, p. 243.
781. DAWKINS 2003, p. 117.
782. WILSON pp. 287 *et seq.*
783. RIDLEY 2003, pp. 186 *et seq.*
784. DAWKINS p. 158; WILSON 2000, pp. 279-280.
785. WILSON 2000, pp. 292-293.
786. WILSON 2000, pp. 282-286.

capacity of those who claim the position of head. The chiefs certainly have privileges, in particular priority and sometimes exclusive access to the females, as well as a major portion of the spoils, but they are subject to constraints, such as the need to interpose themselves between predators and the weakest members of the herd[787]. The rest of the herd members are able to migrate to form a new group if they are not satisfied with the existing situation. If they remain, they respect the dominant position of the chief, while plotting constantly to obtain its reversal[788].

The animals not practicing the system of domination define an exclusive living space which, respected by the other members of the same species, allow them to avoid fatal or biologically expensive conflicts[789]. In this space, which they declare to be their property, by the sounds they make or by the excrement they deposit and in any case by their willingness to attack the invaders, they claim exclusive rights over captured prey, and they copulate freely with invited partners[790].

110. Social insects such as bees, wasps, termites and ants have tighter forms of social organization than those of mammals or cold-blooded vertebrates[791]. The particular feature of the social organization of these insects is the phenomenon of sterile classes, comprising workers and soldiers[792]. The sterile individuals are entirely devoted to their work; life outside the community is impossible for them[793]. Sharing food is the rule. Murders, cannibalism, slavery, infanticide are often seen as regulatory phenomena which aim to maintain order rather than resolve individual conflicts of interest[794]. The var-

787. WILSON 2000, pp. 287 *et seq.*
788. WILSON 2000, p. 290.
789. DAWKINS 2003, p. 158.
790. WILSON 2000, p. 259, 273.
791. WILSON 2000, p. 398.
792. WILSON 2000, pp. 399 et seq.
793. WILSON 2000, pp. 368, 417
794. WILSON 2000, p. 368.

ious economic tasks are divided among individuals either according to the genetic characteristics of each one or according to age and physical development[795]. In ants, the difference between the workers and soldiers is physical, the latter having a more impressive constitution than the former. In some ant species, workers begin first within their cave to engage in domestic work such as care of the new born, cleaning and food management, to move later to outside work, including mainly food collection[796]. Newborns are under the responsibility of the community; they are raised by cooperation between the adults. The young individuals assist the older for a short time with the aim of becoming familiar with the tasks ahead. Specialization is seen in some ants within the nest[797].

Although social insects are physically independent, colonial micro-organisms are organized in such perfect societies that they give rise to a single organization built up of a series of distinct elements[798]. These elements which do not all come from the same parents, abandon their individuality to devote themselves entirely to the good of the entity to which they belong, thereby strengthening the entity's individuality as a single organism[799]. Within the great body, the individual entities specialize in different tasks, some taking on leadership roles, others defence, collection and distribution of food roles, or fertilization and production of new colonies[800].

Cooperation: How Life Uses It to Face Competition

111. The first elements of life, the *replicators*[801], were machines reproducing themselves which could not stop the reproducing

795. WILSON 2000, p. 399.
796. WILSON 2000, p. 412.
797. WILSON 2000, pp. 421 *et seq.*
798. WILSON 2000, p. 383.
799. WILSON 2000, p. 386.
800. WILSON 2000, pp. 386-387.
801. MAYNARD SMITH 1993, pp. 113 *et seq.*

process[802] without ceasing to exist[803]. Their existence was determined by their reproduction[804] which alone could provide them with stability[805]. Errors produced in the replication process caused diversification among replicators[806]. Some non-identical copies had higher capacities compared to the initial replicators[807]. Those who continued to thrive developed particular skills that showed relative strengths compared to others[808]. In a world with limited resources, the satisfaction of the tendency to reproduction needed accurate materials, and these had quickly started to become scarce[809]. Eager for materials needed for their replication, they were thus forced to compete for vital resources[810]. Competition favoured the development of suitable means of aggression and defence. Replicators which managed to survive in the new era were those who adapted themselves to the competitive environment by repelling their adversaries or gaining the ground which had been occupied by them[811]. Nothing seemed able to resist the all-out war which replicators incessantly engaged in with one another for material. In these circumstances, evolution favoured the development of replicators that could cooperate with each other to confront their opponents, and could find ways to control their reproduction in order not to fall victim themselves to their own replicators[812].

112. Sexual reproduction, by the combination of genes lodged within two distinct organisms, facilitated the emergence of new

802. DAWKINS 2003, pp. 78-79.
803. DAWKINS 2003, p. 250.
804. DAWKINS 2003, pp. 103, 125.
805. DAWKINS 2003, p. 31.
806. DE DUVE 2002, p. 85; DAWKINS 2003, p. 36.
807. DAWKINS 2003, p. 25.
808. DAWKINS 2007, p. 683; RIDLEY 2000, pp. 173 *et seq.*; DAWKINS 2003, p. 39.
809. DAWKINS 2003, pp. 127 *et seq.*
810. DAWKINS 2003, p. 39.
811. DAWKINS 2003, p. 40.
812. DAWKINS 2003, p. 75.

mutations, which in turn allowed genes to adapt themselves better to the competitive environment[813]. But that required different forms of sociability with a view to mating and then the rearing of offspring. According to the mode of copulation, and the needs for rearing the offspring, different systems of cooperation between male and female were developed[814]. A child totally dependent on its parents to survive needs at least one of its parents to protect and nourish it. In birds, without internal gestation and lactation, the roles of the father and the mother in rearing and feeding their offspring are interchangeable[815]. Monogamous systems therefore emerged to make both parents work together. In mammalian carnivores, gestation and lactation prevent females from seeking their prey for a relatively long period which makes the contribution of the male essential[816]. However, as the male must have in return an unquestionable assurance of its paternal relationship with the offspring he is going to nourish, monogamous or harem systems arose. In herbivores, which find abundant food without particular effort, females do not have the concern of engaging in raising the offspring and are thus allowed to give priority to the choice of the strongest to fertilize them[817]. Thus, the male which will have the right to fertilize all the females of the herd will be the one which, at the end of a combat between applicants, proves to be the strongest, thereby assuring the females as to the quality of the offspring to which they will give birth.

113. Organisms around us today are those whose genes have undergone appropriate changes allowing them to achieve reproductive success sufficient to ensure their survival. However, viewed from the perspective of observable consequences, all survivors are

813. GRIBBIN 2005, p. 187; DAWKINS 2003, p. 51.
814. DAWKINS 2003, p. 69.
815. DAWKINS 2003, p. 202.
816. DAWKINS 2003, p. 201.
817. DAWKINS 2003, pp. 205, 223.

species whose ancestors had, in terms of the theory of evolution[818], the most effective hereditarily transmissible mutations in respect of their reproduction[819]. The concern to ensure reproduction is the strongest feature of life, stronger yet than the concern for survival[820]. In males, this concern becomes a desire to achieve multiple fertilizations; in females it is a concern for fertilization by the best among the males[821]. However, both have to cooperate in order to achieve their objectives. Formation of harems where the dominant male fertilizes all the females and excludes from access to sex the other males who nevertheless are part of the herd[822], or herds in which a dominant female kills offspring born to her rivals, are systems of reproduction aiming at reproduction success by the selection of the fittest. Concern for reproductive success takes the most astonishing form in the demonstrations of parental altruism. Risking their own lives, parents engage in dangerous activities to save the lives of their offspring[823]. Cries of alarm in front of a threatening predator, insistence on remaining in place to protect offspring despite the approaching predator, priority of nourishing offspring to the detriment of themselves[824], all form an arsenal of tactics which animals invented, thanks to natural selection, to achieve reproductive success.

114. In humans, pregnancy is long, lactation even longer, and the child remains dependent on its parents for years. These biological constraints facilitate the development of monogamy systems of access to sex[825]. A woman does not only seek one robust

818. MAYNARD SMITH 2005, pp. 1 *et seq.*
819. DAWKINS 2003, p. 70.
820. DAWKINS 2003, pp. 134-135, 192.
821. RIDLEY 2003, pp. 209 *et seq.*
822. DAWKINS 2003, p. 219.
823. DAWKINS 2003, p. 143.
824. On altruism and duty see BINMORE 2005, pp. 86-87.
825. RIDLEY 2003, pp. 175-180.

partner to produce healthy offspring. She also seeks a companion who inspires confidence that he will honour a long-term commitment. In the same way, man does not seek from woman only an attractive and fertile partner, but also a companion who will bring into the world children resulting from their union. Natural selection was therefore able to promote *love* more than sexual attraction, as the founder of long-term relationships, suitable for ensuring the protection of children dependent on their parents[826]. The resulting family communities are characterized by an altruistic attitude by the parents towards their children, manifested particularly in food sharing and protective sacrifice vis-à-vis predation[827]. However, the family unit was too small to face food shortage and predation. Natural selection favoured social groups, not necessarily based on kinship, in which as far as food gathering and defence against predators are concerned, there was a distribution of roles and a sharing of burdens and benefits[828]. Humans, with their rationality, do not have to wait for natural selection to drive their genes to optimal social behaviour. Natural selection must undergo multiple failures before seeing the emergence of the best option[829]. The human being, by contrast, is able to anticipate consequences, to set goals, to choose the most appropriate means for achieving them and, in the course of her endeavour, to correct her action or even replace it by another[830]. The human can retain in her memory her failures and her successes and, thanks to language, she can pass her experiences from individual to individual first and then from generation to generation[831]. She can also anticipate the behaviour that other humans

826. RIDLEY 2004, p. 47.
827. DAWKINS 2003, p. 90.
828. DAWKINS 2003, pp. 301, 304.
829. MAYNARD SMITH 2005, pp. 38 *et seq.*
830. DAWKINS 2003, pp. 88-89.
831. DAWKINS 2003, p. 261.

will adopt in relation to her or in response to her behaviour. This ability[832] allows humans to engage in long-term mutually reciprocal relationships and build cooperative social systems which are permanent[833]. Cooperative systems of this type are based on the ability to select a reliable partner[834] and the possibility of imposing sanctions on the partner who does not keep promises made[835].

Order: How It Emerges Spontaneously

115. Order emerges spontaneously as a stabilization process of interacting elements[836]. Forces of attraction and repulsion are being implemented in the interactions of elementary particles until achieving stabilization in a state of equilibrium. Elementary particles remain in provisional equilibrium as long as forces, such as temperature or pressure, remain stable[837]. The solar system is held in balance, as the planets which compose it develop forces of attraction and of repulsion which mutually cancel each other

832. NOWAK 2011, p. 55: *"There is a clear link between this mechanism of co-operation and the evolution of empathy. We need to have a good idea of what is going through the mind of another person in order to understand and appreciate the motivation of a Good Samaritan. (...) We require, in the parlance of the psychologists, a 'theory of mind', that remarkable capacity that enables us to understand the desires, motivations, and intentions of others. This mind-reading ability allows us to infer another's perspective - whether emotional or intellectual".*

833. BALL 2004, pp. 539 *et seq.*; DAWKINS 2003, p. 108.

834. BINMORE 2005, on reputation and trust, pp. 87-88; NOWAK 2011, p. 54: *"If, (...) the world knows that you are good, charitable guy, then you boost your chance of being helped by someone else at some future date. The converse is also the case. I am less likely to get my back scratched, in the form of a favour, if it becomes known that I never scratch anybody else's".*

835. DAWKINS 2003, p. 95.

836. BALL 2004, p. 6; GRIBBIN 2005, p. 3

837. GRIBBIN 2005, pp. 22, 23, 34.

out[838]. Systems that are not held in stable equilibrium giving the impression of being in constant evolution towards new states, also aspire to equilibrium as their movement is characterized by a ceaseless search for stability that is never perfectly attained[839]. Every living organism is such a system[840] as well as systems deriving from living organisms, such as the aggregation of the apparently irregular movements of pedestrians on a sidewalk[841]. Within the market, it is the satisfaction of personal interest which makes individuals engage in competition or which lead them to cooperate until they find a point of equilibrium[842] which satisfies them[843]. Likewise, states in international relations interact with

838. GRIBBIN 2004, pp. 60-61.

839. BALL 2004, p. 128.

840. MAYNARD SMITH 2005, p. 26: *"Life therefore is an active equilibrium between the living organism and its surroundings, an equilibrium which can be maintained only if the environment suits the particular animal or plant, which is then said to be adapted to that environment".*

841. BALL 2004, pp. 207 *et seq.*, 490-491.

842. STARR 2007, p. 237: *"(...) equilibria exist. This is true both in setting where demand and supply are characterized as a point-valued functions and optimizing behaviour is uniquely well defined and where they are characterized as set-valued mappings recognizing the multiplicity of equally profitable production plans a firm may have or the variety of equally satisfactory consumption plans households may consider. (...) The market ensures again the waste of scarce resources"*; p. 238: *"The market can provide the incentives for production and for the desired distribution of any technically feasible output if the income to support it is appropriately distributed. (...) In a large economy, the core, which constitutes the outcome of strategic bar-gaining, is a competitive equilibrium (...). We can interpret this family of results as applying across time and under uncertainty, subject to the availability of well-articulated markets for allocation over time and across uncertain events".*

843 BALL 2004, p. 222: *"Two opposing forces – self interest and competition – suffice to generate a self-regulating steady state, a kind of equilibrium. This is the hidden hand, as Smith put it, that keeps order in the market"*; CASSIDY 2009, p. 30: *"Prices gravitate toward a 'natural price', at which suppliers just cover their outlays for labor, raw material, and rent, as well as making an unexceptional rate of profit. The market system is efficient in that human and physical resources are*

each other seeking the greatest profit for themselves, by making wars or forging alliances, but in the end they stabilize their relationships at a point of equilibrium which, for the time being, seems to them the best possible result[844]. These systems still survive in a state of permanent instability which is due both to the nature of their elements, animated by forces which are constantly moving, and to the number of elements that unceasingly also waxes and wanes in a primarily contingent way. Yet even these systems develop organizational forces that partake of a certain order, despite phases of disruption, transition or disorder[845].

116. There is a necessary quantity of elements allowing order to emerge. When particles in interaction are aggregated in a *critical mass*, complex phenomena begin to emerge in a new order which transcends the individual elements[846]. The laws of Newtonian physics emerge from quantum interactions of elementary particles, and living organisms emerge from chemical interactions: complexity arises from simplicity[847]. When critical mass is reached, the interacting elements begin to regulate their behaviour

---

directed to where they are most needed and prices are tied to costs. It is also self-correcting. If a shortage develops, prices rise and supply expands. If a glut occurs, prices fall and production contracts until supply and demand come into balance".

844. GRIBBIN 2005, pp. 351 *et seq.*, 358.

845. GRIBBIN 2005, p. 126.

846. BALL 2004, pp. 282-284, 286-289; see p. 131: *"Prigogine and his collaborators suggested that dissipative structures are reached when a non equilibrium system is driven to a crisis point called a bifurcation. Close to equilibrium the system might not do anything very remarkable (...). At the bifurcation point, however, the system is abruptly compelled to change its state dramatically"*; p. 155: *"Flocking emerges spontaneously from the birds. It is not programmed in: the rules specify only the motion of individuals. Yet something about the way those individuals interact produces a kind of coherent group behaviour. Emergent properties show that the whole can be more than the sum of the parts".*

847. GRIBBIN 2005, p. 97.

so that order is generated as a new entity compared with the individual elements of which it is composed[848]. As brain and conscience are much more than interactions of neurons, so the individual behaviour of economic operators is more than transactions recorded within a vaster unit, the market[849]. An aggregation of interactive elements becomes a system when specific qualities emerge optimizing energy consumption and seeking relative stability in a state that requires from them the lowest possible energy[850]. Life is a constant evolution in which everyone adapts his weapons to the new weapons used by his opponent. Social animals found a reproductive advantage in their association by economizing and by optimizing their effort[851]. Their social behaviour is the best answer to the problems of adaptation to an environment made up of dangerous predators.

117. The struggle for reproduction is a constant quest for stability in a context where the slightest weakness of the one can turn out to be to the advantage of the other[852]. Whether to live in groups or not is for animals an option to be considered in terms of calculating the benefits and costs. Sometimes these costs are very important: a member of the herd may be obliged to give up his desire to reproduce in favour of the dominant male[853]. But it gains protection against predators, and by its contribution to the collective protection of the herd, it safeguards the offspring of the dominant male. Whether to hunt in groups or not is an option that requires even more subtle calculations than the benefits and costs of group living[854]. Animals form a coalition to hunt when they are catching

848. GRIBBIN 2005, pp. 70 *et seq.* 182-183.
849. BALL 2004, p. 155.
850. BALL 2004, pp. 307, 345.
851. WILSON 2012, pp. 120 *et seq.*
852. MAYNARD SMITH 2005, pp. 26 *et seq.*
853. WILSON 2000, p. 290.
854. BALL 2004, pp. 530-531.

large prey, but prefer to hunt alone to capture small animals. What they expect to obtain from hunting together should generally exceed in nutritional value what they would expect from hunting alone, the cost of hunting and the risk of failure being included in the calculations[855]. Roles are assigned to hunters, and sharing the prey is subject to a combined system of rewards for investment and satisfaction of nutritional needs[856]. The number of children to be born, the modes of fertilization and investment in parental care are subject to the *law of marginal value*, which means that efforts are abandoned gradually when it becomes evident that the investment begins to bring decreasing yields in relation to the energy devoted[857]. The epideictic behaviour of certain animals, their meeting in specific places at regular intervals[858], enables them to have awareness of their number and thus to calculate the optimal level of reproduction in relation to available resources. If the population increases and resources diminish, fertility must fall to avoid fratricidal wars and widespread famine[859]. Some animals leave their young to kill each other to allow the fittest to survive or even themselves eliminate a number of their children to give the rest of their offspring a greater chance of survival[860].

Best Strategy Selection: How Equilibrium Appears as a Logical Requirement

118. Rational choices stabilizing behaviours appear whenever an agent selects a strategy as being the best for him, having regard to the behaviour he expects from the others[861]. In other words, the

855. See *supra* § 95.
856. WILSON 2000, p. 368.
857. DAWKINS 2003, pp. 153 *et seq.*
858. MAYNARD SMITH 2005, p. 199.
859. MAYNARD SMITH 2005, p. 199.
860. DAWKINS 2003, pp. 171 *et seq.*
861. OSBORNE 2004, pp. 45, 120.

behaviour of one of the agents is adapted to the expected behaviour of the others[862]. Life, as explained by the theory of evolution[863], amounts to an infinite series of repetitive games where the mutants, employing new strategies, constantly try to establish balances favourable to them[864]. The best strategy for a living being given the strategy of its opponents is an *evolutionary stable strategy*, that is to say, a strategy which, given the pressures to which it is subject, has proven to be the best to ensure adequate reproduction[865]. Equilibrium, as a solution concept in game theory[866], expresses the idea

862. *"In the game called "the merchants of ice cream", a mayor can assign authorizations to two ice cream sellers to sell their products on a beach. The installation is allowed anywhere on a straight line along the beach and nowhere else. The mayor has selected the two sellers without assigning to them a specific position on the line and he has invited them to indicate to him by irrevocable statement the position of each installation. Both beneficiaries, without communicating to each other, made their statement to the mayor. Both have chosen the middle of the beach. One would expect that they would choose to set up at a certain distance from each other so that they could better serve the people settled at both ends of the beach. But they preferred the centre because each of them having put himself into the other one's shoes, thought that if the two initially shared equally the space by setting up at different points along the beach, his competitor would expand his circle of customers, by displacing daily the mobile installation towards the centre. Thus, he himself, to preserve the same portion of customers, would have no other solution than to also move towards the centre. Finally, the installation in the centre, in the absence of an outside authority which would impose on them the contrary, is the solution which both retailers would select even if it is not the best for their clientele. It is the solution to the problem of the choice of the installation place because it has an essential character: it is the best solution for each one of the two traders with regard to the behaviour expected from the other. None has interest to deviate from this solution because no other solution preserves better his interests. It is thus a stable solution which as such creates an equilibrium in respect to the behaviour which each trader will adopt in relation to another"*; see Jacques-François THISSE, *Théorie des jeux: une introduction*, pp. 22 *et seq.*, text not published.

863. MAYNARD SMITH 2005, pp. 38 *et seq.*

864. DAWKINS 2003, pp. 99 *et seq.*

865. GIBBARD 1996, p. 85; DAWKINS 2003, pp. 103, 289.

866. PETERSON 2009, pp. 212 *et seq.*

of stability between competing interests that are in interaction, in the same way as *evolutionary stable strategy* in biology[867]. But, unlike biology where *natural selection* is the driving force behind the creation of equilibriums[868], in game theory equilibriums are achieved by *rational thinking*.

In game theory, each player pursues her own interest, and as a rational being, she is moved, when choosing her strategies, to maximize that which is of utility to her[869]. Each player knows that the other players are also rational like her, pursuing the same objective of maximizing that which is of utility to them[870]. All have the ability to understand the motivation of others, to *"put themselves in the shoes of others"*, and, for this reason, they are able to anticipate their movements[871]. Under this assumption, game theory tries to conceive strategies for the players which, in the context of interaction, maximize that which is of utility to them[872]. The solution concept for these games therefore results from the application of the best possible strategy in light of the strategy of the other party.

Nash equilibrium[873] is reached by the successive exclusion of possible choices as there successively appears to be a better strategy to apply[874]. The player must put herself in the shoes of the other to anticipate her movement. Each player predicting the choice to be made by her competitor in light of the choice she intends to make, successively rejects one solution after another until she finds a solution which leaves her without regrets should she follow it[875]. The

867. GIRAUD 2009, pp. 29 *et seq.*
868. MAYNARD SMITH 2005, pp. 107 *et seq.*
869. PETERSON, pp. 41, 65, 91 *et seq.*
870. BINMORE 2005, p. 126.
871. GAUTHIER 2006, p. 68.
872. BINMORE 1994, p. 297.
873. OSBORNE 2004, pp. 23, 29-31; GAUTHIER 2006, p. 71
874. GAUTHIER 2006, p. 76. See also fn862.
875. OSBORNE 2004, pp. 385, 377 *et seq.*

concept which dominates the solution is the equilibrium of the respective strategies[876]. It emerges when players realize that their strategies are the *best responses* to the strategy of their co-player and consolidate their behaviour on the basis of that understanding[877].

119. Games that feature players with competing interests are called *zero-sum games*, when the total sum put at stake by players remains the same regardless of the outcome of the game[878]. *Cooperative games* presuppose the possibility of a discussion between the players carried out with a view to establishing an agreement between them on sharing the proceeds of their cooperation[879]. The famous *prisoner's dilemma*[880] is as a game in an area between the

876. GAUTHIER 2006, p. 75 *«Equilibrium is a rationality property of outcomes considered as product of strategies»*.

877. OSBORNE 2004, p. 36.

878. GIRAUD 2009, pp. 35 *et seq.*

879. AXELROD 2006, pp. 3 *et seq*; OSBORNE 2004, pp. 153 *et seq*; GIRAUD 2009, p. 113 *et seq.*

880. GAUTHIER 2006, pp. 79-80; POUNSTONE 1993, pp. 118-119: *"Two members of a criminal gang are arrested and imprisoned. Each prisoner is in solitary confinement with no means of speaking to or exchanging messages with the other. The police admit they don't have enough evidence to convict the pair of the principal charge. They plan to sentence both to a year in prison on a lesser charge. Simultaneously, the police offer each prisoner a Faustian bargain. If he testifies against his partner, he will go free while the partner will get three years in prison on the main charge. Oh, yes, there is a catch... If both prisoners testify against each other, both will be sentenced to two years in jail. The prisoners are given a little time to think this over, but in no case may either learn what the other has decided until he has irrevocably made his decision. Each is informed that the other prisoner is being offered the very same deal. Each prisoner is concerned only with his own welfare – with minimizing his own prison sentence. The prisoners can reason as follows: 'Suppose I testify and the other prisoner doesn't. Then I get off scot-free (rather than spending a year in jail). Suppose I testify and the other prisoner does too. Then I get two years (rather than three). Either way I'm better off turning state's evidence. Testifying takes a year off my sentence, no matter what the other guy does'. The trouble is, the other prisoner can and will*

zero-sum games and those that are cooperative. It is neither one nor the other, but it can become, according to the strategy that players choose, either one or the other. The question at the bottom of the dilemma is the choice between distrust and trust. In the prisoner's dilemma, played as a static game, equilibrium is reached by applying a non-cooperative strategy[881]. But the same game played as an infinitely repeated game reaches equilibrium in the choice of a cooperative strategy, because the pay-offs it brings in the long-term are more than the pay-offs which the opposing strategy brings to the players[882]. Indeed, in the one-shot prisoners' dilemma, the shadow of the future does not weigh within the relations of the players and so players do not have to consider future pay-offs when adopting their strategy. But the game, played in a repetitive way, provides more opportunities for gains to the players when they play a cooperative strategy. However, if one of the players plays *"cooperation"*, while the other does not, the first would be systematically exploited by the second, and pay-offs from cooperation would not be obtained, as was initially expected[883]. That which, on the contrary, makes cooperation possible is the application by both players of strategies of reciprocity where each player plays *"cooperate"* as much as the other plays the same strategy and she starts playing *"defect"* once trust is betrayed[884].

120. Cooperation raises the problem of mutual concessions which are necessary for achieving the agreement to cooperate. A negotiation between persons who are determining the burdens and benefits in connection with their cooperative agreement, takes

come to the very same conclusion. If both parties are rational, both will testify and both will get two years in jail. If only they had both refused to testify, they would have got just a year each".

881. See *infra* §§ 152, 154.

882. See *infra* §§ 156, 157.

883. BINMORE 1994, pp. 189 *et seq.*

884. OSBORNE 2004, pp. 419 *et seq.*

the form of a *bargaining game*[885] insofar as each one of the negotiators applies a strategy aiming at maximizing their benefits[886]. There is a subjective scale of perceived utility which is allotted to each of the participants, quantified however in an inter-subjective manner[887]. On this scale, zero (0) represents a no agreement point and one (1) the terms of agreement satisfying in full the wishes of each of the participants. The space between 0 and 1 represents the utility to be gained from an agreement. The approach of each trader is measured in terms of maximization of profit to be gained from trading and minimization of concessions to be granted on the negotiations. The traders compresse their demand following two convergent principles: to minimize the maximum concessions to be made, and thus to move away as little as possible from item 1; and to maximize the minimum benefits to be gained, thus moving as far as possible from 0. The two movements are obviously carrying them to a point between 0 and 1, representing for each participant the best possible outcome in the negotiation[888].

Negotiation consists of a mixture of proposals and counter-proposals: one of the parties proposes what seems reasonable for the other party to accept, and the other party, in turn, retorts by rejecting the proposal, and so accepting the risk of blocking the negotiations, or by putting forward a new proposal, which will reflect his view of a reasonable agreement. Rational negotiators never forget their personal interest and never make voluntary sacrifices from which the other traders benefit “free of charge”. They always consider the price to be paid compared to the benefits to be gained, having regard to the advantages and sacrifices of their counterparts in the negotiation.

885. BINMORE 1998, pp. 77 *et seq.*
886. PETERSON, pp. 247-251.
887. GAUTHIER 2006, p. 147.
888. GAUTHIER 2006, p. 155.

The key to understanding the process is the idea of concession[889]. Concessions depend on various elements, such as risk aversion of the participants[890], the threat of withdrawal exercised by one party over the other[891], the empathetic perception by one of the negotiators of the behaviour of the other[892]. One principle, however, appears to be more or less constant: the first to concede is the one who has more to lose from a breakdown of negotiations than to gain from not making the concession[893]. The agreement achieved represents the maximization of what everyone could get in terms of individual benefit over the sacrifices regarded in advance as constituting rational concessions. When the negotiations reach that point each will feel satisfied because there was no better solution to be reasonably expected[894]. This *point of equilibrium* is within an area that contains several solutions representing an improvement for the participants, but its essence is that it maximizes the total benefits of each individual participant[895] while requiring the minimum sacrifices from them respectively[896].

889. HARSANYI 2008 pp. 149-159, 200-211, 280-288.
890. McCARTY, MEIROWITZ 2007, pp. 40-46, 278 *et seq.*
891. SAINT-SERNIN 2012, pp. 98 *et seq.*
892. HARSANYI 2008, pp. 130-131; GAUTHIER 2006, pp. 199-200; PETERSON, pp. 179, 183.
893. GAUTHIER 2006, pp. 142-150.
894. GIRAUD 2009, pp. 145-149.
895. VON NEUMANN, MORGENSTERN 2007, pp. 647 *et seq.*
896. NASH 2007, pp. 99 *et seq.*; GIRAUD 2009, pp. 137 *et seq.*

CONCLUDING REMARKS

The Stabiliser of Interactions

121. Anaximander, a Greek pre-Socratic philosopher, asserted that harmony reigns in the world as the result of opposing forces arriving at a state of equilibrium[897]. He conceived justice as the product of a reaction restoring equilibrium between competing forces, each respectively trying to dominate the other[898]. Heraclitus, another Greek pre-Socratic philosopher, observed the links which are formed between opposites and taught that the universe's unity emerges from these links[899]. For Heraclitus, justice was the way followed by nature, so that its various opposing elements exist in equilibrium. Within the dialectical relation of the opposites, Heraclitus found a stable element, the *logos*, the inherent structural principle of the world which produces order[900]. Anaximander and

897. KIRK, RAVEN, SCHOFIELD 1983, pp. 119, 137; p. 118: *"... some other apeiron nature, from which come into being all the heavens and the worlds in them. And the source of coming-to-be for existing things is that into which destruction, too, happens, 'according to necessity; for they pay penalty and retribution to each other for their injustice according to the assessment of Time".*

898. KIRK, RAVEN, SCHOFIELD 1983, p. 120: *"...the prevalence of one substance at the expense of its contrary is 'injustice', and a reaction takes place through the infliction of punishment by the restoration of equality – of more than equality, since the wrong-doer is deprived of part of his original substance, too".*

899. KIRK, RAVEN, SCHOFIELD 1983, p. 192 on the philosophy of Heraclitus: *"The unity of things lies beneath the surface; it depends upon a balanced reaction between opposites".*

900. KIRK, RAVEN, SCHOFIELD 1983, p. 193; p. 187: *"What they should recognise is the Logos, which is perhaps to be interpreted as the unifying formula or proportionate method of arrangement of things, what might almost be termed their structural plan both individual and in sum"*; p. 203: *"Not mere curiosity about nature (although this was doubtless present too) but the belief that man's very life*

Heraclitus had not undertaken scientific experiments to arrive at their conclusions. They expressed an intuition to explain in their minds what they observed in nature. The order around them could only emerge if the divergent or opposing elements of which it is made could be held in equilibrium. The *logos* was to them a logical necessity, a constraint that was required by the structure of being, not a phenomenon induced by observation or experimentation[901]. To put it in modern terms, the fundamental forces of nature[902] should contain in themselves, by a logical necessity that one might infer in an *a priori* manner, the ability to stabilize their mutual interactions of repulsion and attraction at a point of equilibrium, which generates order. *Logos* is the *a priori* and, at the same time, the *sine qua* condition that allows the universe to be made up of divergent elements[903]. In the same way as the physical laws of the universe[904], *logos* is therefore part of a Platonic type world, a world of rules, with the ability to guide the unrolling of our universe's history.

122. We have seen above how order emerges within animal societies[905]. On the one hand, a hierarchical system, based mainly on physical force, produces rights of priority. The regulation of

---

is indissociably bound up with his whole surroundings". Wisdom – and therefore, it might be inferred, satisfactory living – consists in understanding the Logos, the analogous structure or common element of arrangement in things, embodying the μέτρον or measure which ensures that change does not produce disconnected, chaotic plurality. It remains to describe Heraclitus' views about men – their soul, institutions and ideas. But for Heraclitus this subject was in no way separate from the study of the outside world".

901. CORBIN 1969, p. 1123, on Islamic philosophy of science: *"The science of balance tends to enclose all human knowledge".*

902. WEINBERG 1997, pp. 15 *et seq.*

903. HAWKING, MLODINOW 2011, pp. 21 *et seq.*

904. KLEIN 2010, p. 146.

905. See *supra* §109.

behaviour is part of this system, which assigns roles to its members. On the other hand, a system of divided territories sets out areas of exclusive domination. Within their perimeter, the dominant element creates harems or excludes any other animal from hunting. However, the distribution of functions, the assignment of roles, the distinctions between dominant and dominated are not always made on the criterion of power. Other factors exert a crucial influence in this regard. The relationship between mother and child is illustrative. Mothers, and sometimes fathers, provide the necessary care to their offspring and share their food with them. Very often, they adopt altruistic behaviour towards them that leads them even to sacrifice their lives. In societies formed by great apes[906], reciprocal relationships are established in multifarious ways based on the ability to coalesce against the stronger and on cooperation for achieving common goals. Hierarchical and territorial systems, the assignment of roles and functions, physical power or genetic predisposition, generate the order we see in animal societies; in fact, all that may be analyzed either in terms of mutual adjustments made to avoid conflict, or in terms of systems of support and cooperation, for the common good. These adjustments and systems of support and cooperation are practiced because they are integral to the gene pool of the animals as a result of natural selection. Animals have not chosen them as a result of a rational choice, as humans would have done. The evaluation registered in their genes has been performed by the simple fact that the social species we observe have survived the intense competition which any animal species faces on our planet[907]. Biologists, inspired by game theory, have seen in this success the pursuit by those animals that have survived of *evolutionary stable strategies*[908]. Under the priority objective of reproduction, the selected

906. See *supra* §107.

907. See *supra* §113.

908. See *supra* §118.

social behaviours are the best responses to the competitive behaviour of other species. Hence, order in animal societies is not the result of a mere accident. It was generated by an ineluctable constraint to maximize chances of reproductive success. Avoiding conflicts through mutual adjustments; obtaining mutual benefits through systems of reciprocal aid and cooperation are, in this sense, the best responses animals that practice them have used to achieve their main objective.

123. In human societies, rules assign to the individual his property rights, his roles and functions, the extent and the limits of his power and capacities that he can use when dealing with others. If human society exists and humans are not destroyed mutually in a war of all against all, it is because the techniques which we have observed in animal societies that avoid conflicts and foster cooperation, are also practised by humans. What we consider to be a creation of man, law and ethics, have in fact remote genetic origins. However, even if his sociability is of animalist origin, man is able, thanks to his rationality, to reinvent it, to find a rational base to it and to practise it, not as a program which is recorded in his genes, but as an option that is substituted for the natural process of selection[909]. Men live in society because they realize that the benefits they derive from social life are much higher than in a non-social state of life. If they cease believing it, they revolt or, simply, emigrate, seeking elsewhere what is not offered to them in the society where they live. In animals it is natural selection which predisposes to hierarchical and territorial systems; which arrange the roles and functions conditioning the exercise of physical force. In humans, all adjustments of behaviour to avoid conflicts, or promote cooperation as a means of increasing mutual benefits, must be able to be justified or explained in a rational way.

909. See *infra* §129.

124. We saw in the first part of this book, that to convince rational beings to live together in peace, it was necessary to impose on them a law emanating from a higher will or to promise them rewards or threaten them with punishment after death. The ontology adopted facilitates the submission by human beings to laws that are imposed on them. A universe that contains a great governor or life after death compels humans to acknowledge that it is in their interest to respect the word of God. However, as we saw in the second part[910], where men, who must live together, do not share the same ideas on what transcends this world, they are able to reconcile each other's interests on the basis of primary values. The cases which we studied enabled us to note that these values are used as ultimate yardsticks whenever a question is raised on fair distribution[911], remuneration[912] or punishment[913]. In humans, rationality requires the ability to justify the decision made. The cases studied retrace the steps in the reasoning leading to a decision on a matter of justice. The intellectual means used, the conditions laid down, and the techniques employed, all have in common, as we have seen, that they seek to establish *an equilibrium* between interests, represented by different people, which are in conflicting interaction.

We can find here the idea of *logos* discussed earlier[914]. Justice is served when a level of acceptable satisfaction is attained between the interests of some when they are in collision with the interests of others. To do this, justice sets conditions of rationality that we observed by studying the above cases: at the heart of the approach is the search of a point at which the claims of all are satisfied in such a way as to ensure the emergence of the greatest possible de-

910. See *supra* §§ 72-120.
911. See *supra* §§ 95-96.
912. See *supra* § 97.
913. See *supra* §§ 88-89.
914. See *supra* §121.

gree of stability. In game theory, this point is reached when decision makers make a decision that they will not regret[915]. Judges will not regret their decision when the determination they make could not have been improved on; Parliament will have no regrets when it could not have done any better in promoting the legitimate interests at stake. Individuals, faced with a question of justice, will have no regrets when they could not have done any better in seeking to defend their interests.

915. See *supra* §118.

PART III

The Shaping of Fair Balance Solutions

125. Human interests interact either when people get in touch by mere social contacts or when individuals are connected deliberately in common undertakings. The justice issue arising in the first case is to determine to what extent the interests represented by those who interact must shrink to allow peaceful coexistence[916]; while, in the second case, the justice issue which arises is to determine the pay-off accruing to the persons who enter into a cooperative interaction[917]. The problems which arise respectively are, in other words, a coordination of behaviours problem in the first case and a problem of sharing the burdens and benefits of cooperation in the second[918]. The process of conciliation is illustrated by the calculus metaphor in both cases. Two or more opposing interests or values are at stake and justice is assigned the task to indicate the best possible arrangement of them.

Ideologies like Marxism[919] and religions like Buddhism[920] seek to nullify the conditions allowing opposing forces to arise, preaching an ideal state of human life where all needs would be satisfied or there would be no individual needs. Real life however ineluctably raises questions on reconciling opposing interests and values. The duty not to act when doing so harms somebody, may be opposed by the duty to act in order to prevent harms to another[921], while setting

916. See *supra* §§ 92-94.

917. See *supra* §§ 95-97 concerning cooperative ventures and § 120 concerning, among others, exchange of goods and services.

918. GIBBARD 1996, pp. 32, 78, 83.

919. See *infra* §131.

920. See *supra* § 43.

921. SCHOPENHAUER 1991, pp. 131, 133, 140, 156, 161, 162, 180; SARMAS 2011, p. 162; EDMONDS 2014, pp. 28-31.

priorities, in our world of limited resources, is a question of trade-off among concurring or even conflicting objectives[922]. To resolve these problems Jesus preached *"do for others what you want them to do for you"* (Matthew 7, 12); and Kant advised that one should *"[a]ct only on the maxim whereby thou canst at the same time will that it should become a universal law"*[923]. Principles of justice like equality, utility or consent and ethical principles stemming from religions or ideologies, are used to assess in a more or less quantitative way the opposing interests and to conceive step by step how their conciliation can be achieved. In the third and last part of this book we will see where justice's solutions are situated in the whole range of solutions between, on the one hand, ethical standards of altruistic behaviour and, on the other, strategic features of selfish choices.

126. *The Shaping of Fair Balance Solutions* is made up of three chapters. In the first, *Principles of Justice and the Reasons for their Mixing,* we introduce the idea of equilibrium as the indicator of justice into the main theories of justice applicable to societies where people do not share and are not supposed to share the same values and views. In the second chapter, *Metrics and Dialectics for a Reflective Equilibrium,* we present features of equilibrium solutions in order to select among them the one which best transcends individual interests ensuring the most adequate promotion of the collective good. In the final chapter, *Social Institutions as Equilibrium Setting Tools,* we analyse fundamental institutions of society as tools for achieving equilibrium solutions among human interests in interaction.

922. SHAPIRO 2003, p. 102.

923. KANT 1983, p. 136.

7

Principles of Justice and the Reasons for their Mixing

127. Theories of justice consistent with pluralism are those which remain neutral in respect of the various conceptions of good nourished within a society. We may group them under three main ideas: *equality*, when justice is seen as a system of rules likely to secure to each one a certain degree of equal treatment; *utility*, which identifies justice with maximisation of happiness of the greatest number of individuals; and *consent*, which considers that justice is based on rules agreed by free subjects in pursuit of their mutual advantage[924]. Egalitarianism, utilitarianism and contractarianism, inspired respectively by the above ideas, are all theories of justice enshrined in the pro-freedom tradition of Western civilization. However, these theories may legitimately claim to be universal; not in the sense of pretending to replace ethical or religious conceptions of good which a man may hold or a society may select; but in the sense of indicating the best possible way of living together for people not sharing the same beliefs and values, and who have no social solution other than to tolerate or respect each other. Their starting assumptions are different; the means to justice they advocate diverge; their overall objective remains however the same: instituting and preserving a society of free individuals who pursue

924. SHAPIRO 2003, pp. 109 *et seq.*, 115 *et seq.*

their happiness in a way which is mutually compatible. This is the reason why equality, utility and consent are not mutually exclusive. On the contrary, in confronting reality, each one of these principles is forced to fluctuate in such a way as to invade the other's field. In this sense, justice is not specifically to be found only in the idea expressed autonomously by each one of them; justice is to be found in the *rationale* indicating the way in which they coalesce so as to allow a fair balance solution of all interacting interests and values to emerge.

Theories of Justice Compatible with a Pluralistic Society

128. A state adopting a supreme good as its overall objective gives to its legal order the form of a hierarchical structure in which all elements are adjusted to support a common effort. Any institution, any rule, and any behaviour, can be appraised on the basis of whether or not it complies with the sovereign objective[925]. In that scenario justice is a question of adjusting or correcting the elements of the whole within this construction.

For a follower of Plato's ideas, consent, as understood in the West, has no place in a well-ordered society within which everyone must do his duty without having a choice[926]. For a follower of the Brahmin religion[927], equality of human beings would be irrelevant as equal treatment is a principle inconsistent with its vision of a society composed of castes according to the penitence which is reserved for each one. And for a Moslem, the search for happiness wouldn't and shouldn't be measured by utilitarian indicators used in the West to establish the well-being of the people, but by his chances of entering paradise after death[928]. If these three individuals, holders of

925. RAWLS 1997, pp. 437 *et seq.*
926. CLAY 1988, pp. 24-29.
927. See *supra* § 43.
928. See *supra* § 37.

very different philosophical or religious convictions, had to build a society composed of people sharing only their views, they would probably have rejected equality, utility and consent as fundamental values for their society. However, if it were necessary for these three people to live together without doing violence to each other and if, in addition, they were to join together in cooperation, they would have to find principles for living together which, being compatible with their religion or convictions, would have to be capable of being shared by all[929]. Suspicious of one another, these three individuals would certainly have tried to keep the maximum of equality and consent for themselves and would cooperate with each other to promote their personal utilities as defined by them. Democratic societies, in which groups of people who do not share the same convictions have to coexist and work together[930], are organized around ontologically neutral social values such as equality, utility and consent[931].

129. In the West, current philosophical conceptions of the good are fighting against the traditional concept of man as the sovereign being on earth. The animal liberation movement advocates the allocation of rights to animals and preaches that the great apes

929. BADIOU 1997, pp. 105 *et seq.*

930. SHAPIRO 2006, pp. 146-147: *"Rather than think of democracy as a mechanism for institutionalizing the general will, we should recognize its claim to our allegiance as the best available system for managing power relations among people who disagree about the nature of the common good, among many other things, but who nonetheless are bound to live together. To be sure, this view rests on a conception of the common good. But is a comparatively thin one, best captured by the formulation that it embodies what those with an interest in avoiding domination share. Indeed, the possibility of diminishing – if not eradicating – domination is often what draws people to democracy. Confronted with the injustices of apartheid or totalitarian communism, they turn to democracy as the instrument of their emancipation because of its constitutive commitment to non-domination".*

931. FRIEDMAN 2002, p. 12; SANDEL 2012, p. 203.

should be included in the field of humanity, being at the same time critical of human rights as a conception of justice tainted by *"specism"*[932]. Deep ecology[933] raises earth's ecosystem to the dignity of a living being whose preservation is the supreme good; man, in his expansion against nature, is considered as a being whose interests have no moral priority over the interests of other entities of the ecosphere, while capitalism, because of its constant expansion, is condemned as a harmful economic system bringing the earth to disaster[934]. Feminism regards the system of law in place as an emanation of male psychology, which is conflictual and dominating, and advocates a morality based on feelings and a system of justice operating by *ad hoc* solutions[935]. The animal liberation movement, deep ecology and feminism proceed from ideological conceptions of the good that fight against the injustices which occur in the legal systems of the West. They are however ideologies preaching a precise conception of good and, as such, cannot be used as a basis for a justice that is able to incorporate the diversity of the conceptions of good prevalent in pluralistic societies.

Darwinism, with the laws of evolution of the species[936], sociobiology[937], Freudianism[938], and all the political and philosophical theories which see the human being as a mere animal species[939] have not managed to create such a favourable cultural universe as to impose a resolutely deterministic conception of the human species[940]. In democratic societies, human beings are not seen as biological en-

932. SINGER 2009, pp. 140 *et seq.*; JEANGENE VILMER 2008, pp. 45 *et seq.*

933. FERRY 1992, pp. 131 *et seq.*

934. MORIN 1993, pp. 76 *et seq.*

935. KYMLICKA 1999, pp. 255 *et seq.*

936. RIDLEY 2004, pp. 8-16; 2003, pp. 33, 134.

937. WILLSON 2012, p. 169.

938. RIDLEY 2003, p. 283.

939. GUILLEBAUD 2001, pp. 51 *et seq.*; 293 *et seq.*; COMPTE-SPONVILLE, FERRY 1998, pp.102 *et seq.*, 143 *et seq.*; FERRY 1992, pp. 89 *et seq.*

940. BRIGHHOUSE 2004, p. 153; FERRY 1992, pp. 9 *et seq.*; HABERMAS 2002, pp. 30 *et seq.*

tities and their institutions are not considered as tools for reproducing their genes effectively[941]. The crimes of Nazism, state eugenics, racism and genocide exclude the use of this kind of human ontology as a basis for a politically acceptable idea of justice. Within democratic societies, believers, agnostics and atheists, libertarians, socialists and pragmatists, though nursing conceptions of the world or of society that are quite different or opposed, must coordinate their actions under the authority of the same government and cooperate for their mutual benefit.

130. Egalitarianism, utilitarianism and the social contract tradition are conceptions of justice worked out to offer solutions to societies which adhere to the values of freedom and employ the non-authoritarian method to solve the conflicts appearing in them. As freedom is their underpinning value, *equality, utility and consent* do not operate as autonomous imperatives, but as *tools serving liberty*[942]. They are precisely presented not as conceptions of absolute justice ousting any other view, but as necessary instruments capable of efficiently solving freedom maintenance problems which any pluralistic society faces. Their importance, in terms of the approach we are adopting here, is not in their relevance in describing cultural situations in the West. Their interest lies in their abstract and general nature which enables them to appear as models which, detached from place and time, are suitable for resolving problems of justice appearing in pluralistic societies. Of course, it would be hazardous to claim that logically the only conceptions of justice compatible with pluralistic societies are the three mentioned above. However, egalitarianism, utilitarianism and the social contract tradition, at least in the way we understand them here, are *the* mainstream theories of justice, supported by the most influential authors and movements[943].

941. See *infra* §§ 111, 112.

942. GUÉRARD de LATOUR 2011, pp. 165 *et seq.*

943. See *infra* §§ 131, 132, 135, 136, 139, 140.

Equality, Moral Hazard and the Enslavement of the Talented

131. Immanuel Kant advocated the equality of rational beings willing to preserve their moral autonomy. He purified humans from any empirical data[944] and made them the autonomous and rational subjects who should never be used as a mere means by those with whom they share the same autonomy and rationality[945]. A society of such beings is founded on the mutual respect of their freedom so that what each concedes in order to live in society with others is matched by an equivalent sacrifice conceded by the others[946]. Karl Marx claimed that real freedom is only possible in a communist society where the conditions would be established for the equal satisfaction of all essential human needs[947]. He identified justice with the maxim *"from each according to his ability, to each according to his needs"*[948]. According to Marx[949], a man's capacity to create value by his work is alienated by social systems which transform him into a means of production[950]. Marx calls for a revolution which will impose[951] the socialization of all means of

944. FERRY 2006, pp. 95 *et seq.*

945. KANT 1983, pp. 136, 137, 150.

946. BARRY 1995, pp. 191-192.

947. SHAPIRO 2003, on Marx, p. 76: *"Like Hegel, he had a view of short-run disquilibrium and long-run equilibrium in the sense that every hitherto existing mode of production contained internatl tensions or 'contradictions' that must inevitably breed a reaction and replacement by another internally contradictory system, to be replaced again and again until a stable system could be reached. For Marx rather that the Prussian state of nineteenth-century Europe, the stable equilibrium would be a communist utopia ushered in by a socialist state following the overthrow of capitalism. Until that point was reached, history would be a series of unsatisfactory reactions to unworkable tensions, always marked by a contradiction between the relations of production and the forces of production".*

948. RENAUT 2004, p. 138.

949. ARON 2002, pp. 495 *et seq.*

950. SHAPIRO 2003, pp. 71 *et seq.*; ATTALI 2005, pp. 311 *et seq.*

951. SHAPIRO 2003, pp. 85 *et seq.*

production and consequently the eradication of all exploitation of man by man[952]. Jean-Paul Sartre, for his part, is impelled by his primary conception of man as the only being on earth that freely determines his essence, to advocate equality in order to create a society of free people. Sartre, however, understood that the absolute freedom with which man is endowed cannot be maintained if any man, acting in bad faith, disregards the consequences of his acts to others[953]. If we choose to behave in a certain way, we must in good faith allow others to behave in the same way[954]. Thus, responsibility, based on the principle of non-contradiction[955], leads to the adoption of moral norms which, by being consistent with each other, permit the emergence of a social order ensuring equal freedom for all individuals[956].

132. Published in 1973, when the Cold War was at its height, John Rawls's *Theory of Justice* offered American liberals assurances that it was possible to preach within the capitalist world an ideal of social equality perfectly consistent with the market economy[957]. Rawls' starting point is his intuition that nobody deserves their physical, psychic and mental capacities and the chance granted them to live in a given society[958]. When privileged and unprivileged persons engage in a cooperative venture the former, having greater capacities and thus more means of contribution, claim a proportionately greater part of the value generated by the

952. MARX ENGELS 1966, pp. 31 *et seq.*
953. SARTRE 1996, p. 39; see also p. 31: *"l'homme est libre, l'homme est liberté … l'homme est condamné à être libre"*.
954. SARTRE 1996, p. 61.
955. SARTRE 1996, p. 68.
956. SARTRE 1996, p. 71.
957. SHAPIRO 2003, p. 136.
958. Paul, *First Epistle to Korinthians*, 4.7: *"For who regards you as superior? What do you have that you did not receive? And if you did receive it, why do you boast as if you had not received it?"*

cooperation. However, not deserving the gifts on which their capacities of contribution are based, the inequity of departure affects the equity of a sharing proportionate to the contributions which will result from their gifts.

Rawls proposes an experiment of thought as a basis of impartial justice. He invites us to put ourselves under a *veil of ignorance* that blinds us to the conditions that make up our situation[959]. He considers that rational beings under such a veil of ignorance would adopt as basic principles of justice[960], first, a rule on freedom, granting to each the largest basic liberties compatible with the basic liberties of the other[961]; and, secondly, a rule on distribution of economic and social benefits to all requiring that unequal treatment in this matter should be possible only if it is justified as a means of improving the conditions of the less advantaged[962].

The second Rawlsian principle of justice says in substance that capitalism should be tolerated if it allows transfers of wealth from the most to the least fortunate. In the underlying structure of the second principle there is a negotiation idea guided by the strategic objective of *maximizing the minimum*, that is to say, making the position of the less privileged the best possible[963]. This rule of *"maximin"* is also the point of contention generated by Rawls's theory. Scholars find it doubtful whether rational subjects acting under the starting conditions posed by Rawls, would adopt a strategy of *maximin*, which is in fact a recognition of a right of veto on the part of the least favoured to the progress of the most favoured[964]. They argue that rational beings under such conditions would select a complex utilitarian strategy consisting in maxi-

959. RAWLS 1999, pp. 15 *et seq.*; BARRY 1989, pp. 322-333; SHAPIRO 2003, p. 119.

960. RAWLS 1999, pp. 52-56.

961. RAWLS 2008, p. 69; RAWLS 1993, pp. 155 *et seq.*; BINMORE 1994, p. 145; see also ELEFTHERIADIS 2008, p. 155-170.

962. RAWLS 2008, p. 78; BARRY 1989, pp. 226 *et seq.*

963. GILBOA 2010, p. 74; SHAPIRO 2003, p. 133.

964. BARRY 2004, pp. 53 *et seq.*

mizing collective utility and minimizing individual concessions to society[965].

133. What matters for Kant is the creation of a system of equal freedoms and rights, in which all would have the same opportunities to thrive as autonomous beings. For Marx, true freedom could appear only in a classless society where humans are not alienated by working conditions and some are not subjugated, because of economical inequalities, by others. Sartre realised that economic conditions were essential in a society of equal beings and, for this reason, he conceded to the communist movement the transitory task of releasing humans from their subjugation to social classes. The objective of all was ultimately real freedom, but each in his own way considered that real freedom was not achievable without equality. Rawls, within the Kantian tradition, formulates his principles of justice to enable social cooperation based on the effective equality of all. He recognizes, however, that an absolutely egalitarian society would eventually turn against freedom because it would take enforcement actions to maintain equality, and moreover would lead to collective impoverishment if the most talented had no incentive to employ their gifts for the benefit of society. In order to reconcile the equality which he preaches with freedom and utility, he introduced his second principle of justice by which he conceded to the most gifted the possibility to grow rich subject to the condition of alienating from their property that which would serve the least privileged. According to Rawls, political authorities should consciously give preference to policies which improve the life of the less well-off, even if these policies do not optimize national wealth as a whole.

134. The two Rawlsian principles of justice reflect the two different directions the egalitarian tradition has followed. The first

965. SHAPIRO 2003, pp. 141 *et seq.*; GAUTHIER 2006, p. 322.

illustrates the political movement which focused on equality of rights, equality before the law and non-discrimination of whatever kind in societal matters[966]. The second principle reflects the requirements of equality in real life conditions for which social reformist movements, left parties and radicals are fighting[967]. Although Rawls gives absolute priority to the first principle over the second, he nonetheless understands that it is impossible to preserve equality in social conditions without affecting liberty as such. The two main concerns of Rawls in the implementation process of his second principle of justice thus illustrate the main problems any egalitarian idea of social justice has to face[968]: moral hazard[969] and restriction of freedom. In a society where everyone has the same rights to social goods, there are limited incentives for individual effort[970], while, at the same time, gifted individuals are constantly obliged to work not for their own benefit, but rather for the benefit of others[971].

966. Kant, Mill, Locke; see §§ 131, 135, 139.

967. Marx, Bentham, Rousseau; see §§ 131, 135, 139.

968. WALZER 1997, pp. 23 *et seq.*; STIGLITZT 2012, p. 78: *"I and, as far as I know, most progressives – do not argue for full equality. We realize that that would weaken incentives. The question is, How seriously would incentives be weakened if we had a little bit less inequality?"*; p. 106: *"(...) inequality is the inevitable consequence of any incentive system, (...) They then maintain that there is a trade-off between efficiency and equality. While different people may differ in how much efficiency one would be willing to give up to get more equality in the view of the Right the price we have to pay for any more equality in America is just too great. Indeed, it's so high that even the middle and the bottom, especially those who depend on government programs, would likely suffer; with a weaker economy, incomes for all would be down, tax revenues would be lower, and government programs would have to be cut".*

969. GILBOA 2010, p. 132.

970. GILBOA 2010, p. 132.

971. HAYEK 1994, p. 129; SPAPIRO 2003, p. 144.

Maximizing Utility, Lack of Information and Uncertainty

135. David Hume[972], in his *Enquiry Concerning the Principles of Morals* claims that *"wherever disputes arise, either in philosophy or common life, concerning the bounds of duty, the question cannot, by any means, be decided with greater certainty, than by ascertaining, on any side, the true interests of mankind"*[973]. The interests of mankind are, according to Hume, the individual interests of all the individuals who make up society. Justice and morality emerge from the mutual respect by persons for each other's basic interests[974]. According to Hume, this mutual respect restrains men from interfering with the goods of others in the same way as they expect others to adopt the same attitude of restraint[975]. For the father of classical utilitarianism, Jeremy Bentham, the morality of an action is measured compared to its consequences for the good of the humanity. *"An act,* he wrote[976], *which seems beneficial in its immediate when its results are seen in their entirety and are coldly calculated, may after all be pernicious. Similarly, an act, whose consequences seem harmful at first, may, well*

972. BARRY 1989, pp. 145 *et seq.*

973. HUME 2002, p. 552.

974. PLATO, *Republic*, book 2, 359 a, b: *"(...) to do injustice is, by nature, good; to suffer injustice, bad (...). And so when individuals (...) have had experience of both (...), they think that they had better agree among themselves to have neither; hence there arise laws and mutual covenants; and that which is ordained by law is called by them lawful and just. This they affirm to be the origin and nature of justice; it is a (...) compromise, between the best, which is to do injustice and not be punished, and the worst, which is to suffer injustice without the power of retaliation (...) justice, being in the middle between the two".*

975. HUME 1993, p. 90: *"I observe that it will be of my interest to leave others in possession of their goods, provided that they act in the same way with me. They are aware to have a similar interest to regulate their conduct"*; see SHAPIRO 2003, pp. 19 *et seq.*

976. BENTHAM 2006, p. 125.

balanced, be proven beneficial". Called the *"calculus of utility"*, the technique of Bentham to measure utility consisted, first, in drawing up an inventory of all the interests potentially affected by a decision to be taken; second, in adding, expressed respectively in positive or negative arithmetical values, all pleasure and suffering that the envisaged decision might produce; and, finally, in weighing on a balance of, on the one hand, the pleasures and, on the other, of the sorrows expressed in a quantitative way, in order to select the most useful decision to make[977]. John Stuart Mill's[978] starting point was the assumption that state authorities were in no better position to define utility for the individual than individuals themselves. He suggested the "*harm principle*" to justify state action in limiting freedom of individuals: individuals living in society interact with each other in a way which may cause harm to others and the role of the state is to intervene whenever necessary to prevent or punish harmful actions[979]. If the harm threshold is crossed, then utilitarian considerations to resolve or regulate conflicting utilities come into play[980]. According to Mill, *"if the utilitarian principle is good at something, it should allow us to weigh these conflicting utilities, to make the balance and well determine the area in which either has preponderance*[981]. In this respect, Mill was a *rule utilitarian*[982]: he thought decisions should be made about the net effects of classes of actions and policies and not about each action or policy taken individually.

136. John C. Harsanyi, a modern representative of utilitarianism[983], argues that individuals evaluate social interactions using

977. BENTHAM 1907, pp. 30, 31.
978. J.S. MILL, 1968, p. 57.
979. J.S. MILL 1983, pp. 163-164.
980. SHAPIRO 2003, p. 61.
981. J.S. MILL 1983, p. 77.
982. SHAPIRO, p. 61.
983. BARRY 1989, pp. 17 *et seq.*; 76 *et seq.*; BINMORE 2005, pp. 147 *et seq.*

either an individual or a collective code. The first enables a person to appraise social situations compared to her own interest, the second compared to social well-being[984]. Ethics is the field where the individual ceases thinking of increasing her personal utilities and places herself in the position of an impartial and impersonal observer[985]. If she has to evaluate from this impersonal and impartial point of view a social situation, she must make the effort to temporarily forget her own position. To do so, she should allow the same probability of being in the position of any person[986]. The possibility of making *interpersonal comparisons of utility* remains open according to Harsanyi in so far as the differences in behaviour and in preferences expressed by the various individuals are controlled by the same basic psychological laws. Thus, if the individual who likes to eat beef and hates to eat fish, imposed her preference on the exclusively fish consumers, the latter would be worse-off than before[987]. According to Harsanyi[988], an individual must assess the personal position of another individual on the basis of the preferences of this other individual[989]. Assessments of this nature are possible only if the appraiser develops *empathetic qualities*[990]. She must determine a social situation by using the code of appraisal of others and not her own code[991]. In this respect, Harsanyi claims that the differences of the individuals are determined by three variables of causality: the biological heritage, the personal history of each one, and her environment[992].

984. HARSANYI 2008, pp. 10-11.
985. HARSANYI 2008, p. 10.
986. HARSANYI 2008, p. 48.
987. HARSANYI 2008, p. 52.
988. HARSANYI 2008, pp. 51-55.
989. HARSANYI 2008, p. 54.
990. HARSANYI 2008, p. 51.
991. HARSANYI 2008, p. 56.
992. HARSANYI 2008, p. 58; BUCHANAN, TULLOCK 2004, p. 74: *"Essential to the analysis is the presumption that the individual is uncertain as to what his own precise role will be in any one of the whole chain or later collective choices that*

Harsanyi considers that individuals, when in the position of the impersonal and impartial observer, look at the alternative social situations before them as *risky ventures*[993]. A rational subject, writes Harsanyi, who is in such a situation of uncertainty will make a rational choice only if she chooses the project that maximizes her expected utility[994]. In other words, making moral judgments means that a person evaluates social situations in terms of *maximizing the average utility*, whatever her position in the alternative situation she assesses.

137. Hume argued that men were able to establish justice by mutual respect for their rights even without state intervention and Bentham acknowledged that equal distribution of utilities was more likely, than any other kind of distribution, to increase overall well-being[995]. Mill turned utilitarianism into a liberal doctrine by limiting state intervention to cases where men are doing harm to each other[996]. Utilitarian thinkers consider the quest to maximize global utility as the basic moral principle, without however

will actually have to be made. For this reason he is considered not to have a particular and distinguishable interest separate and apart from his fellows. This is not to suggest that he will act contrary to his own interest; but the individual will not find it advantageous to vote for rules that may promote sectional, class, or group interests because, by presupposition, he is unable to predict the role that he be playing in the actual collective-decision process at any particular time in the future. He cannot predict with any degree of certainty whether he is not more likely to be a winning or a losing coalition on any specific issue. Therefore, he will assume that occasionally he will be in one group and occasionally in the other. His own self-interest will lead him to choose rules that will maximize the utility of an individual in a series of collective decisions with his own preferences on the separate issues being more or less randomly distributed".

993. HARSANYI 2008, pp. 22-24.
994. HARSANYI 2008, p. 50.
995. SHAPIRO 2003, pp. 21-25.
996. SHAPIRO 2003, p. 61.

neglecting either freedom or equality. Inequalities and limitations of freedom, when a certain threshold is exceeded, start to become counterproductive and so affect the global utility distributed within the population[997]. Bentham conceived a calculus to find out what global well-being requires and Mill was in favour of calculating global utility outcome when individuals, by their mutual interactions, are producing harm to one another. Harsanyi realised that any calculus of utility was inescapably affected by lack of sufficient information to make a fully enlightened judgment[998]. He perceived therefore the rules of justice as patterns of behaviour to be chosen under conditions of uncertainty and argued in this respect that rationality required those ones to be selected which are expected to maximize average utility. However, for Mill the average utility was expected to be maximised by the protection of individual freedoms, and Bentham, for his part, defended a rather economic conception of utility, praising wealth redistribution policies as a means of increasing global utility.

138. There are two contending views of injustice to which two different conceptions of utility correspond[999]. The first stems from malevolent acts calling for individual redress and, the second, from social institutions producing structural disadvantages that require sustained action by government if they are to be addressed effectively. *Free market utilitarian thinkers* limit state intervention in preventing or repressing harm caused to citizens by human malevolence[1000]. Conversely, *reformist utilitarians* praise an extensive role by the state to eradicate structural disadvantages[1001]. They consider that state action should be used to reverse social trends which

997. See *supra* § 60.
998. HARSANYI 2008, pp. 9-11, 94.
999. SHAPIRO 2003, p. 67.
1000. SHAPIRO 2003, p. 55.
1001. SHAPIRO 2003, pp. 26-36.

negatively affect access by the neediest individuals to utility resources. However, the policies that reformist utilitarians advocate are affected by what besets any calculus of utility: first, the lack of all the information necessary for calculating adequately the consequences which these policies will have in the future[1002]; and, second, ignorance of individual preferences as interpersonal comparisons of utility turn out to be extremely difficult, if not impossible[1003]. Using probabilistic approaches in order to remedy these failures is certainly the appropriate choice. But, in real life, applying a probabilistic approach to fill such a significant gap in knowledge often comes close to wishful thinking[1004].

The Social Contract Theories, Free Riders and Externalities

139. Thomas Hobbes argued[1005] that reason requires each person, acting in his own interest, to abandon a portion of his liberty, provided that others do the same, in order for his survival and his well-being to be defended by means of the state[1006]. *A commonwealth is said to be instituted,* Hobbes has written[1007], *when a*

1002. GILBOA 2010, p. 6.

1003. BINMORE 2005, pp. 27 *et seq.*; 121 *et seq.*

1004. ALCHIAN 1950, p. 219: *"In general, uncertainty provides an excellent reason for imitation of observed success. Likewise, it accounts for observed uniformity among the survivors, derived from an evolutionary, adopting, competitive system employing a criterion of survival, which can operate independently of individual motivations. Adapting behavior via imitation and venturesome innovation enlarges the model. Imperfect imitators provide opportunity for innovation, and the survival criterion of the economy determines the successful, possibly because imperfect, imitators. Innovation is provided also by conscious wilful action, whatever the ultimate motivation may be, since drastic action is motivated by the hope of great success as well as by the desire to avoid impending failure".*

1005. HOBBES 1982, p.150.

1006. HOBBES 1982, p. 141.

1007. HOBBES 1651, pp. 64-65.

multitude of men do agree, and covenant, everyone with every one, that to whatsoever man, or assembly of men, shall be given by the major part the right to present the person of them all, that is to say, to be their representative; every one, (...), shall authorize all the actions and judgements of that man, or assembly of men, in the same manner as if they were his own (...)." According to John Locke, men pass from the state of nature to the state of government in order to address the shortcomings of the state of nature[1008]. In doing so, they have as their main objectives the preservation of their life, their health, their freedoms and their goods[1009]. The civil authority which is thus established by contracting individuals assumes a limited power which is to be used exclusively for the purpose for which it was instituted[1010]. Jean-Jacques Rousseau, for his part, considered that man living in society is free when he obeys a law in the creation of which he had participated. He is equal to any other as he is endowed with the same right to the formation of the general will and takes part in it in the same measure as any other member of society[1011]. The *social contract* gives to the political body full power over the person and the goods of the associates. This power is however limited by its own nature: submitted to the general will, it proceeds only by decisions which have a general character and which, directed to all, express the common interest of all[1012].

140. Jürgen Habermas, a modern representative of the social contract tradition[1013], sees at the origin of human society, men and women invested with subjective rights, appropriate to their nature as moral beings[1014]. They create a state to protect their rights and

1008. LOCKE 243, p. 253.
1009. SHAPIRO 2003, pp. 110-115; RUSSSELL 2003, pp. 606-610.
1010. SHAPIRO 2003, pp. 14-17; RUSSSELL 2003, pp. 613-616.
1011. RUSSELL 2003, pp. 669-670.
1012. GAUTHIER, 2006, pp. 313-318.
1013. HABER 2001, p. 195.
1014. HABER 2001, pp. 195 *et seq.*

agree not to allow any restriction of them without a rationally held discussion in which their arguments will be duly heard[1015]. Human rights are of a moral nature and become legal only when the state gives to them the fundamental character desired by the subjects of law. Democracy and human rights are, in regard to one another, enabling conditions[1016]. There can be no democracy without respect for freedom of conscience, and there can be no human rights without a democratic government to determine their contents and limits. The validity of a law must perpetually be justified on the basis of rational arguments, and when these arguments lose validity the legislator must repeal or modify the law[1017]. Judges do not have any democratic authority to replace the democratic procedure for adopting the law by using voluntarist interpretations. Their function is to monitor discussions on human rights and to declare any act adopted without an *appropriate procedure of discussion* to be contrary to human rights[1018]. Hence, Habermas recommends the abandonment of any *essentialist conception of justice*[1019]. Social morals cannot lay claim, in the multicultural societies of today, to any kind of universality. The rule of law can only be produced by a process within which any person concerned can give approval following a discussion held on the basis of rational arguments[1020]. Democratic law is the product of a perpetual tension between the world of facts which, by way of the official institutions, sets up claims to validity[1021], and the world of rational minds, which verify and legitimate these claims. Inherent in the law is the rational adhesion of the people to whom the law is applicable[1022].

1015. HABERMAS 1997 pp. 135 *et seq.*
1016. HABERMAS 1997 pp. 477 *et seq.*
1017. HABERMAS 1997 pp. 290 *et seq.*
1018. HABERMAS 1997 pp. 276 *et seq.*
1019. HABERMAS 1992 pp. 16, 111, 149; ROSENFELD 2000, pp. 103 *et seq.*
1020. HABER 2001, p. 168; HABERMAS 1986 p. 88.
1021. HABERMAS 1997 pp. 15 *et seq.*
1022. HABERMAS 1986, pp. 86-89.

141. Hobbes argued for a social contract under which all natural rights of the contractors were entrusted to the sovereign in order to be fully protected by him. Locke, opting for a limited state, argued for a social contract under which only a part of the natural rights of citizens were transferred to the state under conditions put in place in order to preserve liberty. Rousseau preached a social contract creating a democracy which, by expressing the general will, would preserve to all equal liberty. In all three authors the social contract, a legal tool binding actual citizens in an exchange exercise, was considered the foundation of justice[1023], the fundamental reference to judge the rightness of social behaviour. Habermas presented a social contract version not as an historical event which occurred once and has hitherto produced its effects, but as a process producing *fair balance solutions* every time individuals are in disagreement on a question of justice. He argued that rational beings are able, even if they do not share the same beliefs and values, to identify progressively, under the conditions of a fair discussion, the points which prevent them from agreeing and then, by a process of mutual concessions, to find an outcome of consensual approval.

142. Rawls is considered by a large number of distinguished scholars to be the modern representative of the social contract tradition, and Hume's argument on the implied agreement of members of a society not to harm each other is seen as structured on contractarian assumptions[1024]. Social contract tradition is however differentiated here from egalitarianism and utilitarianism by the mere fact that in its substance, as it appears from Habermas's argument,

1023. PHARO 2001, pp. 33-35.

1024. BUCHANAN, TULLOCK 2004, pp. 241-242: *"The essence of the contractual conception of the collectivity, quite independent of the empirical validity of this construction, involves the mutuality of gain among all members of the group"*. See also HAMPTON 1995, pp. 386-389.

it proceeds from a clearly procedural conception of justice without aiming, as the other two conceptions do, ultimately to satisfy substantive requirements such as equality or utility[1025]. Freedom could certainly be considered to be the end-objective towards which contractarian theorists are aiming. But, first, freedom is pervasive in all three conceptions of justice we have presented here as the underlying ultimate value; and secondly, in the social contract tradition, liberty is realised by the social contract procedures so that there is no distinguishing feature as between liberty and social contract except that the first is the outcome of the second.

143. Social contract theories assume that all citizens participate or are willing to participate in the contracting process. For this reason, whatever the nature of the contract, whether it is hypothetical, historical or even a requirement of reason, social contract theorists face two serious difficulties raised by *free riders* and *externalities*. Free riders are people who, for their own reasons, refuse to participate in the social contract process, specifically preferring free riding[1026]. They may be members of terrorist organisations or simply citizens not paying taxes. Forcing free riders to participate in the contracting process is abandoning the main feature of any social contract as an agreement based on unanimous consent. Externalities are side-effects produced by the implementation of the

1025. BUCHANAN, TULLOCK 2004, p. 271: *"Instead of initially developing a social-welfare function which unambiguously orders all social situations, we start from the presumption that we are quite ignorant as to what is 'better' or 'worse' for the group. Falling back on the Pareto criterion for assessing changes, we admit as 'better' only those changes that are observed to be approved unanimously by all members of the group. Any changes that secures unanimous support is clearly 'desirable', and we can say that such a change is 'in the public interest'. (...) The 'public interest' becomes meaningful only in terms of the operation of the rules for decision-making, and these rules can be evaluated only over a long and continuing series of separate issues".*

1026. SHAPIRO 2003, pp. 233-234.

social contract on goods or interests not subject to the contractual obligations[1027]. They include pollution produced to a neighbour community[1028] or extinction of the common fisheries stock owing to extreme individualistic practices[1029]. Ignoring the side-effects on goods and interests unprotected by the social contract is to accept a narrow-minded self-interest conception of the social contract developing unsocial egoistic features.

Free market theorists advocate, in the case of free riders, *Pareto optimizing solutions*[1030], where any legitimate change should maximize the utility of at least a fraction of the population without affecting the interests of others, and, in the case of externalities, limitations on or extensions to property rights to protect goods and interests affected by side-effects of a social contract[1031]. Other theorists advocate that free riders be compensated[1032] for freely submitting themselves to the social contract discipline by allocating to them what should be unreasonable for them not to accept[1033]. Others, animated by a more robust conception of state action, either consider that free riders should be obliged to adhere to the social contract as it is in their real interest to do so, or see externalities as market failures and call for state intervention to regulate markets or replace them in regard to the provision of public services[1034]. In other terms, in confronting reality, social contract theorists have to resolve a number of practical issues which oblige them to admit the mixing of their principle of justice with the other competing principles.

1027. KAY 2004, pp. 249-252; CASSIDY 2009, p. 339; SHAPIRO 2003, pp. 233-234.

1028. GILBOA 2010, p. 129, KAY 2004, pp. 254-255.

1029. BINMORE 2005, pp. 7, 14.

1030. BINMORE 2005, p. 7; SHAPIRO 2003, pp. 46-55; BARRY 1989, p. 13.

1031. CASSIDY 2009, pp. 113-121, 127-128.

1032. NOZICK 1988, pp. 104 *et seq.*; SHAPIRO 2003, pp. 128-129.

1033. SHAPIRO 2003, pp. 112, 113, 139-141. See *infra* § 180 on expected costs to achieve consensus.

1034. RUBINI 2011, pp. 39-43.

Mixing the Principles of Justice

144. A few decades ago, India and China, the most populous countries in the world, suffered from extreme poverty and lacked serious growth prospects. This is no longer the case. Both have introduced important capitalist reforms and, becoming actors in global trade, have seen their gross national product increase annually at spectacular rates. Broad layers of their populations are enjoying better living conditions. Admittedly, a class of newly rich has appeared whose incomes present abyssal differences compared to those of the classes which did not benefit yet from the changes. But, the phenomenon of enrichment of these two nations is undeniable.

Under Rawls's egalitarian principle, individuals in India and China would have chosen collective enrichment only when it could be beneficial to the least privileged. However, it is doubtful that with the brake imposed by this principle on the enrichment of a country, India and China, if they had adopted it, would have achieved the economic performances which they are currently demonstrating. Harsanyi applies, in the choice of policies to follow, a test similar to that of the veil of ignorance. In order to make choices of really impartial policies, he invites us to forget our identity temporarily in this respect and to place ourselves in the shoes of those likely to be affected by them[1035]. But, as we saw above, he does not apply the Rawls' criterion of *maximin* to make his choice under such uncertainty. Thus, as regards the recent economic development of India and China, he would have acknowledged an increase in the average utility within the population as a whole, leading to the validation of the economic policies followed by these two countries during recent decades. Under a social contract approach, individuals draw from cooperation utilities which they would not have if they did not engage in cooperative undertakings.

1035. See *supra* § 137.

Admittedly, the sharing of benefits and burdens is agreed following a negotiation[1036] where each one takes part with all his strengths and weaknesses. This does not necessarily prejudge the unfairness of the division. For, on the one hand, coalitions are always possible, allowing the poor, normally numerous, to unite against the richest and, on the other hand, withdrawal is still an option, and therefore, it is in the interest of those among them who wish cooperation to continue not to misuse their strong position in order not to see their counterpart desist at the first opportunity. Thus, just as in ancient Rome, where patricians knew how to make to plebeians the concessions that were strictly necessary in order not to upset the established order[1037], so a contractarian, in the case of the development of India and China, would advise the parties involved on making the necessary concessions which, without slowing down the process of national enrichment, would guarantee the stability of the social contract against popular rejection which could occur as a consequence of intolerable inequalities.

145. A society is a cooperative venture that coexists and competes with other societies of the same type living in interaction. Amerindians lost the war against the Spanish empire not because their society was unjust, but because they did not have guns[1038]. The Soviets disappeared because they could not follow the Americans in the arms race while preserving an acceptable standard of living for their people. Rawls applied his principles to a society whose defence effort does not impact on the implementation of the principles of justice prevailing within it. It was the concern for fair sharing that prevailed. Thus, Rawls's second principle of justice would force the talented to work mainly to improve the lives of the poor. However, a society which enters into competition with other

1036. See *supra* § 120.

1037. See *supra* §§ 33, 34, 35.

1038. FERGUSON 2011, p. 100.

societies cannot concern itself only with questions of production and distribution of utilities[1039]. Equality, utility and consent have, in their specific implementation, to be constantly reconciled, in a competitive world, with the need for continuous adaptation to the requirements of competition. Every society must look at what happens to its competitors and develop, in this respect, a suitable strategy to ensure that it can survive and endure. Such a strategy will necessarily affect the setting of the equilibrium indicator for fair distribution of utilities inside the country. Efforts by a government to maximize national wealth in order better to carry out national defence programs will require incentives to be given to the most gifted, thus increasing the level of social inequalities. If, on the other hand, the government wishes to cement national unity, it will adopt a policy of redistribution of wealth in favour of the disadvantaged, making them feel more integrated within the nation[1040].

In principle, utilitarians give preference to solutions which establish equilibrium at a point where average utility is at the maximum while respective sacrifices reach the minimum. Contractarians, on the contrary, pursuing the stability of the cooperation contract, give preference to solutions which maximize the minimum utility that each individual can draw from the joint venture. Egalitarians, finally, give preference to solutions of equity under conditions of equality at the beginning while inequalities are tolerated, in order to improve the position of the least favoured. Contractarians and egalitarians are thus quite satisfied with a society where a *proportional equality* prevails, provided that the ideal of

1039. NOWAK 2011, p. 93: *"Croup selection makes no assumptions about whether individuals are cooperative or selfish, let alone whether genes themselves are truly selfish. Instead, it simply says that intense between-group competition will favour mechanisms that blur the distinction between group and individual welfare if they improve performance or fitness at the group level. For group selection to occur we need competition between groups and some coherence of groups".*

1040. LANE 2007, pp.117-119.

arithmetic equality is constantly pursued, though never realy attained[1041].

146. It is difficult to foresee with which kind of specific solution each one of the three main traditions on justice will come up. Their principles of justice will certainly be combined, but in which proportion it is not possible abstractly to determine. As we have seen[1042], there is a conservative and a liberal strategy when adapting principles of justice to reality[1043]. Humans are not optimistic to the same degree when it comes to trusting other humans or government. By their education, social experience or even their genes[1044],

1041. PLATO, *Laws*, book 6, 757 a, b, c: *"(...) there are two equalities called by the same name, but are in reality (...) the opposite of one another; one of them (...) is the rule of measure, weight, and number, which regulates and apportions them. But there is another equality, (...) it gives to the greater more, and to the inferior less in proportion to the nature of each; and, above all, greater honour always to the greater virtue, and to the less, less; and to either in proportion to their respective measure of virtue and education. And this is justice (...)".*

1042. See *supra* §§ 134, 138, 143.

1043. See *supra* §§ 135,139, 143.

1044. HAIDT 2012, p. 278-279: *"After analysing the DNA of 13,000 Australians, scientists recently found several genes that differed between liberals and conservatives. Most of them related to neurotransmitter functioning, particularly glutamate and serotonin, both of which are involved in the brain's response to threat and fear. This finding fits well with many studies showing that conservatives react more strongly than liberals to signs of danger, including the threat of germs and contamination, and even low-level threats such as sudden blasts to receptors for the neurotransmitter dopamine, which has long been tied to sensation-seeking and openness to experience, which are among the best-established correlates of liberalism. (...) Even though the effects of any single gene are tiny, these findings are important because they illustrate one sort of pathway from genes to politics: the genes (collectively) give some people brains that are more (or less) reactive to threats, and that produce less (or more) pleasure when exposed to novelty, change, and new experience. These are two of the main personality factors that have consistently been found to distinguish liberals and conservatives. A major review paper by political psychologist John Jost found a few other traits, but nearly all of them are conceptually related to*

some are *risk averters,* while others are *risk takers*[1045]. The first are reluctant to go along with changes and when they see change as inevitable they ask for guarantees against unforeseen consequences. The others readily contest the solutions of the past and see fewer disadvantages when replacing them with new solutions.

The European Court of Human Rights refuses to substitute its own assessment on the elements of the case for a great number of assessments made by the national authorities, by recognizing, what the Court calls, a *margin of appreciation*[1046]. Its case-law on the margin of appreciation reflects the much broader idea that par-

---

threat sensitivity (e.g., conservatives react more strongly to reminders of death) or openness to experience (e.g., liberals have less need for order, structure, and closure)". BUCHANAN, TULLOCK 2004, p. 111: *"Thus the community of homogeneous persons is more likely to accept less restrictive rules even though it can 'afford' more restrictive ones. By contrast, the community that includes sharp differences among individual citizens and groups cannot afford the decision-making costs involved in near-unanimity rules for collective choice, but the real fears of destruction of life and property from collective action will prompt the individual to refuse anything other than such rules. (...) Regardless of the compromises on decision-making rules that may be adopted, the relative costs of collective organization of activity can be expected to be much greater in a community lacking some basic consensus among its members on fundamental values. (...) Many activities that may be quite rationally collectivizes in Sweden, a country with a relatively homogeneous population, should be privately organized in India, Switzerland, or the United States".*

1045. McCARTY, MEIROWITZ 2007, pp. 40-46, 278 *et seq.*

1046. ECHR,10 April 2007, *Evans* v. *U.K.*, § 77: *"A number of factors must be taken into account when determining the breadth of the margin of appreciation to be enjoyed by the State (…). Where a particularly important facet of an individual's existence or identity is at stake, the margin allowed to the State will be restricted (…). Where, however, there is no consensus within the member States of the Council of Europe, either as to the relative importance of the interest at stake or as to the best means of protecting it, particularly where the case raises sensitive moral or ethical issues, the margin will be wider (…). There will also usually be a wide margin if the State is required to strike a balance between competing private and public interests or Convention rights".* See also ECHR, 16 Dec. 2010, *A B and C* v. *Ireland*, §§ 231-239; 18 March 2011, *Lautsi* v. *Italy*, §§ 68-71.

liamentary majorities and national supreme courts' judges should enjoy a certain degree of freedom when dealing with principles of justice[1047]. Cultures, ideologies and personal attitudes determine collective choices of social values, and consequently influence the relevant elements by which a right balance is established. As communitarians argue[1048], the point of equilibrium, or indicator of justice, is not to be determined on the basis of purely rationalist arguments excluding the moral tradition proper to a given society. Every society and every nation builds its equilibrium points on the basis of elements generating consensus that are embedded in the collective consciousness.

1047. See *infra* § 167.

1048. SANDEL 2007, pp. 315 *et seq.*; SHAPIRO 2003, pp. 169-174; KYMLICKA 1999, pp. 217 *et seq.*

8

Metrics and Dialectics for a Reflective Equilibrium

147. John Rawls praised *"Reflective Equilibrium"* as the method appropriate to establishing principles of justice. His equilibrium was *reflective* in the sense that it was not intuitive but based on a retraceable intellectual process, and it was *equilibrium* because there was coincidence between the premises used for the judgments on justice and the principles of justice drawn from these premises[1049]. It is the fundamental thesis of this book that although the premises of

1049. BRIGHTHOUSE 2004, pp. 12-13: *"Theories of justice tell us what principles should guide us when designing social institutions, reforming them and living within them. How do we establish conclusions about these matters? The method that most of the philosophers discussed in the following pages follow is what John Rawls has called the method of reflective equilibrium. This method invites us to develop a theory of justice in the following way. We list our considered judgements about particular cases, and look at whether they fit together consistently. Where we find inconsistencies, we reject those judgements in which we have least reason to be confident (for example those in which we have reason to suspect there is an element of self-interest pressing us to the conclusion we have reached). We also list the principles we judge suitable to cover cases, and look through those principles for inconsistency, again rejecting those concerning which we have least reason to be confident in our judgements. Then we look at the particular judgements and the principles in the light of one another. Are there inconsistencies? Do some of the principles look less plausible in the light of the weight of considered judgements, or vice versa?"*

justice's decisions are indeed subject to beliefs not entirely controlled by rationality, decisions on justice's issues are, on the contrary, established following an intellectual process which is governed by reason. Interests and values entering into interaction are not always stabilised in an equilibrium of justice via consciously taken decisions on justice. Patterns of coordinative or cooperative relations may have been produced by traditional practices, implicit agreements or even mere coincidence. But when it comes to assessing the rightness of these patterns from justice's point of view, a decision on justice has to be made in the sense of a judgement retracing the consistency between the premises we would have used and the conclusions we would have drawn. Justice's vehicle is a decision, the domain of which is the area of human interactions. Stabilising interactions is the desired outcome of an operation seeking to do justice, but not any kind of outcome; only the optimal one. Reciprocity offers a pattern for optimal solutions in a wide range of interactions without, however, being in a position to cover all possible interactions satisfactorily. Justice is not only about adjusting conflicting interests; it is also a question of maintaining an order within coordinative and cooperative relations which makes everyone involved feel that their interests are receiving the best possible treatment. Metrics for the assessment of these interests and the dialectics for their conciliation are necessary in order to establish adjustments indicating the way to follow for producing the optimum outcome from the interactions.

The Decision as Adjustment

148. At the sight of the snake, chimpanzees remain standing on their feet and do not move, while they climb a tree when they feel the threat of a tiger and they hide to avoid eagles. In these cases, they perceive a threatening reality, they evaluate their reaction to it and they select an appropriate behaviour[1050]. Their reac-

1050. BERTHOZ 2003, pp. 120-122.

tions are certainly determined and limited by automatisms encrusted in their brains. Their behaviour, however, manifests the taking of a decision to act. In it, we can see the objective pursued of avoiding the danger and, ultimately, of surviving. We also see an operation of the memory acquired by their species to assess the danger of the snake, the tiger or the eagle. We see, finally, the weighing of the actions available and the choice of the most adequate answer in relation to the nature of the threat. In domestic animals also, certain actions are acquired and depend clearly on the will of their master, as well as on the level of their training[1052]. When humans decide as rational beings, they weigh the relevant elements and choose the action to perform or to omit on the basis of the objective connected to their activity[1053]. The analysis of the situation is conducted by identifying the relevant elements, whether factual or ethical[1054], evaluating them, assigning to them positive or negative values[1055], and finally deciding[1056] on the basis of how strong or weak are the risks envisaged and the benefits expected[1057].

149. Life encases living beings in its laws[1058], but human beings have the power, thanks to their rationality, to replace nature and invent their own laws. Life that determines their being pushes them to perform basic life functions: to procreate; to be nourished, housed, and defended against predators. The reality they observe provides them with useful information in this respect. A description of reality, such as *"the fire burns the human body"*, is information

1051. DE WAAL 2006, p. 235; BERTHOZ 2003, p. 108.
1052. BERTHOZ 2003, pp. 340, 345.
1053. KOSSLYN, MILLER 2013, pp. 27-40.
1054. See *supra* § 74.
1055. See *supra* § 77.
1056. See *supra* § 86.
1057. See *supra* § 80.
1058. See *supra* §§ 112, 113.

which contributes to protection against burns. Humans verify the accuracy of the description of reality that reached them, and once its truth is validated, they include it in their memory as an indicator of conduct towards fire. They cannot then avoid saying: *"If this is true, then, to avoid burns, I should not put my body in contact with fire"*. They will thus transform a description of reality into a pattern of behaviour applicable to them, which they will even try to transmit to the persons close to them out of a concern to protect them from fire. In this example, truth is integrated within a human decision process first, to transform, in conjunction with the basic needs of humans, the description of reality into useful information for survival, and then to trigger behaviour in humans by transforming the information into a prescription. Descriptions of reality such as *"uncontrollable social unrest may be caused, if murderers are not punished"* or *"if a murderer is not punished, more murders are likely to be committed"* constitute information to be delivered to society with a view to providing the means to decide on what to do with murderers. A prohibition of murder would mean that the social body has found the above descriptions of reality presented as accurate and that it expects, by the punishment of murderers, to avoid the evils produced when murderers are not punished[1059].

150. Truth is related to a decision that man has to make. In the human mind, truth is not only the right correspondence between what someone has in contemplation and the material world[1060], but also an element of analysis in the decision-making process. A truthful statement of fact, combined in the individual's mind with the requirements arising from his interests, will indicate to him, using his intelligence, the right decision[1061]. Thus, the search for truth is a

1059. ELEFTHERIADES 2008, pp. 86-91.

1060. BADIOU 1988, pp. 365 *et seq.*; ENGEL, RORTY 2005, pp. 20-26, 34-37, 47-48, 62-69; WITTGENSTEIN 2005, p. 37 § 4.25.

1061. CHANGEUX 2002, pp. 132-134; BERTHOZ 2003, p. 79.

question which is determined by the interest concerned, whose importance imposes a more or less demanding investigation, and the degree of the risk of error which can be tolerated[1062]. In other terms, the degree of certainty required to ensure the truthfulness of a description of reality is a matter of evaluating, on the one hand, the risk of error and, on the other hand, the sacrifices to be accepted in order to limit this risk to the minimum[1063].

Men need to know the truth in order to assign values to their surrounding world. This is the reason why men search the ultimate meaning of reality as a whole[1064]. A fundamental meaning of the reality gives a sense that enables values to be assigned to all situations in which man is involved, and thus allows the distinction to be made between what is good and what is bad, even when basic practical information is lacking[1065]. In other words, the reference to a fundamental meaning offers to men the ultimate metrics of evaluation necessary to make rational choices in all respects[1066].

151. A decision on justice issues is primarily a decision[1067], having however a particular identity which distinguishes it: its sphere of action is where there is an interaction between persons representing different interests which have to be adjusted[1068]. A lawmaker must, in order to make the right rule, carry out an evaluation of the social interests which she wishes to regulate, based on an order of values which is prescribed to her by the context within which she operates. The judge, no matter in which legal order she operates, examines the facts of the dispute on the basis of the eval-

1062. ENGEL, RORTY 2005, p. 43.

1063. SARMAS 2011, pp. 128-129.

1064. See *supra* §§ 15, 18, 23, 37, 40, 43.

1065. CHANGEUX 2002, pp. 327, *et seq.*, 400 *et seq.*; KAHN 2007, pp. 108 *et seq.*, 113 *et seq.*

1066. HEISENBERG 1990, pp.290-291; WHITE 2006, pp. 81-83; see *supra* § 160.

1067. BERTHOZ 2003, p. 334.

1068. GILBOA 2010, p. 5.

uations already carried out by the legislator and expressed in the form of legal norms, in order to measure the value which the legal order assigns to the claims of the litigating parties before her. Two persons who negotiate in order to agree on the clauses of a contract, refer to their order of values and arrive at an agreement only when a common value is allotted to the subject-matter of their negotiation which corresponds to what is, for each party, preferable compared to what in their view is to be avoided.

Not any decision which can be described as right is necessarily a decision on justice. There are decisions that are right, such as the decision to go on vacation earlier or later or to stop smoking or overeating. A decision on justice is not merely a right decision; it is the decision which settles questions concerning interests or values, by seeking to establish the fair price, or adopt the correct rule, or impose an appropriate correction.

Game Theory's Equilibriums

152. The *prisoner's dilemma* features two selfish players, invested with different interests[1069]. Each of them has two options: either denounce the other or remain silent. According to the game[1070], there is no mechanism available to players for binding commitments or to address mutual threats. There is no way for each one of them to foresee what the other player will do, based on elements of analysis such as players' profile or reputation; nor is there any means available to players for eliminating the other or escaping the interaction. Finally, there is no possibility of the players changing the benefits resulting from the movements available to them. The only options available to them are indeed to denounce or to remain silent[1071]. If individuals in a prisoner's

1069. See *supra* § 119.

1070. BINMORE 2005, pp. 63 *et seq.*; POUNSTONE 1993, pp. 101 *et seq.*

1071. POUNDSTONE 1993, p. 120.

dilemma interaction coordinate their behaviour for the mutual defence of their interests (cooperation), each gets a pay-off equivalent to three points, and together they totalise six points. If both behave distrustfully to each other (defection), each gets a point and together they have two points. In the event that one chooses to defect, and the other to cooperate, the first gets five points and the second zero.

Persons in a prisoner's dilemma cannot make their choice without regard to what they think the other individual with whom they interact will do[1072]. If a player thinks the other player will defect, she can only opt for desistance too, because, if she cooperates, with the other withdrawing, she will get the lowest price. On the other hand, if the player thinks that the other player will cooperate, she will defect, because thus she obtains the highest price among all the prices available to the players. In any hypothesis, *"defect"* is the best option for both, with each getting one point rather than three in the case of cooperation where together they would total six. The conclusion to be drawn is clear. Rational beings acting in a situation like that described in the prisoner's dilemma do not receive the optimum potentially available from their interaction[1073].

The prisoners above are in a situation very common to a great variety of social interactions[1074]. They are forced to interact, so they cannot isolate themselves, but they have the freedom to decide on the form of interaction, cooperation or defection. By making a rational choice, they decide to defect because cooperation is, in any case, not the best option for them. The solution in the prisoner's dilemma is a stable and rational solution, respectful of the freedom of participants, ensuring furthermore equal treatment for each participant, as each obtains the same reward. Even if we presume that the dilemma occurs in a state of *moral vacuum*, the solution

1072. BINMORE 2005, p. 126.
1073. POUNDSTONE 1993, p. 126.
1074. BINMORE 2005, p. 67.

of mutual defection presents nothing fundamentally immoral, since neither of the players betrayed the confidence of the other. Both simply chose, freely and rationally, not to cooperate. What makes us feel uncomfortable, however, in the given solution is that the two players with the option they made, are in worse state compared to the one in which they would be if they had cooperated. Not only that, but if they had cooperated, the profit which would have been generated would be cumulatively the highest of all the hypothetical situations considered, namely six points[1075].

153. The so-called *ultimatum game*, also studied by game theory, also leads to socially paradoxical conclusions[1076]. Two people use the following procedure to divide a pie. The first person offers to the second a part of a pie. If the second person accepts the offer, the first receives what is left of the pie. If the second person rejects the offer, both receive nothing. Each person is interested only in the portion of the pie that she receives without taking care of what will happen to the other person, and each person is interested in getting the largest piece of the pie that is possible. In this game the second person has two options available: either accept the offer made to her by the first person, or reject it. If she rejects it, she gets nothing and therefore would not be satisfied, since, on the basis of the starting assumptions, she will be inclined to take the largest part of the cake that is possible. The first person has an infinite range of choices as to the offer to make, but does not have the capacity to take the final decision. Thus, the piece of the pie she will obtain depends on the choice that the second person will make.

The first player wishing to avoid getting nothing, if her offer is rejected, must be available to offer any division of the pie other than that which would result in her getting nothing. However, the first player knows that she can make to the second player an offer so

1075. BINMORE 2005, p. 66.

1076. OSBORNE 2004, pp. 181-187.

infinitesimally small as to be next to zero, being sure that the second player will accept it as it maximizes her utilities compared to what she would have if the offer were rejected. The second person is therefore compromised in her choice of strategy. Rejecting any offer is not the best strategy, because then she gets nothing. She must thus be resigned to accepting any offer except zero.

The stabilization of this interaction cannot be obtained differently than by the first player offering zero, because thus she will have no regrets, and by the second player accepting any offer, because thus she does not exclude the possibility of obtaining something, even if she knows that she will get nothing[1077]. This solution certainly leaves a bitter taste. In a game where one proposes and the other accepts or rejects, the player who proposes, in the end obtains everything. The prisoner's dilemma, which does not lead to a socially optimal solution, at least provides an egalitarian solution. In the ultimatum game the solution is provocatively unequal.

154. The prisoner's dilemma and the ultimatum game constitute abstract formulations of very common social situations in which the options made by free and rational agents stabilize human interactions to reach socially appropriate equilibriums. In the first case, the actors involved in the interaction would be better off if they could cooperate, but as they do not trust each other, they choose to defect. In the second case, the first player knowing the context of the options available to the other player makes the latter get nothing, getting everything herself. Social situations involved in the two games cover very different assumptions[1078]. A person who wonders whether or not to comply with the terms of a contract is faced with a prisoner's dilemma if the pay-off of defection outweighs the benefits of keeping her commitment. States face the same dilemma when they wonder if they can trust their

1077. OSBORNE 2004, pp. 181 *et seq.*
1078. POUNDSTONE 2003, pp. 253 *et. seq.*

potential adversaries or should arm themselves better, even if it means an unnecessary arms race[1079]. Social situations concerned in the ultimatum game are less extensive but not less important. They concern economic relations in which an actor, owner of the capital or the means of production, has the opportunity to make offers to workers and the latter have no other option but to accept or reject[1080].

155. Most of the social models that we have examined in the historical part of this book, from the Pharaoh's empire[1081] to the latest Western dictatorships[1082], interfered with the mechanism of social relations we have seen above to modify pay-offs of each available movement so that anti-social options become inappropriate[1083]. If, for example, the government agency imposes a penalty for mutual defection so as to make it completely unproductive and, using the supervision of a tyrannical and intrusive police, ensures the relentless repression of the recalcitrant, the prisoner's dilemma solution can no longer operate[1084]. It is the same with the ultimatum game's solution when the social system is so designed as to make it impossible for the first player (the capitalists) to oppress the second (the workers) and replaces their respective power with a system whose shares are determined by a third party and imposed on the two actors unilaterally[1085]. For a government agency to intervene in social relationships in order to modify the benefits the actors can expect from their interactions is not in itself condemnable, provided that this intervention only aims at releasing an optimization of the benefits which the actors can obtain without any deterioration of the essential components of the mechanism of in-

1079. POUNDSTONE 2003, pp. 153 *et. seq.*
1080. POUNDSTONE 2003, pp. 305 *et seq.*
1081. See *supra* §§ 14, 15, 16.
1082. See *supra* §§ 59, 60.
1083. BINMORE 2005, p. 178.
1084. GAUTHIER 2006, pp. 157 *et seq.*
1085. BINMORE 1994, p. 32.

teraction[1086]. However, the experience of history[1087] does not indicate that this way was followed by the models studied. Their interventions broke the mechanism of stabilization of the interactions between representatives of interests to replace it with a hierarchical system of priority rights based on race or class superiority, or supported by religion, morals or ideology which suspended the freedom of choice of individuals whose interests were affected. Deviation from the solutions suggested by game theory to conceive other equilibriums has had a big price in terms of freedom.

Emergence of Generalized Reciprocity

156. During the First World War, enemy soldiers showed considerable restraint on the western front, a line from France to Belgium, which covered more than five hundred miles. Small enemy units were face to face with each other for a long period and troop rotation was slow, as advances due to successes of war stagnated. The enemy units thus observed one another. At the beginning, pauses in engagements were held for periods of rest which occurred at the same hour on both sides. Breaks began to be held during periods of bad weather. During Christmas a marked fraternization took place. No agreement bound the two sides to observe the truces. During meals, Christmas time or miserable weather, enemy units could, without violating any explicit obligation, have used their arms against the enemy. It was observed that attacks during periods in which breaks were observed, prompted the enemy suffering these attacks to reply with a ferocity two or three times greater than the assaults[1088]. The enemies mutually ob-

1086. BINMORE 1994, p. 68.

1087. See *supra* § 60.

1088. AUMANN 2006, pp. 354-355: *"The fundamental insight is that repetition is like an enforcement mechanism, which enables the emergence of cooperative outcomes* in equilibrium – *when everybody is acting in his own best interests. Intuitively, this is well-known and understood. People are much more cooperative in long-term relationship. They know that there is a tomorrow that inap-*

served pauses in combat engagements, and were punished accordingly, if the break was not observed[1089]. There was an implied agreement between the soldiers on both sides: provided that there was no battle ordered by the high command, the units that stood face to face in the trenches would rather prefer to *"live and let the others live"*[1090]. For a war, it was a surprising result. The high commands of both armies, when they realized what was happening to their troops, took measures to break the implicit agreements by ordering their subordinates to constantly attack the enemy and by speeding up troop rotations[1091].

157. Reciprocity observed long-term increased the price of cooperation to a level higher than the price of defection. Whenever the soldiers cooperated, they did not count only the immediate pay-off which their restraint from firing back would bring them, but also any pay-off which the same behaviour would offer them in the future. Fire-back could in the short term be profitable, but in the long-run, its pay-off was exceeded by the pay-off from cooperation. This led to cooperative behaviour, by stabilizing voluntary and rational social interactions at an equilibrium based on reciprocity[1092]. The conditions for the emergence of this equilibrium were, first, the sustainability and intensity of interactions be-

---

propriate behaviour will be punished in the future. A businessman who cheats his customers may make a short-term profit, but he will not stay in business long. (...) In brief, for any game G, we have THE FOLK THEOREM: The cooperative outcomes of G coincide with the equilibrium outcomes of its super-game G. Differently put, repetition acts as an enforcement mechanism: It makes cooperation achievable when it is not achievable in the one-shot game. Of course, the above caveat continues to apply: In order for this to work, the discount rates of all agents must be low; they must not be too interested in the present as compared with the future".

1089. AXELROD 2006, pp. 76-82

1090. AXELROD 2006, pp. 73 *et seq.*

1091. AXELROD 2006, p. 82.

1092. AXELROD 2006, pp. 169 *et seq.*

tween the same individuals, and, secondly, the maintenance of a chain of interactions which made cooperative behaviour profitable in the long-term. The behaviour of the troops had the effect of changing the nature of the game that players were supposed to play. There was no longer a zero-sum game, *"you kill me or I'll kill you"*, but a game in which the victory of the one did not mean the defeat of the other. *"Live and let the others live too"* is a game where all players benefit.

Game theory explains this phenomenon as a *repeated prisoner's dilemma*[1093]. The soldiers on either side indeed had benefits similar to those of the players in prisoner's dilemma. It would certainly be preferable for them were the enemy not to fire back when they used their arms. However, if neither fired, this would be preferable than for both to use their arms. Lastly, both parties would prefer mutually to refrain from using their arms, than to engage in hostilities without knowing in advance who would be the winner among them, getting randomly the price of temptation and naivety[1094]. We could expect antisocial behaviour, the preference for using arms, to prevail as the dominant strategy for both sides. However, what had changed the game, producing the emergence of a mutual behaviour of cooperation, was duration. The soldiers played the prisoner's dilemma game in a reiterated way and, therefore, they were able, in the series of games which followed, to punish desistance and reward cooperation in order to channel the behaviour of their enemies into the path of mutual respect.

This shows that building a good reputation[1095] as a player who works with those who are cooperative or defect from those who betray trust is essential[1096]. A person who has a reputation for consistently defecting, will discourage individuals who could be

1093. BINMORE 1994, p. 58.
1094. AXELROD 2006, p. 75.
1095. OSBORNE, RUBINSTEIN 1994, pp. 238-242.
1096. AXELROD 2006, pp. 150-158.

willing to cooperate with her[1097]. In the same way, a person who has a reputation for cooperating unconditionally will be subject to exploitation by those who do not hesitate to defect when this is more advantageous to them than to cooperate[1098]. *Reputation* allows the community of cooperators to identify cooperative individuals and at the same time to isolate or punish non-cooperative individuals[1099].

158. Cooperators are not altruistic. They pursue the satisfaction of their self-interest, being, however, convinced that in the long-run they are better-off by cooperating in a loyal way than by playing free riders or cheating. This is the reason way, for their part, they engage among themselves in a game of negotiation to get the greatest benefit from their cooperation. Cooperators seek to maximize the minimum of their benefits while minimizing the maximum profit that their counterparts seek to draw. There are weak and strong in such a relationship. The strong are those who, because of their physical or mental abilities, are certain that their contribution in the joint venture will be more substantial. They

1097. BINMORE 1994, p. 97; NOWAK 2011, p. 77: *"For my research on the Prisoner's Dilemma, I decided to use a simple approach. (...) I programmed a computer to find out what happened in what I called the spatial Prisoner's Dilemma, using a four-color code to help reveal what was going on"*; p. 78: *"(...) blue for cooperators because it is the colour of heaven; red for defectors, because it is the colour of the other place, I selected green to be a cooperator that had previously been a defector, and yellow vice versa"*; p. 79: *"In this milling universe of unpredictability and chaos there was one fixed point. (...), there were several interesting conclusions to be drawn. (...), once you move from a well-mixed population of defectors and cooperators (a soup) to a heterogenous population with ghettoes of cooperators and defectors (a pizza) the trajectories of evolution can be very different and cooperation is able to emerge and to thrive, even in the absence of complicated strategies"*; p. 80: *"This is the take-home message of my work. Clusters of cooperators can prevail, even if besieged by defectors"*.
1098. AXELROD 2004, pp.146-149.
1099. DE WAAL 2009, pp. 169 *et seq.*; NOWAK 2011, pp. 75-80.

therefore ask to have a bigger piece of the "pie". The weak are those who will in any event have less to bring. But they do not lose the strength of their arguments. Being cooperative, the negotiators do not go so far as to engage in a zero-sum game. They know that if they cooperate to generate the maximum possible value due to their cooperation this can bring only mutual profit to them. Thus, they play the empathetic game, each one putting herself in the shoes of the other, to get closer, by mutual concessions, to the point where their agreement will be possible[1100]. The stronger party thinks: *"my abilities are superior and I would contribute a larger share to the common result, but the profit distributed to my counterpart should not be so little that she will feel offended in her dignity in respect to me"*. And the weaker party thinks: *"my counterpart has plenty of capacity freely offered to her by nature, but does not deserve more than me; if, however, she decided to cooperate with me, she should not feel exploited by me, otherwise she will not offer the maximum of what she could offer in my interest"*. Each one for herself, the cooperators anticipate the empathetic reflexions of their counterparts arriving finally at a stable point, necessarily formed by mutual concessions. At this point, each party feels that she is not drawing the full benefit she could draw. But, comparing the respective utilities and the sense of dignity of the parties, the solution achieved offers to each one the least sacrifices and the most profits[1101].

Metrics for Trade-Off Exercises

159. To the extent that the community of cooperators provides its members with a comparative advantage in respect of a community of selfish members[1102], it becomes a magnet to new mem-

1100. BINMORE 2005, pp. 126-127.

1101. See *infra* § 178.

1102. BUCHANAN, TULLOCK 2004, p. 18: *"The market and the State are both devices through which co-operation is organized and made possible. Men co-*

bers who, themselves, although basically selfish, will have to play the cooperative game, create a reputation as true collaborators and thus reap the benefits of reciprocity[1103]. There would need to be a change of scale in this evolution, when the community of cooperators, feeling strong enough[1104], decides to protect its members against free riders and cheats[1105]. Reciprocal relations, based on the reputation of loyal cooperation, therefore generate an order of stable behaviour founded on the assumption that cooperation is the pattern of social conduct to follow[1106]. Selfish individuals or simply free and rebellious minds are forced to submit themselves to the *rules* followed by the community of cooperators[1107].

Such rules, no matter if they come from morality or the state[1108], combine two opposing characteristics[1109]. They have, firstly, a certain degree of abstraction converting potentially affected individ-

operate through exchange of goods and services in organized markets, and such co-operation implies mutual gain. The individual enters into an exchange relationship in which he furthers his own interest by providing some product or service that is of direct benefit to the individual on the other side of the transaction. At base, political or collective action under the individualistic view of the State is much the same. Two or more individuals find it mutually advantageous to join forces to accomplish certain common purposes. In a very real sense, they exchange inputs in the securing of the commonly shared output".

1103. FUDENBERG, TIROLE 1991, pp. 367-391; NOWAK 2011, p. 54: "*Thanks to the power of reputation, we help others without expecting an immediate return. If, thanks to endless chat and intrigue, the world knows that you are good, charitable guy, then you boost your chance of being helped by someone else at some future date. (...) Indirect reciprocity now means something like 'if you scratch your back, my good example will encourage others to do the same and with luck, someone will scratch mine".*

1104. HAUSER 2006, pp. 214 *et seq.*

1105. See *infra* § 143.

1106. BINMORE 1998, pp. 263 *et seq.*; BINMORE 1994, pp. 97 *et seq.*

1107. NOWAK 2011, p. 204.

1108. STRANGAS 1988, pp. 32 *et seq.*, 622 et seq.; NOZICK 1998, p. 42.

1109. GAUTHIER 2006, p. 157 *et seq.*

ual interests into social values in such a way that they cannot be reduced to individual cases. And, secondly, they comprise a degree of specification sufficient to serve as a guide to individuals in choosing a course of action. A rule thus establishes a pattern of human behaviour in which interacting social values, which integrate individual interests, are adjusted to the community's benefit. This has an important consequence for individuals. When social values integrating individual interests get the best possible treatment, each individual can get, in her turn, the best possible treatment of her interests as reflected in social values. Undue burdens are not imposed on her and she obtains the benefits she deserves while her counterparts have been charged with the burdens they merit and have been offered the benefits to which they were entitled. This *equilibrium of burdens due and benefits merited for all*, achieved via rules generating an order of predictable behaviours, is what moral and state authorities are called on to establish and maintain as justice in their respective areas of power[1110].

160. Ideology, religion, mysticism and ethics influence minds in the direction of convincing them that the equilibrium established by the political regime was the best possible as it best fits the interests of all[1111]. Discriminatory hierarchy and cruel tyranny could be fully justified and even considered as an incarnation of the idea of justice in the eyes of those subjected to ontological myths justifying hierarchies and tyrannies[1112]. Each in the specific position assigned to her, within such a social order, receives what she deserves and can only acknowledge that she

1110. STIGLITZ 2012, p. 104: *"In Russia under communism, the widespread sense by workers that they were not being adequately played a major role in the collapse of their economy. As the old Russian adage had it, They pretended to pay us, and we pretended to work".*

1111. See *supra* § 68.

1112. See *supra* §§ 60, 65, 67.

deserves no better. The distribution of benefits and burdens is considered fair because the principle governing distribution secured to each, having regard to the ideological foundations of the society, is the best possible treatment of her interests. Thus, the *cosmological model* has integrated justice in a global order, containing nature and society, and has transformed persons into instruments for maintaining that order[1113]. The *theological model* made justice a matter of God and turned humans, anxious to avoid the anger of God or to earn rewards from him, into servants of the divine will[1114]. The *democratic model*, finally, separated divine and cosmological matters from regulatory operations by raising the individual, rational and intelligent agent, as the only master of her fate[1115]. Within the cosmological and theological models of justice, an authoritative morality indicates the good on the basis of stable and unchallengeable metrics for performing weighing operations. But, in the democratic model, evaluation criteria are at the mercy of humans whose interests are at stake.

161. When the ideological constructions subsuming individuals in a system of which they become functional instruments collapse, each individual, subjected to the obligations imposed on her by society, asserts rights against society. Equal to others, and autonomous in her own rationality to pursue her happiness, the individual would under no circumstances make sacrifices to society without obtaining compensation. Compared to others with whom she is declared equal, she asserts her right not to be subjected to undue burdens and not to be deprived of her deserved benefits.

Democratic societies have crystallized a broad consensus around core practical goods which all individuals are supposed to share, such as life, bodily integrity, personal autonomy, access to

1113. See *supra* §§ 65, 67.
1114. See *supra* §§ 65, 67.
1115. See *supra* §§ 66, 67.

property, recognition and respect by others[1116]. Individual claims arise in respect of these goods whose satisfaction in their entirety is impossible as they are conflicting or even contradictory[1117]. Justice in a pluralistic society arranges social interactions to provide the best possible treatment to individual interests. Just as two interacting individuals need mutual concessions in order to pursue a line of conduct which avoids conflicts, so it is necessary for communities of individuals to establish rules to regulate behaviour and prevent or resolve conflicts. In democratic societies[1118], where nobody is recognised as inherently superior to the other, an arithmetically *equal treatment* of all is a logical requirement. *Utility* may move equality towards proportionality when to impose burdens on some and offer benefits to others appears necessary in order to preserve and promote social welfare. Each adjustment to proportional treatment should however be treated as made in the mutual interest and thus should be subject to the *consent* of those affected by it. Within a democratic society, law fixes the right proportion of equality, utility and consent within rules of conduct by which individual competing claims are expected to be reconciled into an order of freedom.

Dialectics of Reconciliation

162. Decisions of justice settle questions concerning interests or values in interaction, seeking to stabilise human relations in an order where patterns of behaviour are foreseeable[1119]. Whatever the form or the character of such decisions, there are two elementary requirements which, by their very nature, they have to meet. They must be consistent to each other, creating an order of mutually compatible human behaviour; and they should take care of all interests

1116. See *supra* § 64.
1117. SHAPIRO 2003, p. 102.
1118. See *supra* § 146.
1119. BERTHOZ 2003, p. 334.

involved in a way that no better treatment of them could arguably be possible. Decisions on justice thus aim to combine the appropriate defence of interacting specific interests within a general order of harmonized human behaviour. This is the reason why justice's decisions have to be produced on the basis of a process within which interests are not treated separately, but in relation to each other and the treatment each one receives is a function of its consistency with the order of foreseeable behaviours in which it is enshrined. In other words, justice decisions are produced by a *dialectical process*, which subjugates competing forces into a harmonized synthesis.

Two clearly distinguished exercises can be identified in this process. The first concerns interests and values and its objective is to produce an *evaluation* of the interacting interests which *reflects* the hierarchy of values on which the order of foreseeable behaviours is based. The objective of the second exercise is to point to the *decision* which, better than any other possible decision, *satisfies* all the values and interests involved in the interaction[1120]. Both exercises cannot practically proceed otherwise than by trying successively several solutions until the most adequate emerges as a stabiliser of interactions. This is why they could be conceptualized as balancing exercises aiming at applying a *reflective equilibrium* approach.

163. The first balancing exercise aims, as it has just been suggested, in producing an evaluation of the interacting interests which reflects the hierarchy of values on which the order of fore-

1120. The research of KOSSLYN and MILLER (2013, pp. 27-40) reveals that the brain is composed of two parts, a bottom-brain system and a top-brain system. The bottom-brain system organizes signals from the senses, comparing what is being perceived with the informations stored in memory, and then uses the comparisons to classify objects and interpret events in order to allow us to confer meaning on the world. The top-brain system uses the results gotten from the operations of the bottom-brain system to formulate plans, to figure out what goals we should achieve, and to compare what is happening with what was expecting, adjusting the ongoing plans accordingly.

seeable behaviours is based. *Differentiation* places justice's problem against a background[1121] that will serve to deconstruct the case into its elementary pieces. This background, offering the necessary metrics, can be a moral theory, such as that advocated by utilitarianism[1122], or a legal system consisting of a hierarchy of rules[1123], or even a great ontology, such as that of a religion which sees in a holy book the potential source of regulating any matter of justice[1124]. Whatever this background, it must assign values to the claims raised by the interests involved and thus support a weighing exercise. There may be no specific quantitative value, to be allocated to each of the elements entering into the weighing process[1025]. Each one should obviously receive a certain positive or negative value, but one cannot express this in arithmetical terms. Three requirements, however, must be observed: first, all relevant elements should be identified and evaluated; secondly, the positive or negative value allocated to them should be consistent with the metrics by which the evaluator operates; and, third, the evaluator must be in a position convincingly to justify the judgments she has made.

Differentiation is followed by the exercise of *integration*. It is not enough to unravel a situation into its primary elements in order to apply the weighing metrics to them. A balancing exercise is still needed, allowing a hierarchy to be established among the interacting interests in the case under discussion. After all appropriate considerations, the order of priority given to each interest at stake is tested for its *consistency* with the principles to be observed, the likely *consequences*, and the reaction of *rejection* or *acceptance* by those to whom the solution will be applied. This ensures that the

1121. WITTGENSTEIN 1961, p. 210, and 2001, p. 75, § 241; GRAYLING 1988, p. 84; GIBBARD 1996, pp. 246 *et seq.*; GLOCK 2003, pp. 250 *et seq.*

1122. See *supra* §§ 118-119.

1123. See *supra* § 103.

1124. See *supra* §§ 15, 23.

1125. See *supra* §§ 77, 86, 103, 146; see also FAIGMAN 1994, pp. 753 *et seq.*

order to be established following the balancing exercise is the best possible for each of the values and interests involved.

164. The aim of the second balancing exercise is to point to a decision which, better than any other, satisfies all the values and interests involved in the interaction. This decision will assign to each of the claims under the previous operation the protection they deserve. A differentiation and integration exercise also applies here. The *differentiation* is necessary to establish the range of all conceivable decisions which could resolve the conflict[1126]; and the *integration* to make the choice of the decision which better than any other reconciles all interests and values involved[1127]. For a decision to reconcile, as needed, the competing elements involved, it is necessary to try all potential solutions, to find the one which better meets the conditions required. An undeserved harm must be stopped[1128] or compensated for[1129], punishment must be proportionate[1130], safeguards must accompany interferences[1131], and the dominant position accorded to a value must be accompanied by appropriate safeguards for the protection of other conflicting values[1132]. A decision therefore crystallizes a point of equilibrium: each one of the claims raised has been assessed on the basis of the applicable evaluation criteria, the interests have received the treatment they deserve and, finally, by the decision to be taken, the parties will receive what each can reasonably expect.

Two hypotheses may be envisaged in this context. The first concerns solutions simply regulating behaviours with no other objectives than to avoid conflicts and maintain current order. The sec-

1126. KAST 2002, pp. 24, 28.

1127. ALEINIKOFF 1987, pp. 943 *et seq.*; KAST 2002, pp. 46, 54, 58. This is an algorithmic like process; see CORMEN 2013, pp. 25-59; PAPADIMITRIOU 2007, pp. 29-49.

1128. See *supra* § 73.

1129. See *supra* § 78.

1130. See *supra* § 79.

1131. See *supra* § 82.

1132. See *supra* § 76.

ond covers cases where a specific objective is pursued, with priority being conferred on one of the competing values. Road regulations illustrate the first hypothesis, when the authorities, by introducing traffic rules, have no other objective than to facilitate vehicular traffic in the public domain. A scheme is established prioritizing drivers' rights and obligations according to the circumstances, the overall objective being to maintain order in the use of the roads. The second hypothesis may be illustrated by reference to a case where the authorities, worried by the increase in traffic accidents due to drivers' alcohol consumption or to cars' excessive speed, decide to put in place a deterrence system. Measures like alcohol tests or flashing of cars when speed limits are exceeded are obviously intrusive to the private life of drivers but, in light of the legitimate objective pursued, may be accepted as reasonable limitations of the drivers' rights if they are proportional to the level necessary to achieve the objective pursued[1133]. In the first hypothesis, the differentiation process identifies the various elements comprising the interaction and allocates to them the positive or negative value dictated by the general coherence objective pursued. In the second hypothesis, however, attainment of the specific objective pursued necessitates the deployment of a specific proportionality assessment to limit collateral burdens on the values and interests involved[1134].

165. Under the approach advocated here, there cannot be *categorical rules* or any kind of *absolute rights*. Every decision on justice proceeds, directly or indirectly, from balancing exercises and is formulated in such a way as to reflect and respect them. Moral imperatives contained in holy books and legal requirements expressed in statutes are usually formulated in a categorical manner, not allowing any balancing with competing considerations. The prohibition of torture, and of inhuman and degrading treatment, is formulated in Ar-

1133. KOLM 1996, pp. 160-161; ROUTHGARDEN 2007, pp. 461-486.

1134. See *supra* §§ 80, 83, 86.

ticle 3 of the European Convention on Human Rights, as a categorical rule, and the European Court of Human Rights has consistently stated that this right is absolute as it is not allowed to be balanced, with regard to its limitation, against any other right or value recognised by the Convention. This right is indeed absolute[1135]. But only for those who are intended to apply Article 3 of the Convention. The drafters of Article 3 were not bound by such a categorical rule when reflecting on its content. Following however a balancing exercise they conducted at their level of decision making, they decided to avoid any risk-taking as to the protection of individuals against ill-treatment, and thus introduced a *per se* rule imposing the absolute respect of the right on all levels of decision making bound by that Article.

We find categorical rules at any level of a pyramidal order of norms[1136]. In order to be formulated or at least evaluated in their

1135. ECHR, 1 June 2010, *Gäfgen* v. *Germany*, § 87: *"The Court reiterates that Article 3 of the Convention enshrines one of the most fundamental values of democratic societies. Unlike most of the substantive clauses of the Convention, Article 3 makes no provision for exceptions and no derogation from it is permissible under Article 15 § 2 even in the event of a public emergency threatening the life of the nation (...). The Court has confirmed that even in the most difficult circumstances, such as the fight against terrorism and organised crime, the Convention prohibits in absolute terms torture and inhuman or degrading treatment or punishment, irrespective of the conduct of the person concerned (...). The nature of the offence allegedly committed by the applicant is therefore irrelevant for the purposes of Article 3 (...)".*

1136. STUCKE 2009, pp. 1384-1385: *"For example, a* per se *price-fixing claim under section 1 of the Sherman Act requires proof of an agreement. But even under some lower courts' more "structured" rule of reason, antitrust plaintiffs (...) and defendants must engage in an elaborate four-part minuet. As under the* per se *rule, plaintiffs must also prove an agreement under the rule of reason. But they must then, first, establish that the challenged restraint has had substantial adverse effects on competition, such as increases in price, or decreases in output or quality. In the absence of direct evidence of these anticompetitive effects, plaintiffs can demonstrate the likely anticompetitive effects of a restraint by showing the defendants' "market power" as inferred from their high market share within a properly defined product and geographic market. Such a market definition, in turn, entails issues of cross-elasticity of demand, as well*

rightness, all such rules are subject to balancing exercises by which they have to demonstrate that the point of equilibrium they incorporate is the best possible in view of any other alternative to be considered[1137]. In democratic societies, respect for human dignity and personal autonomy are not only legal principles but also paramount moral values. However, this does not mean that, even if expressed categorically, they do not require justification having regard to the alternatives which could be advanced against them.

---

as supply substitutability into those markets, and ease of entry. But that is just the opening of a four-step routine. After plaintiffs meet their initial burden, the second step shifts the burden of production to defendants to provide a procompetitive justification for the challenged restraint (including the extent to which the restraint increased productive efficiencies, lowered marginal costs, and yielded procompetitive benefits to consumers). If the defendants offer procompetitive business justifications, plaintiffs can, in the third stage, respond by showing the defendants' procompetitive justifications as pre-textual, that lesser restrictive alternatives exist for the challenged restraint, or that the restraint is not reasonably necessary to achieve the procompetitive objectives. If plaintiffs' rule of reason claims survive to this point, plaintiffs must, in a fourth step, show that the restraint's anticompetitive effects outweigh its procompetitive benefits. The fact-finder then engages in a "careful weighing of the competitive effects of the agreement – both pro and con – to determine if the effects of the challenged restraint tend to promote or destroy competition."; see also FAIGMAN 1994, pp. 783-784; TSAKYRAKIS 2009, pp. 468 *et seq.*; PETERSEN 2013, pp. 1387 *et seq.*

1137. See U.S.A. Supr. Court, 25 June 2008 (modified October 1, 2008), *Kennedy* v. *Louisiana*, IV: *"It is an established principle that decency, in its essence, presumes respect for the individual and thus moderation or restraint in the application of capital punishment. (...) To date the Court has sought to define and implement this principle, for the most part, in cases involving capital murder. One approach has been to insist upon general rules that ensure consistency in determining who receives a death sentence (...). The tension between general rules and case-specific circumstances has produced results not all together satisfactory. (...) This has led some Members of the Court to say we should cease efforts to resolve the tension and simply allow legislatures, prosecutors, courts, and juries greater latitude. (...) For others the failure to limit these same imprecisions by stricter enforcement of narrowing rules has raised doubts concerning the constitutionality of capital punishment itself. (...) Our response to this case*

Justice may be the *feeling* of satisfaction approved by all involved in social interactions. It is, also, a *conviction* based on *rational assessment* that all have received the best possible treatment of their interests[1138].

---

law, which is still in search of a unifying principle, has been to insist upon confining the instances in which capital punishment may be imposed. (...). We find it difficult to identify standards that would guide the decision maker so the penalty is reserved for the most severe cases of child rape and yet not imposed in an arbitrary way. Even were we to forbid, say, the execution of first time child rapists, (...), or require as an aggravating factor a finding that the perpetrator's instant rape offense involved multiple victims, the jury still must balance, in its discretion, those aggravating factors against mitigating circumstances. In this context, which involves a crime that in many cases will overwhelm a decent person's judgment, we have no confidence that the imposition of the death penalty would not be so arbitrary as to be "freakis[h]," (...) We cannot sanction this result when the harm to the victim, though grave, cannot be quantified in the same way as death of the victim. It is not a solution simply to apply to this context the aggravating factors developed for capital murder. The Court has said that a State may carry out its obligation to ensure individualized sentencing in capital murder cases by adopting sentencing processes that rely upon the jury to exercise wide discretion so long as there are narrowing factors that have some 'common-sense core of meaning (...) that criminal juries should be capable of understanding.' (...) As noted above, the resulting imprecision and the tension between evaluating the individual circumstances and consistency of treatment have been tolerated where the victim dies. It should not be introduced into our justice system, though, where death has not occurred".

1138. BERTHOZ 2003, pp. 304 *et seq.*

9

Social Institutions as Equilibrium Setting Tools

166. Social institutions, such as those examined in this chapter, were not deliberately designed by human intelligence to satisfy justice requirements. Family, state authorities, punishment, free market and democracy, all have undergone a long evolutionary process to regulate patterns of behaviour by attributing mutually compatible roles and socially useful functions. Law and morals deal with these institutions in different ways, from fully supporting their operation, to condemning at least some of them. In the final chapter of this book, we will conduct an analysis of fundamental social institutions in order to see how, in the sharing of burdens and benefits, they try to secure to all the best possible treatment of interests. We will first address the family as a union of individuals which stabilizes sex relationships by creating the necessary conditions for the companions' engagement in the care of children. We will then consider the state as a tool allowing humans to be free from the arbitrary power of the stronger, and to obtain the benefits of engagement in cooperative ventures. We will thereafter address accountability as the basis of the observance of obligations that humans assume to one another. We will also approach the free market as a mechanism satisfying efficiently the material needs of humans and will consider to what extent the distribution of goods provided by it may be considered equitable.

Finally, we discuss democracy as an institution reconciling conflicting interactions in such a way as to produce social stability combined with the unremitting pursuit of equity.

Family: Reconciling Altruism and Self-Interest

167. Two people want to go to a concert. Two concerts are available to them: Bach or Stravinsky. The first person prefers Bach, the second Stravinsky. If they go out alone, they are not happy. They thus prefer going to the concert of the composer they like the least rather than going alone to that of the composer they love. In this game, the worst solution would be for both players to go out alone and the best would be to go to the concert of the composer they prefer. But as they prefer different composers, they will never be both fully satisfied. To transfer this game to the setting of family relationships, X and Y prefer to live as couple and therefore they reject the solution to live apart. But, in their lives as a couple, each member of the couple may have divergent preferences. X prefers to pursue his career and leave housework to Y, whereas Y would also like to have a career, sharing equitably the domestic tasks with X. The *"battle of the sexes"* has two stable points of equilibrium which, once chosen by the players, neither will deviate from: the Bach-Bach option or the Stravinsky-Stravinsky option. If the players opt for Bach-Bach or Stravinsky-Stravinsky, neither will dare to deviate to increase her earnings, because unilateral deviation will create a Bach-Stravinsky or Stravinsky-Bach pairing either of which are, as we have seen, the solutions least preferred by the players. Once the choice made, the balance created by the Bach-Bach or Stravinsky-Stravinsky options consequently remains stable.

This *"battle of the sexes"*[1139] game spotlights the quest for equilibrium within family relations. Social conditions were such that the balance operated in favour of men at the expense of

1139. GIRAUD 2009, p. 128.

women; women, systematically disadvantaged because of their gender, had no choice but to submit to the asymmetrical relationship that gave them a subordinate role in the couple.

168. For access to sex and reproduction, many solutions are possible and some of them present significant advantages over the others. The solution, for instance, followed by some mammals to give access to sex only to the male that defeated other male competitors, ensures procreation with the strongest genes[1140]. Parents' ignorance of the identity of their offspring, advocated for the guardians by Plato in his *Republic*, ensures equal opportunity for every child[1141]. The monogamist family offers sexual exclusivity between spouses, thus affording equal satisfaction of the needs of all, without wealth, beauty or strength being able to deprive the less fortunate of the possibility of founding a family. Family channels sexuality and the desire to procreate in ways which render the use of force inappropriate, releasing energy to be devoted to other activities as necessary to mankind as the satisfaction of immediate sexual needs.

In the traditional Western-type family, children were raised through the efforts and care provided by the spouses according to a division of labour based primarily on gender. Parents and children were linked by a bundle of rights and obligations, their sacrifices being compensated by adequate benefits. The man was assured of regular access to sex and he was sure of being the only one to fertilize his wife. In return, he had to limit his freedom of choice concerning sexual partners and share his resources with his wife and children. The woman, for her part, was assured of finding the companion who satisfied her need to procreate and, in addition, would take care of her during the long and delicate period when she had to deal almost exclusively with her new-born. She

1140. WILSON 2000, p. 483.

1141. PLATO, *Republic*, book 5, 457d, 462 d, 464-465 d.

was, in return, sacrificing her freedom to live an independent social life, and her genetic interest in being fertilized by the most robust male[1142]. People living under the influence of the generally accepted ideas at that time, could satisfy within a family what was regarded as their fundamental needs, such as they perceived them. Their faith requiring them to prepare their souls for the *Last Judgment*, fidelity, abstinence and sacrifice, were considered by them to be the best way to achieve this[1143]. Society subjected them to the family duties of monogamy, specification of roles based on gender and the giving of priority to children. Such a family ensured the succession of the generations in the established order and raised children who carried on the social values by which their parents were inspired.

169. Secularization of societies, gender equality, and respect for private life have led to a profound questioning of the concept of the traditional family and a redefinition of the roles of father and mother in respect of their children. A new balance is sought to integrate a woman into society on an equal footing with man, along with people who are willing to develop freely their sexual orientation without infringing the freedom of others, and parents who are not willing to stay locked up in a hypocritical family framework. The woman was the main victim of the traditional family in an unbalanced relationship as regards the burden placed on the spouses in the care of their offspring. Before marriage, she had to protect her virginity, a sign of her morality, or, at least, contain her sexuality to prevent pregnancy, while the man was free and even encouraged to have sexual experiences before marriage. Within marriage[1144], the wife had to take care of unpaid household work and thus be deprived of her own income, to devote herself to the care and education of children, unable

1142. MOLLER OKIN 2008, pp. 116 *et seq.*
1143. Alain CORBIN 2008, pp. 255-267.
1144. MOLLER OKIN 2008, pp. 306 *et seq.*

to exercise a professional activity which would have allowed her to be recognized by one of her social qualities other than as mother or wife. Thus women were subject to an obligation of conduct that deprived them of personal autonomy and freedom of choice, and transformed them into human beings having, by their nature[1145], to carry out subordinate tasks compared to those which men were to undertake[1146]. The prohibition of abortion, women's confinement to domestic tasks, and a virtual ban on divorce, were justified by the need to protect birth, education and child development. There was however an imbalance which was immediately striking. In the tripartite relation of woman, children and man, it was the woman who had to carry the main part of the load and the man who remained the principal recipient. As long as the man had the difficult tasks of going to war or performing hard agricultural work, which decreased his life expectancy compared to women, women's withdrawal into domestic tasks was understandable. In modern times, this withdrawal became a fundamental injustice perpetuating a domination which, in light of the changes in ethics, lifestyles and mentalities that had occurred, no longer appeared to be justified.

For a society free of gender prejudices, playing the so-called *mixed strategies* game in the *"battle of the sexes"*[1147] offers a solution that brings stability gains to players while maintaining an equal respect for their preferences. Instead of playing consistently selfishly or systematically altruistically, the players decide to play alternately Bach-Bach and Stravinsky-Stravinsky, offering the possibility of sharing the gains of cooperation[1148]. A model couple is based on mutual concessions when each one is animated by the idea of keeping to her or his own advantage the maximum possible of benefits without jeopardising the sustainability of the couple[1149].

1145. GILLIGAN 2008, pp. 107 *et seq.*
1146. GILLIGAN 2008, pp. 171 *et seq.*
1147. OSBORNE 2004, pp. 113-114.
1148. MYERSON 1997, pp. 155 *et seq.*
1149. OSBORNE 2004, p. 208.

The State: Neutralizing Arbitrary Force

170. There was once a small tribe of primates whose strongest member, the alpha, excluded other males of the tribe from access to the females and claimed priority to the best part of the booty. The males were frustrated, but felt too weak to challenge him; the females suffered, but did not have the means to react, and had nothing else to do but submit. Until they realized that, by acting together, they gained the power they needed to free themselves. The original moment of humanity could be considered this revolutionary reaction[1150] against the strong, supported by a morality against selfishness. Men freed from the domination of the strongest seek happiness under conditions of equilibrium of power between individuals who are pursuing their own benefit in mutually profitable undertakings. Seen from this perspective, the *social contract* is an acknowledgment that each individual permanently consents to the society that provides her with sound reciprocal relationships with others[1151]. Neutralizing arbitrary force, inspired by an ethical ideal, as a means of resolving conflicts in society, is the primary task which the state assigned to itself.

Reciprocity presupposes autonomous wills, possessing the freedom to decide after weighing the pros and cons for their own interests in relation to what is at stake. Associative life and trade operate on the presumption that those who join forces or exchange goods will not be tempted to subject the other contracting party to violence or to take away her property by cheating. If human will is subjugated by threats of violence, if there is cheating or any other kind of abuse, the conditions of reciprocity are not met, and thus justice based on agreement of wills cannot emerge. Criminal and civil law, in protecting people or property, assign rights and duties in order to maintain a balance between people who respect each

1150. BARRY 1989, pp. 320-322.

1151. HAMPTON 1995, pp. 382-384.

other and engage in fair relations. Social welfare institutions and all kinds of services available to the public also seek to preserve the opportunity for all to engage in sound reciprocal relationships.

171. Primitive communities took up arms and formed coalitions with other communities, in order to build up the necessary strength to oppose and overcome their attackers[1152]. The same force was subsequently deployed in sedentary societies against those who did not respect the internal order of society, and tried to get more than they were due, using violence or cunning[1153]. The force of the state was thus opposed to those who, by abusive means, tried to obtain more than they should. It became the protective force of the weak – widows, orphans, foreigners, old, and the sick –, against those who would take advantage of the inability of the weak to put up any resistance, so becoming prey to unscrupulous individuals. The state imposed the restitution of that which had been violated, although guaranteed by established order. State justice ensures that the disrupted order will be restored as it should be, without the opposing parties being able to use their respective strength in order to force an outcome according to their wishes[1154]. In its deployment within society, state power opposed all those who would use arbitrary force to appropriate property not belonging to them or to draw any benefits to which they would otherwise have no claim. The power of order is applied to neutralize the power of the arbitrary or to restore, as required, the order that has been disrupted by arbitrary power. Starting as a preventive, defensive or corrective force against the attackers and cheats, state power was also deployed against the aggressive forces of nature to remedy ills, to prevent natural disasters, and to prepare against natural threats[1155]. However, such a

1152. See *supra* § 12.
1153. See *supra* § 19.
1154. BINMORE 2005, p. 178.
1155. See *supra* § 25.

force, employed by the will of the ruler, could easily be turned against those whom by definition it should serve. Then it is the arbitrary power of the state which is being exerted against the interests of its own subjects, and it is the reaction to this arbitrary power which produced the revolt of the subjects who, pitting their own force against the force of state arbitrary power, gave birth to democracy[1156].

172. In order to neutralize force and combat the egoistic impulses of the strongest, mankind invented myths, cosmological explanations and divine interventions[1157]. The men, who invented cooperation against the dominant force of the alpha, when they became ageing fathers, invented morality as a means of inhibiting the parricidal impulses of their sons[1158]. Their concern was still the same: to neutralize force as a means of distributing goods and to replace it by consent manifested in a context facilitating mutual advantage. As consent cannot be always achieved on the basis of rationalist considerations, it was necessary to recruit morality and with it myths and gods to persuade partners to respect the rules of the social game[1159]. However, morals which initially had the role of containing egoistic impulses themselves became a means of oppression in the hands of the dominant minorities, in order to secure the maintenance of their power. The brutal physical force of the egoistic alpha male or of the rebellious son was replaced by perfidious means of domination which became increasingly sophisticated. The risk of blindness due to misconceptions that manipulate the mind is in our days stronger. The original alpha male can thus be seen now in the figure of the greedy financier, who, by the policies he imposes on the industrialists creates unemploy-

1156. BINMORE 1994, p. 33.
1157. See *supra* § 65.
1158. FREUD 2001, pp. 11 *et seq.*, 35 *et seq.*
1159. See *supra* § 161.

ment, or in a government which, by virtue of its military power, intends to rule all nations, or in a culture which considers itself in possession of a unique truth. This is why the quest for justice consists in constantly maintaining symmetrical relations between individuals looking for their mutual benefit in a changing context. The structure however which creates the equilibrium remains the same: no matter the prevailing ethos, it is identified with the order that emerges from the neutralization of arbitrary force and selfishness.

Accountability: Supporting the Network of Reciprocities

173. The discussion on free will goes back to the relationship between man and God: God, by creating the world, in the way he did, predestined man to salvation or perdition as he knew at the origin of time what each one of us would become, and created the world in such a way as to enable this to happen. In the era of experimental science, God has been replaced by the principle of causality: man is determined by natural laws which govern him[1160]. The idea man has of his freedom of choice is an illusion. In fact, his choices are determined by a multitude of factors, physical and social, that influence his will and incline it in favour of one or the other option. A calculator, with the powerful ability to capture and process all relevant data in this regard, would be able to predict his choices. The discovery of quantum physics and the random behaviour of elementary particles called into question the principle of causality[1161]. However, natural selection, psychoanalysis, genome studies and cognitive science dealt a fatal blow to the idea of man, being equipped with a soul, and free will[1162]. Some genes started to be held responsible for certain kinds of de-

1160. KAHN 2007, pp. 196 *et seq.*, 212 *et seq.*

1161. BOHR 1991, p. 174.

1162. KAHN 2007, p. 216; KARLI 1995, pp. 1 *et seq.*

viant behaviour[1163]. The conclusions of these discoveries have invaded modern political thought, including the concepts of justice. If individuals cannot be held responsible for the gifts and handicaps that nature has assigned to them randomly, or if enhancement of individuals' capacity is dependent on socio-cultural factors beyond their control, it would be unfair to distinguish between individuals on the basis of their unmerited gifts and, therefore, law should be purified from classifications, or should even seek to counter inequalities, based on such conditions[1164].

174. In contemporary Western science, the human being is a product of natural selection and, as such, is subject to the constraint of the ceaseless combat for adaptation and of survival[1165]. However, in this fight, he does not stand alone. He fights in coalition with others. Human beings are tied together in a symbiotic and reciprocal relationship in which they take on roles, create expectations of one another, and give and take. Physical strength and the threat of its exercise are not the only regulatory elements of social coordination. Feelings of pity, sympathy or empathy, produce a similar regulating effect. They avoid making others suffer because to see them suffering normally causes feelings of embarrassment to them, and even remorse when they consider themselves responsible for this suffering[1166]. Feelings which impede, obstruct, or threaten social links are detected and condemned[1167]. Envy, jealousy, selfishness, lack of compassion are treated as antisocial states of mind, and persons who show them in their behaviour risk social downgrading[1168]. Individuals who do not coordinate their behaviour with others as their social environment expects them to do, run the risk of losing the

1163. EVERS 2009, pp. 71 *et seq.*
1164. SHAPIRO 2003, p. 141.
1165. See *supra* § 114.
1166. HAUSER 2006, pp. 214 *et seq.*
1167. GIBBARB 1996, pp. 366 *et seq.*
1168. GIBBARB 1996, pp. 160 *et seq.*

recognition status others had allocated to them. Even if there is no risk of the use of physical force to restrain or punish him, social disapproval or exclusion are sufficient threats to make an individual reconsider his behaviour[1169]. Hence, fear of physical and moral reprisals lead them to regulate their behaviour to one another in order to avoid the inconveniences they would have to suffer if they do not. Their intellectual abilities allow them to envision the hostile reactions that their behaviour could provoke[1170]. They can get into the minds of their interlocutors, measure their reliability, and gather information on them before engaging in a reciprocal relationship with them. They predict, in other words, what reactions they will generate in others because of their behaviour and, according to a calculation of benefits and risks, they will give up or persevere in their projects.

Expectations of others are projected on to every one of us and when we deviate from these expectations we take the risk of provoking in others reactions of resentment against us. In a society governed by a social contract, parties are willing to take retaliatory measures against cheats, by isolating them from the social fabric as elements not worthy of confidence. Thus, the deserters have to calculate, on the scale of utilities to be drawn up, not only the specific utility they expect to gain from cheating, but also the global impact that such a defection risks having on their reputation[1171]. By means of these social sanctions it is possible to force contractors to honour the contracts themselves and to persuade free riders to desist from their strategy of isolation.

175. Socrates did not want to leave Athens[1172] as his disciples suggested he should in order to avoid the death sentence, because he

1169. See *supra* §155.

1170. See *supra* §114.

1171. BINMORE 2005, p. 178.

1172. See the *Critias* of PLATO, in *The Last Days of Socrates*, Penguin Books, 2003, pp. 71 *et seq.*

had considered, taking to its extreme the idea of reciprocity, that it was his civic duty towards Athens, a city from which he had received so many advantages since he was born, to remain there and suffer the sentence imposed on him by his city, even if, in the sense we understand it today, he was a victim of injustice. Man is placed in a network of reciprocities, and draws from it profit for himself, but, in exchange, is bound by a series of obligations he has to fulfil. As he expects others to meet their obligations to him, so he must keep the promises he has given to others. To achieve this, he must foresee the consequences, bad and good, and be organized to avoid them. If, to settle a debt, one starts to worry at the time of maturity, it is usually too late. It is necessary to save money for reimbursing it in a spirit of discipline and precaution. From the time when an obligation is clear and the sanction accompanying it predictable, a person has to be organized to control his behaviour so as to respect it.

It is in this sense that we deal with human accountability, freedom of choice and free will: *ex ante* rather than *ex post*. We don't try to understand, after the contravention occurred, how the perpetrator managed to get into that situation. We try to ensure that a man with an average capacity to control his behaviour can manage to avoid it[1173]. Not to accept human accountability, in the terms stated here, is to deny the possibility of any reciprocal link. If we generally waive our responsibility, claiming that we are not fit to receive sanctions, others could also say to us that they are not fit to fulfil their obligations towards us either[1174].

Free Market: Maximizing Economic Efficiency

176. We presented above the game known as the *ultimatum game* where two people share a cake, the first having the capacity to make

1173. Mathieu 18, 8 à 9, *"If your hand or your foot is for you an occasion of sin, cut them and throw them far from you"*; voir aussi Marc 9, 43 à 49.
1174. BERTHOZ 2003, pp. 317 *et seq.*

a proposal for sharing and the second to accept or to reject the proposal[1175]. According to the rules of the game, if the second person rejects the proposal, both players get nothing. In this game, as we have seen, the equilibrium consists, for the player who makes the offer, in obtaining all and, for the player who receives the offer, accepting any proposal. If the ultimatum game provides paradoxical solutions, this is because the conditions initially set for the players are far away from social reality. As presented, the ultimatum game is a zero-sum game, having two players with opposing interests without any capacity of negotiation between them. However, we will cease having such a game if we accept that the game can be played several times and that the parties have the possibility of making counter-proposals. Thus, imagine that this game is played in real life by two coalitions, the first of which, made up of the capitalists, proposes an offer, and the second, that which receives or rejects the offer, comprises workers[1176]. The object is the distribution of the profits of industrial production and the two coalitions are entirely free to defend their own interests without intervention by a third party, for example the state, in favour of one or the other. As Marx said[1177], it is in the interest of the capitalists, concerned to maintain, if not to increase, the level of production, to grant to the workers in remuneration what is biologically necessary for them to preserve their productive forces and an additional supplement to stimulate them to increase their productivity to the level desired. As for the workers, we can assume that their ultimate will is summed up in their desire to get all the gain, but for such a solution they need radical upheavals which would modify substantially the rules of the game or even destroy it.

In democratic societies, public policies seek, more or less, to maximize the minimum level of utilities available to the least

1175. See *supra* § 153.

1176. OSBORNE 2004, pp. 465 *et seq.*

1177. SHAPIRO 2003, pp. 86 *et seq.*

favoured and, at the same time, to minimize the maximum level of utilities available to the most fortunate. A society which maximizes the minimum received by the poor placates them in order that they should not rebel against their status of inferiority; a society which minimizes the maximum enjoyed by the rich imposes a charge on the rich as the price of benefiting from the development in society of their capacities. The least gifted have no interest in engaging in a cooperative venture with the most gifted if they do not draw from it an advantage which seems to them reasonable. It is in the logic of living together that all participants may mutually offset the disadvantages of life in society against its advantages. The most gifted are, certainly, owners of their capacities, but, to develop them and draw a personal advantage from them, it is necessary that this development occurs in an organized society[1178]. The least gifted may find it beneficial to benefit from the development of the capacities of the most gifted, provided that this is done in the latter's interest too. And, to make the most gifted work for the benefit of the least, the first should obviously be offered the necessary incentives[1179].

1178. ALCHIAN, DEMSETZ 1972, p. 778: *"The economic organization through which input owners cooperate will make better use of their comparative advantages to the extent that it facilitates the payment of rewards in accord with productivity. If rewards were random, and with-out regard to productive effort, no incentive to productive effort would be provided by the organization; and if rewards were negatively correlated with productivity the organization would be subject to sabotage. Two key demands are placed on an economic organization-metering input productivity and metering rewards".* STIGLITZ 2012, p. 92: *"For one thing, the government sets the basic rules of the games. It enforces the laws. More generally, it provides the soft and hard infrastructure that enables a society, and an economy, to function. If the government doesn't provide roads, ports, education, or basic research – or see to it that someone else does, or at least provides the conditions under which someone else could – the ordinary business cannot flourish".*
1179. See *supra* §§ 96-97.

177. The chief who wants for his village[1180] stable solutions of fair division cannot ignore ambient morals in the society in which he operates. His own ideas about justice or injustice count for as much as he shares them with those he leads. He can certainly use public coercion to impose them on his people. But if he cannot manage to secure that they pass into the collective consciousness as ideas of justice, he will one day have to decide whether to strengthen his means of coercion at the risk of upsetting the balance of power over which he presides, or to take note of his failure and change his policies. Free market theorists praise capitalism as the fundamentally stable economic system which has the natural capacity by means of the price mechanism to stabilize offer and demand at the most efficient level[1181]. Marxists, on the contrary, see in capitalism a fundamentally unstable system in continuous crisis which can be surmounted only by unethical means, such as wars, colonialism or massive unemployment[1182]. The collapse of socialist regimes in Europe led to admit that the right distribution of goods within a society presupposed the choice by this society of an effective economic system, able to produce the wealth to which the members of society aspired. In the decade following the collapse of European communism, market economy was imposed in the form of global capitalism. The broadly shared belief in its efficiency was such that the critics of the market economy were hardly perceptible, the discussion on justice in the economic field having been limited to improvements of the capitalist system. The idea of efficiency prevailed over the idea of justice or, in other words, justice seemed a principle subordinated to the requirement

1180. See *supra* § 97.

1181. BUCHANAN, TULLOCK 2004, p. 25: *"Differences in utility functions stem from differences in taste as much as anything else. The class status of the individual in the production process is one of the less important determinants of genuine economic interest".*

1182. CASSIDY 2009, pp. 49 *et seq.*

1183. DWORKIN 1996, pp. 334 *et seq.*

of efficiency[1183]. Phenomena related to climate change, itself largely attributed to industrial activity, or to the debt crisis of sovereign states have changed the situation[1184]. Capitalism, once predominating against socialism owing to its efficiency in producing wealth, is now criticized for producing so much growth as seriously to undermine the future of human life on the planet[1185]. In a globalized economy subject to the contingencies of the financial markets[1186], capitalism is also criticized for imposing its dictates on democracies, which are no longer able to regulate the functioning of the markets[1187].

178. The ultimatum game, played experimentally with real players, did not give the results predicted by game theory. It was observed that players who receive the offer prefer to reject it when it is not sufficient, up to either about one third of the sum to be divided, or up to a significant proportion of their annual income[1188]. Utilitarians who profess the idea that a rational being, in a situation of uncertainty, prefers a solution that increases his utility, cannot, if they do not broaden their concept of utility[1189], understand such behaviour. This behaviour is however fully rational. The human being, as a product of natural selection, carries in him in an instinctive way, the concern of comparing his state with that of his neighbour. In a world with limited resources, the capacity of some to control these resources is very often equivalent to the impossibility of others to access them. If, therefore, a person sees that, under the distribution of wealth, her neighbours are getting such a share as to result in a weakening of her own position in society, she would prefer both herself and her neighbours, to re-

1184. JONAS 1990, pp. 312-316.
1185. JONAS 1990, pp. 261 *et seq.*
1186. VALDEZ, MOLYNEUX 2010, pp. 263 *et seq.*; FERGUSON 2012, pp. 49 *et seq.*
1187. ROUBINI 2011, pp. 13 *et seq.*; STIGLITZ 2010, pp. 184 *et seq.*, 12 *et seq.*
1188. OSBORNE 2004, pp. 183-185.
1189. See *supra* §§ 136-138.

ceive nothing at all[1190]. To this first explanation based on comparative advantages, another may be added based on reputation. If the party receiving the offer played this game to an audience which is her social environment, she would have an interest, for the sake of her own reputation and that of her family, in not accepting an offer so low as to be considered humiliating by the public who observe her[1191]. Her pecuniary utilities could be increased by accepting a humiliating offer, but her reputation as a human being worthy of respect would suffer from it and, altogether, the total utilities obtained would not be to her advantage[1192].

The united workers would thus not accept a share which would place them in a position of general inferiority compared to the capitalists and would be perceived as humiliating by their social environment. The capitalists, using their empathetic abilities, are certainly able to understand the wishes of the opposite coalition. But, instead of reaching a compromise acceptable to all, they prefer to exploit the context which surrounds the game and thus limit the possibilities of choice of their counterpart. By a misuse of religion, they present their wealth as a gift from God

1190. SHILLER 2012, pp. 187 *et seq.*

1191. FUDENBERG, TIROLE 1991, pp. 367 *et seq.*

1192. BUCHANAN, TULLOCK 2004, p. 238: *"One of the great advantages of an essentially economic approach to collective action lies in the implicit recognition that political change, at all levels, is basically equivalent to economic exchange. By this we mean simply that mutually advantageous results can be expected from individual participation in community effort. Much of the debate surrounding the majority-rule doctrine seems to deny this possibility implicitly, even if such a denial is not explicitly stated. In this sense the discussion seems closely akin to the medieval arguments about the just price. If, in market or exchange transactions, the loss to one trader must be offset by gains to the other, some rational basis for philosophical argumentation about the justice of prices would be present. However, the simple fact is, of course, that in normal trade all parties gain; there exist mutual gains from trade. The great contribution of Adam Smith lies in his popularization of this simple point, but the full import of this conception for democratic political theory does not seem to have yet been appreciated".*

awarded to them for their merits; by the threat of external enemies and the diffusion of a nationalist ideology, they seek to give the impression that the overall economic efficiency of the nation is more important than the sharing of gains in production; by excessively free international trade, they deprive national workers of a real power to engage in effective negotiations. The fundamental idea which hides behind the ultimatum game and which makes it so attractive is that the party who has the power to accept or to reject the offer has no interest in being comparatively weaker or undergoing a humiliation by the acceptance of an offer which confers a big advantage to the person making the offer[1193]. Any associative undertaking is founded on this simple idea. The weaker party will not join the stronger only to increase her comparative weakness or to be humiliated. She will find another solution, such as the total rejection of the game[1194].

Democracy: Consenting to Burdens and Benefits

179. The weighing of interests within a judicial procedure is carried out by means which both serve to neutralize the arbitrary forces which can be developed in such a procedure, and allot to each interest involved the weight attached to it by the legal order.

1193. STIGLITZ 2012, p. 105: *"Economists talk about the importance of relative income and relative deprivation. What matters (for individual's sense of well-being, for instance) is not just an individual's absolute income, but his income relative to that of others. The importance of relative income in developed countries is so great that it is a completely unsettled question among economists whether there is any long-run relationship between GDP growth and subjective well-being in those countries. Individuals' concerns with their consumption relative to that of others – the problem of 'keeping up with the Joneses' – helps explain why so many Americans live beyond their means – and why so many work so hard and so long"*.

1194. BUCHANAN, TULLOCK 2004, p. 241-242: *"The essence of the contractual conception of the collectivity, quite independent of the empirical validity of this construction, involves the mutuality of gain among all members of the group"*.

Courts and judges are required to be independent and impartial in order to prevent the most powerful party in the proceedings from exerting improper influence on the balance of justice in regard to the factors to be considered. The conflict is resolved on the basis of generally applicable rules as the weighing of interests is not left to the discretion of judges but is carried out under rules indicating the course of conduct suitable for ensuring respect for the values at stake. The procedure for the adoption of a legislative rule presents similar features. In whatever political or constitutional context we place ourselves, there is always a question of prevention, correction or improvement of a social situation revealing an interaction of interests which, to be settled, requires the relevant elements to be evaluated with a view to the optimum decision. A rational decision maker, whether he is the philosopher king of Plato[1195], or the most despotic tyrant, cannot avoid taking this route. They may be arbitrary in the marshalling of the evidence, immoral in their assessment of it, or even stupid in the choice of the decision, but, using the rationality with which they are endowed, they cannot avoid following the same course.

Similar features are also present in the democratic process of adopting a law. However, the difference here is that the procedure described above is decentralized with several actors intervening to influence it. In an undemocratic regime the route to be taken is centrally controlled. In a democracy the process is uncontrolled without being disorganized and arbitrary. Constitutional norms and political customs indicate the framework in this respect, but the people and institutions involved are free to use multiple means of influence other than those which are regulated by legal acts. Each person who feels affected by the decision to be taken may intervene by mobilizing all means of influence which seem good, provided that they do not infringe the law.

1195. KOURÉ 1962, p. 128.

180. Legislative choices made within a democracy are reversible following the same process that produced them. They are reversed when experience shows that their application is not producing the desired effects or when the moral and political conceptions which used to sustain them cease to do so. The non-final nature of the choices in democracy allows the debate which is engaged around a rule not to have the character of the search for an absolute standard of behaviour to be established forever. These characteristics exert a great influence on the effectiveness of the rule adopted and the stability which results from it for the whole order into which the rule is integrated. The experimental character of the quest for the best rule to be adopted allows corrections and successive adaptations, sometimes even, if necessary, disruptions and radical alterations, whereas opening of the procedure to the greatest number of participants makes it possible for decision makers to have regard to the fullest information on what is at stake.

Furthermore, decision making by majority is, for the democratic process, a practical method to close the debate in the least inappropriate way. Majority rule and direct or indirect representation are not of the essence of democracy[1196]; they are accommoda-

1196. BUCHANAN, TULLOCK 2004, p. 71: *"The rational individual will also recognize that time and effort will be required on his part to participate in all such decisions and these costs will mount as the share of the group requires for decisive action is increased. Therefore, insofar as he is able to foresee the impact of such decisions, he will try to choose a decision-making rule that will minimize the total expected costs that he must occur, both the costs imposed in him by the collective decisions taken adversely to his own interests and those which he will incur as a decision maker."*; p. 77: *"The analysis has shown that the rule of unanimity does possess certain special attributes, since it is only through the adoption of this rule that the individual can insure himself against the external damage that may be caused by the actions of other individuals, privately or collectively. However, in our preliminary analysis, once the rule of unanimity is departed from, there seems to be nothing to distinguish sharply any one rule form any other. The rational choice will depend, in every case, on the individual's own assessment of the expected costs. Moreover, on a priori*

tions to which a calculus exercise has been applied, ensuring the best possible treatment of the interests involved in the most efficient manner[1197]. The essence of democracy is the fair treatment of all interests affected by a state decision[1198]; in this respect, majority rule and participation offer an efficient way to take a decision, better integrating and managing the competing expectations[1199]. Unanimity, absolute or relative majority, delegation to technocrats, adoption by referendum or parliamentary process are all, with their various possible specifications, tools to be selected depending on the various conditions which affect the decision on justice to be taken[1200].

181. The equation which democracy has to solve is how to reach a decision that seems fair to all those whose interests are affected, although it is taken by means of a procedure that is determined by the ratio of forces deployed in the arena of political struggles. The role of political parties in this process is crucial. Political parties crystallize common experiences and preferences based on interests, beliefs and ideologies which allow hypotheses to be formed and choices to be made, in circumstances where there is no information or unpredictability prevails[1201]. Thus, the political programmes of parties and their election platforms set objec-

---

grounds there is nothing in the analysis that points to any uniqueness in the rule that requires a simple majority to be decisive. On balance, 51 per cent of the voting population would not seem to be much preferable to 49 per cent."; p. 85: "*Indeed, the essence of the collective-choice process under majority voting rules is the fact that the minority of voters are forced to accede to actions which they cannot prevent and for which they cannot claim compensation for damages resulting. Note that this is precisely the definition previously given for externality*".

1197. BUCHANAN TULLOCK 2004, pp. 47-57.

1198. SHAPIRO 1999, p. 37.

1199. SHAPIRO 2003, pp. 221-222.

1200. SHAPIRO 2006, pp. 16-19, 66-67.

1201. See *supra* § 146.

tives and recommend appropriate means by substituting for lack of information and unpredictability, their convictions about the meaning of life and their intuitions on the course of events yet to occur. The implementation of their programmes, once they have formed the government, allows the validity of their predictions to be verified, with democratic debate and rotation of parties in government making corrections a substantial element. The point of equilibrium achieved by this process can be maintained until the change of majority or, even, until the majority who supported it realizes that the solution it itself had chosen was not the right one. Thus, the right point of equilibrium is also sought in time, each majority refining its targeting, so that the solution is increasingly improved.

182. The democratic process illustrates what we have described throughout this book as the production structure of justice. The relevant elements[1202] are gathered, within the democratic process, in a decentralized way by the manifestation of the interests affected by the process. The weighing of these elements[1203] is carried out within a procedure where public discussion obliges the participants to exchange arguments in such a way as not to allow the opponent to reject them easily. Pluralist democratic societies, without essentialist conceptions of good[1204], are mixing equality, utility and consent to a point of equilibrium where both fairness and efficiency are satisfied[1205]. Progressive parties give preference to minimizing inequalities and centre-right parties are positioned more on the side of maximizing wealth[1206]. But, under the democratic system where freedom prevails[1207], left and right are con-

1202. See *supra* § 74.
1203. See *supra* § 77.
1204. See *supra* § 129, 140.
1205. See *supra* § 145, 161.
1206. See *supra* § 145.
1207. See *supra* § 64, 142.

stantly forced to compromise in their ideological positions. The point of equilibrium established in a democracy is still fragile and lasts only until a pressing social need[1208] necessitates its replacement by a new one. As in life, organisms that survive must constantly seek, in an inescapably competing world, biologically stable equilibriums[1209], so in democracy equilibrium intended to serve, as well as may be, all interests, is always subject to constitution and reconstitution, without ever being declared final. Democracy, allowing solutions to be determined by a process of adjustment until the point of equilibrium is reached, mirrors the selecting structures we see in nature[1210].

1208. ECHR, 18 Mai 2004, *Plon* v. *France*, § 55; U.S.A. Supr. Court, 22 Jan. 1973, *Roe* v. *Wade*, VIII: "*Where certain fundamental rights are involved, the Court has held that regulation limiting these rights may be justified only by a compelling state interest*".

1209. See *supra* § 118.

1210. HAYEK 1982, pp. 35 *et seq.*

CONCLUDING REMARKS

The Invariable Structure

183. Solutions of justice are conveyed in different vehicles[1211], depending on the level of issues. *Macro-justice* solutions are normally conveyed in constitutions or international conventions, *meso-justice* solutions in legislative texts, and *micro-justice* solutions in contracts, court judgments or administrative decisions. Vehicles may differ, but the substance in a procedure to decide on issues of justices remains the same. The two balancing exercises we have seen in this part of the book, with their components, the differentiation and the integration process, are applicable to any kind of justice operation, irrespective of its object, coordination or cooperation, or its nature, distribution or retribution. Whether a legislator dealing with conflicting interests or a judge deciding on a case, a philosopher reflecting on the conditions of a fair society or a newspaper reader reacting to information, the way they follow in their mind to decide on an issue of justice is similar. Without differentiating, the normative and factual reality of a case is too compact to be accessible to the human capacity for appreciation. And without integration within a decision marking the end of the balancing processes, all

1211. KOLM 1996, p. 10: *"(...) it turns out to be crucial to distinguish macro justice, which concerns the most general principles of justice in a society notably as concerns the overall distributive justice of the allocation of resources, from micro-justice concerned with the multifarious issues of specific or local justice, and from meso-justice which refers to issues that are specific but sufficiently important to have a global impact (for instance, concerning education and social policies). The basic point is that the problem of macro-justice will turn out to be roughly solved in theory, as a mix between process-freedom, income justice and the satisfaction of basic needs, in proportions that depend on the state of the society considered, and after the respect of basic human rights".*

the selecting, assessing and weighing activity is useless as no solution is given to the coordination or cooperation issue at stake[1212].

A quest for *reflective equilibrium* underlies the balancing exercises. Various kinds of decision solving the problem of justice are tested by verifying successively their consistency with the order of values in which it will be integrated, their consequences when applied to the real world having regard to the risks which they may generate and finally their acceptability by all stakeholders[1213]. Human discretion plays a prime role in the weighing of the various elements in play[1214]. Here as well, discretion goes hand in hand with guarantees against arbitrary decisions and the reflective equilibrium ensures that the decision selected is not arbitrary but based on transparent reasoning in which all crucial elements coming into play have been identified and duly assessed.

184. In the process described, two distinct imperatives are articulated in such a way that it becomes almost impossible to separate them: rationality, on the one hand, and ethics, on the other. Proportionality is the rational requirement and fulfils a utilitarian function. As soon as objectives are set, we must seek the appropriate means to achieve them. To provide less than what is appropriate will make it impossible to achieve them; to provide more will be an unnecessary waste of resources which could be devoted to other goals. The characteristic of the human being, as we have seen[1215], is to set himself, through his developed intelligence, the objectives to

1212. See *supra* § 164.

1213. SCALIA, GARNER 2012, p. 59: *"Principles of interpretation are guides to solving the puzzle of textual meaning, and as in any good mystery, different clues often point in different direction. It is a rare case in which each side does not appeal to a different canon to suggest its desired outcome. The skill of sound construction lies in assessing the clarity and weight of each clue and deciding where the balance lies".*

1214. See *supra* § 146.

1215. See *supra* § 113.

be achieved and to seek to meet them by mobilizing necessary and sufficient means. When human beings, in pursuit of their ends, employ means which interfere with the interests of others, proportionality ceases to have a merely rational nature. It is transformed to an ethical requirement in regard to selection of the most appropriate means. It is not enough for the means selected to be adequate. They must also not do unnecessary harm to others, or, in other words, any harm to others must be justified compared to the good they are intended to produce[1216]. The idea of equilibrium conditions this process. When each person whose interests have been affected in the process of pursuing a goal, feels, based on fundamental values to which society adheres, that she has received the best possible treatment in regard to the treatment of others, her behaviour becomes stable and an order based on mutual agreement is generated[1217].

185. We have seen above that principles of justice compatible with democratic societies, such as equality, utility and consent, when applied in practice, develop flaws which either contradict the idea of justice they serve, or offend freedom, the ultimate objective they are supposed to pursue. Egalitarianism has to fight against moral hazard creating parasites and enslaving the talented[1218]; utilitarianism has to overcome lack of information in regard to consequences and the making of interpersonal comparisons of utility[1219]; and contractarianism has to find workable solutions for integrating free riders and resolving the problem of externalities[1220]. Furthermore, principles of justice are to be applied not in virtual societies, sterilised from the external world, but in com-

1216. See *supra* §§ 128, 159, 160.
1217. See *supra* § 162.
1218. See *supra* § 134.
1219. See *supra* § 138.
1220. See *supra* § 143.

petitive environments where freedom within a society cannot be preserved without national autonomy or independence[1221]. Thus, an effort to ensure equality may undermine wealth creation and consequently effective national defence; a priority given to increase national wealth may create inequalities disrupting social peace; and an insistence on consensual solutions may interfere with the process of taking decisions at the right moment. When it comes, however, to dealing in practical terms with these flaws, egalitarianism, utilitarianism and social contract tradition have no better choice than to mingle their areas of operation, the one being inspired by values credited to the other[1222]. To create incentives to work, egalitarians have to introduce proportionate methods of wealth distribution[1223]. To promote average utility, utilitarians have to accept egalitarian distributions[1224]. Contractarians will adopt policies of putative consent inspired by egalitarian and utilitarian considerations to integrate socially irresponsible individuals into the social contract framework[1225]. Justice puts in place the dialectic by which the problem of mingling equality, utility and consent into a workable equilibrium is possible.

186. We believe in the West that this equilibrium is determined by man alone on the basis of an intellectual process to guide our minds to this point. We have established bodies, such as parliaments and courts, which in an inter-subjective way establish this point of equilibrium. Each of us, also, may use his own rationality, to consider within himself the appropriate point of equilibrium for the relevant elements that come into play. The theories of justice that we have presented offer a framework within which

1221. See infra § 163.
1222. See infra § 163.
1223. KOLM 1996, pp. 36-37, 75-76, 128-130.
1224. KOLM 1996, pp. 54-55, 120-121.
1225. See *supra* § 143.

the underlying structure of justice can be comprehended, but it would be wrong to grant them a political.weight which they do not claim. These theories do not claim to replace parliaments and the courts with mathematicians able to handle arithmetical formulas[1226]. It is easy to see why. Coherence, as a requirement of justice[1227], assumes that an intelligent being can conceive all the possible implications of the introduction of a new rule or the taking of a new decision on justice's issues. Whether such rules or decisions are compatible with the other elements within which they are to integrate, is a matter of will rather than logic. Proportionality[1228] is neither subject to the laws of an unremitting determinism. To come to a conclusion about the utility of a measure presupposes, generally, projections into the future, calculations on probability concerning the risks surrounding an operation. To come to a conclusion about the advantages or the disadvantages of an option to be undertaken, when necessary for the sake of justice, is often unavoidably a wager on the future. Democratic consent[1229], ensuring acceptance by the people of what is decided for them, is, for these reasons, of overriding importance.

Humanity, in its search for justice, has tried to avoid consent or to dissimilate it either by recourse to mystical authorities and their peremptory tests of consistency or by subjecting itself to tyrannical authorities which, under the threat of repression, silence the judgment of their subjects on the utility of measures taken. Contemporary democracies do not live under the illusion of believing that justice is conceived and delivered in a world of certainty. Thus, courts established to decide on observance of principles of justice are composed in such a way that their members may reflect differ-

1226. DERRIDA 1994, p. 53.
1227. See *supra* § 83.
1228. See *supra* § 80.
1229. See *supra* §§ 180-182.
1230. See *supra* §§ 92-94.

ent views on consistency, while parliamentary majorities, subject to their regular renewal, vote on measures which they consider useful, though the opposition may be of the contrary view. In the democratic world, justice is as it is, not by decree of authority, but by the will of those to whom its requirements will apply.

INDEX

BIBLIOGRAPHY

ALCHIAN (Armen)
Uncertainty, Evolution, and Economic Theory
in The Journal of Political Economy, vol. 58, pp. 211-221 (1950)

ALCHIAN (Armen A.),
DEMSETZ (Harold)
Production, Information Costs, and Economic Organization
in The American Economic Review, vol. 62, pp. 777-795 (1972)

ALEINIKOFF (Alexander)
Constitutional Law in the Age of Balancing
in The Yale Law Journal, vol. 96, pp. 943-1005 (1987)

AMAR (Akhil Reed)
America's Unwritten Constitution
Basic Books, 2012

ANGÉLIS (Nicolas K.)
Être et justice chez Aristote
L'Harmattan, 1999

ARISTOTLE
Ethicha Nichomachea
Oxford Classical Texts, 1920

ARMSTRONG (Karen)
Islam
A Short History
Phoenix, 2003

ARON (Raymond)
Le marxisme de Marx
Le Livre de Poche, 2002

ATKINSON (A. B.)
Income Tax and Top Incomes over the Twentienth Century
in Revista de Economía Pública, 168, pp. 123-141 (2004)

ATTALI (Jacques)
Les Juifs le Monde et l'Argent
Histoire économique du people juif
FAYARD, 2002

ATTALI (Jacques)
Karl Marx ou l'esprit du monde
Le Livre de Poche, 2005

AUMANN (Robert)
War and Peace, a Working Paper
in Center for the Study of Rationality, 428, pp. 350-358
Hebrew University of Jerusalem, 2006

AXELROD (Robert)
The Evolution of Cooperation
Basic, 2006

BADIOU (Alain)
Saint Paul
la fondation de l'universalisme
PUF, 1997

BADIOU (Alain)
L'être et l'événement
Seuil, 1988

BALL (Philip)
Critical Mass
Arrow Books, 2004

BARRY (Brian)
Theories of Justice
University of California, 1989

BARRY (Brian)
Justice as Impartiality
Clarendon, 2004

BASHAM (Arthur L.)
La civilisation de l'Inde ancienne
Arthaud, 1988

BELLINGER (Gerhard)
Encyclopédie des religions
Le Livre de Poche, 2000

BENTHAM (Jeremy)
Déontologie, ou, la Science de la morale.
Encre Marine, 2006

BENTHAM (Jeremy)
An Introduction to the Principles of Morals and Legislation
Clarendon Press, 1907

BERGERON (Louis),
RONCAYALO (Marcel)
Le monde et son histoire
Les révolutions européennes et le partage du monde contemporain
Robert Laffont, 1985

BERTHOZ (Alain)
La décision
Odile Jacob, 2003

BESSONE (Magali)
La Justice
Flammarion, 2000

BINMORE (Ken)
Game Theory and the Social Contract
vol. 1, *Playing Fair*
MIT Press, 1994

BINMORE (Ken)
Game Theory
and the Social Contract
vol. 2, *Just Playing*
MIT Press, 1998

BINMORE (Ken)
Natural Justice
Oxford University Press, 2005

BOESCH (Christophe)
L'homme, le singe et l'outil: question de cultures?
in *Aux origines de l'humanité*
Le propre de l'homme,
pp. 175 *et seq.*
Fayard, 2003

BOHR (Niels)
Physique atomique et connaissance humaine
Gallimard, 1991

BRAITHWAITE (R. B.),
Theory of Games as a tool for the Moral Philosopher
Cambridge University Press, 1955

BREHIER (Louis)
Les institutions de l'empire byzantin
Albin Michel, 1949

BREYER (Stephen)
Pour une démocratie active
Odile Jacob, 2007

BRIGHOUSE (Harry)
Justice
Polity, 2004

BUCHANAN (James M.),
TULLOCK (Gordon)
The Calculus of Consent
Liberty Fund Indianapolis, 2004

BURN (A. R.)
The Pellican History of Greece
Penguin Books, 1988

CALDER (Norman)
Law
in *History of Islamic Philosophy*
Routledge, 2003

CAMPS (Gabriel)
Introduction à la préhistoire
Librairie Académique Perrin, 1982

CAQUOT (André)
La religion d'Israël
in *Histoire des religions* I*,
pp. 359-461
Gallimard, 1970

CASSESE (Antonion)
The general Assembly: Historical Perspective
in *The United Nations and Human Rights*, pp. 25-54.
Clarendon Paperbacks, 1995

CASSIDY (John)
How Markets Fail
Penguin Books, 2009

CHANGEUX (Jean-Pierre)
Du vrai, du beau, du bien
une nouvelle approche neuronale
Odile Jacob, 2008

CHAUVIN (Rémy)
Les sociétés animales
PUF, 1999

CHENG (Anne)
Histoire de la pensée chinoise
Seuil, 1997

CHRISTOFFERSEN (Jonas)
Fair Balance: Proportionality, Subsidiarity and Primarity in the European Convention of Human Rights
Martinus Nijhoff, 2009

CLARK (Grahame),
PIGGOT (Stuart)
Prehistoric Societies
Penguin Books, 1990

CLASTRES (Pierre)
La société contre l'État
Minuit, 1974

COMPTE-SPONVILLE (André), FERRY (Luc)
La sagesse des modernes
Robert Laffont, 1999

CORBIN (Alain)
L'harmonie des plaisirs
Perrin, 2008

CORBIN (Henri)
La philosophie islamique, Des origines à la mort d'Averroës
in *Histoire de la philosophie,*
I, vol. 2, pp. 1054-1187
Gallimard, 1969

CORMEN (Thomas H.)
Algorithms Unlocked
The MIT Press, 2013

DAVIDSON (Donald)
Actions et événements
PUF, 1993

DAWKINS (Richard)
Le gène égoïste
Odile Jacob, 2003

DAWKINS (Richard)
Il était une fois nos ancêtres
Une histoire de l'évolution
Robert Laffont, 2007

DE DUVE (Christian)
A l'écoute du vivant
Odile Jacob, 2002

DE JASAY (Anthony)
Justice and Its Surroundings
Indianapolis Liberty Fund, 2002

DE LUMLEY (Henry)
La Grande Histoire des premiers hommes européens
Odile Jacob, 2007

DE ROMILLY (Jacqueline)
Pourquoi la Grèce?
Le Livre de Poche, 1992

DE ROMILLY (Jacqueline)
La Grèce antique à la découverte de la liberté
Le Livre de Poche, 1989

DE WAAL (Frans)
L'Age de l'empathie
Leçons de nature pour une société plus solidaire
Les Liens Qui Libèrent, 2010

DE WAAL (Frans)
De la réconciliation chez les Primates
Flammarion, 2002

DE WAAL (Frans)
Our Inner Ape
Riverhead Books, 2006

DE WAAL (Frans)
Primates and Philosophers
How Morality Evolved
Princeton University Press, 2009

DE WAAL (Frans)
Le bon singe
les bases naturelles de la morale
Bayard, 1997

DELMAS-MARTY (Mireille)
Le relatif et l'universel
Seuil, 2004

DELSOL (Chantal)
La grande méprise
Justice internationale, gouvernement mondial, guerre juste ...,
La table ronde, 2004

DEPUTTE (Bernard),
VAUCLAIR (Jacques)
Le long apprentissage de la vie sociale Ontogenèse comportementale et sociale chez l'homme et le singe
in *Aux origines de l'humanité,*
Le propre de l'homme,
pp. 245 *et seq.*
Fayard, 2003

DERCHAIN (Philippe)
La religion égyptienne
in *Histoire des religions* I*,
pp. 63-140
Gallimard, 1970

DERRIDA (Jacques)
Force de loi
Galilée, 1994

DESCOLA (Philippe)
Par-delà nature et culture
Gallimard, 2005

DIMITRAKOPOULOS (Ioannis)
Individual Rights and Liberties Under the U.S. Constitution
Koninklijke Brill NV, 2005

DREYFUS (F.-G.)
Histoire universelle
De la révolution française au monde contemporain,
Larousse, 1998

DWORKIN (Ronald)
Law's Empire
Hart Publishing, 2012

DWORKIN (Ronald)
Freedom's Law
The Moral Reading of the American Constitution
Oxford, 2012

EDMONDS (David)
Would you Kill the Fat Man?
Princeton University Press, 2014

ELEFTHERIADIS (Pavlos)
Legal rights
Oxford University Press, 2008

ENGEL (Pascal),
RORTY (Richard)
À quoi bon la vérité?
Grasset, 2005

EVERS (Katinka)
Neuroéthique
Quand la matière s'éveille
Odile Jacob, 2009

FAIGMAN (David)
Measuring Constitutionality Transactionally
in Hastings Law Journal,
vol. 45, pp. 753-784 (1994)

FARAGO (France)
La Justice
A. Colin, 2002

FAVIER (J.)
Histoire universelle
Du Moyen Âge au siècle des Lumières
Larousse, 1998

FAVRE (Henri)
Les Incas
Que sais-je?
PUF, 2003

FERGUSON (Niall)
Civilization
in Penguin Books, 2011

FERGUSON (Niall)
The Great Degeneration
How Institutions Decay
and Economies Die
Allen Lane, 2012

FERRY (Luc)
Le nouvel ordre écologique
Grasset, 1992

FERRY (Luc),
COMPTE-SPONVILLE (André)
La sagesse des modernes
Robert Laffont, 1999

FERRY (Luc)
La sagesse des Mythes
Apprendre à vivre 2
Plon, 2008

FINNIS (John)
Natural Law and Natural Rights
Clarendon Press, 1986

FREUD (Sigmund)
Totem et Tabou
Payot & Rivages, 2001

FRIEDMAN (Milton)
Capitalism and Friedom
University of Chicago Press, 2002

FUDENBERG (Drew),
TIROLE (Jean)
Game Theory
MIT Press, 1991

GAUTHIER (David)
Morals by Agreement
Clarendon, 2006

GIBBARD (Allan)
Sagesse des choix, justesse des sentiments
une théorie du jugement normatif
PUF, 1996

GIBBON (Edward)
Histoire du déclin et de la chute de l'empire romain
Byzance de 455 à 1500
Robert Laffont, 1983

GILLIGAN (Carol)
Une voix différente
Pour une éthique du "care"
Flammarion, 2008

GIRAUD (Gaël)
La théorie des jeux
Flammarion, 2009

GLOCK (Hans-Johann)
Dictionnaire Wittgenstein
Gallimard, 2003

GLOTZ (Gustave)
La cité grecque
Albin Michel, 1968

GRANET (Marcel)
La pensée chinoise
Albin Michel, 1988

GRAYLING (A. C.)
Wittgenstein
Oxford University Press, 1988

GRIBBIN (John)
Deep Simplicity
Penguin Books, 2005

GRIMAL (Nicolas)
Histoire de l'Egypte ancienne
Le Livre de Poche, 1988

GROSS (OREN)
The Process of Balancing
in Tulsa Law Review,
vol. 45, pp. 733-744 (2010)

GUÉRARD de LATOUR (Sophie)
La société juste
Égalité et différence
Armand Colin, 2011

GUILAINE (J.)
Histoire universelle
Des origines à la fin des grands empires
Larousse, 1998

GUILLEBAUD (Jean-Claude)
Le principe humanité
Seuil, 2001

GUILLEMAIN (B.)
Histoire universelle
Du Moyen Âge au siècle des Lumières
Larousse, 1998

GURNEY (O. R.)
The Hittites
Penguin Books, 1990

HABER (Stéphane)
Jürgen HABERMAS
une introduction
Pocket la découverte, 2001

HABERMAS (Jürgen)
Morale et communication
Flammarion, 1986

HABERMAS (Jürgen)
L'éthique de la discussion
Cerf, 1992

HABERMAS (Jürgen)
Théorie de l'agir communicationnel
Fayard, 1997

HABERMAS (Jürgen)
L'avenir de la nature humaine
Vers un eugénisme libéral?
Gallimard, 2002

HAIDT (Jonathan)
The Rihteous Mind
Why Good People are devided
by Politics and Religion
Pantheon Books, 2012

HAMPTON (Jean)
Contract and Consent
in *A companion to contemporary Political Philosophy,*
pp. 386-389
Blackwell, 1995

HARSANYI (John)
Rational Behavior and Bargaining Equilibrium in Games and Social Situations
Cambridge University Press, 2008

HAUSER (Marc)
Moral Minds
How Nature Designed Our Universal Sense of Right and Wrong
Harper Collins, 2006

HAYEK (F. A.)
The Road to Serfdom
Routledge, 1994

HAYEK (F. A.)
Law, Legislation and Liberty
Routledge and Kegan Paul, 1982

HAWKING (Stephen), MLODINOW (Leonard)
Y a-t-il un grand architecte dans l'Univers ?
Odile Jacob, 2011

HEISENBERG (Werner)
La partie et le tout
Le Monde de la physique atomique
Flammarion, 1990

HOBBES (Thomas)
Leviathan
London, 1651

HOBBES (Thomas)
Du citoyen
Flammarion, 1982

HOMO (Léon)
Les institutions politiques romaines
Albin Michel, 1970

HUME (David)
Enquiries concerning Human Understanding, and concerning the Principles of Morals
Clarendon Press, 1975

HUME (David)
An Enquiry concerning the Principles of Morals
in SCHNEEWIND (J.B.)
Moral Philosophy from Montaigne to Kant,
pp. 552 *et seq.*
Cambridge University Press, 2002

IMBER (Colin)
The Ottoman Empire
Palgrave, 2002

JACOBY (Susan)
Wild Justice
the Evolution of Revenge
Harper & Row, 1984

JANKÉLÉVITCH (Vladimir)
Le Paradoxe de la Morale
Seuil, 1989

JEANGÈNE VILMER
(Jean-Baptiste)
Éthique Animale
PUF, 2008

JESTIN (Raymond)
La religion sumérienne
in *Histoire des religions* I*,
pp. 154-202
Gallimard, 1970

JOURCIN (A.)
Histoire universelle
De la révolution française au monde contemporain
Larousse, 1998

KANT (Emmanuel)
Fondements de la métaphysique des mœurs
Librairie Delagrave, 1983

KARLI (Pierre)
Le Cerveau et la liberté
Odile Jacob, 1995

KAST (Robert)
La théorie de la décision
La Découverte, 2002

KATSIMANIS (Kyriakos)
Étude sur le rapport entre le beau et le bien chez Platon
thèse dactylographiée
Paris-Sorbonne, 1976

KAY (John)
The Truth about Markets
Penguin Books, 2004

KELLY (Alfred H.),
HARBISON (Winfred A.),
BELZ (Herman)
The American Constitution
Its Origins and Development
vol. 1 and 11
Norton and Company, 1991

KIRK (G. S.),
RAVEN (J. E.),
SCHOFIELD (M.)
The Presocratic Philosophers
Cambridge University Press, 1983

KLEIN (Étienne)
Discours sur l'origine de l'univers
Flammarion, 2010

KOLM (Serge-Christophe)
Modern Theories of Justice
MIT Press, 1996

KOSSLYN (Stephen M.),
MILLER (G. Wayne)
Top Brain, Bottom Brain:
Surprising Insights Into How You Think
Simon and Schuster, 2013

KOURÉ (Alexandre)
Introduction à la lecture de Platon
Gallimard, 1962

KRAMER (Samuel Noah)
L'histoire commence à Sumer
Flammarion, 1994

KUHN (Harold William),
NASAR (Sylvia)
The Essential John Nash
Princeton University Press, 2007

KYMLICKA (Will)
Les théories de la justice
une introduction
La Découverte, 1999

LAFFORGUE (G.)
Histoire universelle
Des origines à la fin des grands empires
Larousse, 1998

LANE (Ruth)
The Game of Justice
a Theory of Individual Self-government
State University of New York, 2007

LE POURHIET (Anne-Marie)
Droit constitutionnel
Économisa, 2008

LEDERMAN (Leon M.)
Une sacrée particule
Si l'univers est la réponse, quelle est la question?
Odile Jacob, 1996

LEFEBVRE (René)
La justice
Ellipses, 2000

LÉVÊQUE (P.)
Histoire universelle
Des origines à la fin des grands empires
Larousse, 1998

LEWIN (Roger)
L'évolution humaine
Seuil, 1991

LOCKE (John)
Traité du gouvernement civil
Flammarion, 1982

FUKUYAMA (Francis)
The Origins of Political Order
Profile Books, 2011

McCARTY (Nolan),
MEIROWITZ (Adam)
Political Game Theory
an Introduction
Cambridge University Press, 2007

MALINOWSKI (Bronislaw)
Trois essais
sur la vie sociale des primitifs
Payot, 2001

MARITAIN (Jacques)
Christianisme et démocratie
suivi de *Les droits de l'homme*
Desclée de Brouwer, 2005

MAYNARD SMITH (John)
The theory of evolution
CANTO, 2005

MEULEAU (Maurice),
PIETRI (Luce)
Le monde et son histoire
Le monde antique et les débuts du Moyen Âge
Robert Laffont, 1971

MILL (John Stuart)
Utilitarianism on Liberty
Essay on Bentham, together with Selected Writings of Jeremy Bentham and John Austin
Fontana Press, 1962

MILL (John Stuart)
L'utilitarisme
in Garnier Flammarion, 1968

MILL (John Stuart)
On Liberty
Penguin Books, 1983

MILZA (P.)
Histoire universelle
De la révolution française au monde contemporain
Larousse, 1998

MOLLER OKIN (Susan)
Justice, genre et famille
Flammarion, 2008

MOLYNEUX (Philip),
VALDEZ (Stephen)
An Introduction to Global Financial Markets
Palgrave Macmillan, 2010

MONTET (Pierre)
L'Égypte éternelle
Marabout, 1970

MORIN (Edgar)
Terre-patrie
Seuil, 1993

MORINAIS (M.)
Histoire universelle
Du Moyen Âge au siècle des Lumières
Larousse, 1998

MYERSON (Roger B)
Game Theory
Analysis of Conflict
Harvard University Press, 1997

NASH (John)
Two-person Cooperative Games
in the essential: John Nash
(edited by H. Kuhn and S. Nasar)
Princeton University Press, 2007

NIETZSCHE (Friedrich)
La généalogie de la morale
Gallimard, 1988

NIETZSCHE (Friedrich)
Par-delà bien et mal
Prélude d'une philosophie de l'avenir
Gallimard, 1975

NOUGAYROL (Jean)
La religion babylonienne
in *Histoire des religions* I*,
pp. 203-249
Gallimard, 1970

NOWAK (Martin),
HIGHFIELD (R.)
Super Cooperators
Canongate, 2011

NOZICK (Robert)
Anarchie, État et utopie
PUF, 1988

OSBORNE (Martin),
RUBINSTEIN (Ariel)
A Course in Game Theory
MIT Press, 1994

OSBORNE (Martin)
An Introduction to Game Theory
Oxford University Press, 2004

PAPADIMITRIOU (Christos)
The Complexity of Finding Nash Equilibria
in *Algorithmic Game Theory*
Cambridge University Press, 2007

PETERSEN (Niels)
How to Compare the Length of lines to the Weight of Stones: Balancing and the Resolution of Value Conflicts in Constitutional Law
in German Law Journal,
vol. 14, pp. 1387-1408 (2013)

PETERSON (Martin)
An Introduction to Decision Theory
Cambridge University Press, 2009

PHARO (Patrick)
Le sens de la justice
Essais de sémantique sociologique
PUF, 2001

PICQ (Jean)
Une Histoire de l'État en Europe
Pouvoir, justice et droit du Moyen Âge à nos jours
Sciences Po Les Presses, 2009

PIETRI (Luce),
MEULEAU (Maurice)
Le monde et son histoire
Le monde antique et les débuts du Moyen Âge
Robert Laffont, 1971

PIETRI (Luce),
VENARD (Marc)
Le monde et son histoire
La fin du Moyen Âge et les débuts du monde moderne
Robert Laffont, 1971

PILLORGET (S.)
Histoire universelle
Du Moyen Âge au siècle des Lumières
Larousse, 1998

PLATO
Crito
in *Platonis Opera*
I, I pp. 45-54
Oxford Classical Texts, 1995

PLATO
Platonis Rempublicam
Oxford Classical Texts, 2003

PLATO
Leges
in *Platonis Opera V*
Oxford Classical Texts, 1922

POSNER (Richard)
The Economics of Justice
Harvard University Press, 1983

POTOK (Chaim)
Wanderings
History of the Jews
Fawcett Crest, 1992

POUNDSTONE (William)
Prisoner's Dilemma
Anchor, 1993
RAWLS (John)
A Theory of Justice
Harvard University Press, 1999

RAWLS (John)
La justice comme équité
Une reformulation
de Théorie de la justice
La découverte, 2008

RAWLS (John)
Théorie de la justice
Seuil, 1997

RAWLS (John)
Justice et democratie
Seuil, 1993

REICHHOLF (Josef H.)
L'émergence de l'homme
Flammarion, 1990

RENAUT (Alain)
Qu'est-ce qu'une politique juste
Essai sur la question du meilleur régime
Bernard Grasset, 2004

RENQUIST (Willial H.)
The Notion of a Living Constitution
in Texas Law Review,
vol. 54, pp. 693 *et seq* (1976)

RICHE (P.)
Histoire universelle
Du Moyen Âge
au siècle des Lumières
Larousse, 1998
RIDLEY (Matt)
Genome, the Autobiography
of a Species
Fourth Estate, 2000

RIDLEY (Matt)
The Red Queen
Harper Perennial, 2003

RIDLEY (Matt)
The Origines of Virtue
Penguin Books, 1997

RIDLEY (Matt)
Nature via Nurture
Harper Perennial, 2004

ROBERTS (J.M.)
History of the World
Penguin Books, 1995

RONCAYALO (Marcel),
BERGERON (Louis)
Le monde et son histoire
Les révolutions européennes et le partage du monde contemporain
Robert Laffont, 1985

RONCAYALO (Marcel)
Le monde et son histoire
Le monde contemporain
Robert Laffont, 1985

ROSEN (Lawrence)
The Justice of Islam
Comparative Perspectives on Islamic Law and Society
Oxford University Press, 2000

ROSENFELD (Michel)
Les interprétations justes
Bruylant, 2000

ROUCHE (M.)
Histoire universelle
des origines à la fin des grands empires
Larousse, 1998

ROUTHGARDEN (Tim)
Routing Games
in *Algorithmic Game Theory*
Cambridge University Press, 2007

RUBINI (Nuriel)
Crisis Economis
Penguin Books, 2011

RUSSELL (Bertrand)
History of Western Philosophy
Routlege, 2003

SAINT-BONNET (François),
SASSIER (Yves)
Histoire des Institutions
avant 1789
Montchrestien, 2004

SAINT-SERNIN (Bertrand)
Précis de l'action
Cerf, 2012

SANDEL (Michael J.)
Justice
A Reader
Oxford University Press, 2007

SANDEL (Michael J.)
What Money Can't Buy
The Moral Limits of Markets
Allen Lane, 2012

SARMAS (Ioannis)
Liberté d'expression
et diffamation
Une étude de jurisprudence
à partir des théories de la justice
Ant. Sakkoulas, 2011

SCALIA (Antonin),
GARNER (Bryan A.)
Reading Law:
The Interpretation of Legal Texts
THOMSON/WEST, 2012

SCHMIDT (Christian)
La théorie des jeux
Essai d'interprétation
PUF, 2001

SCHOPENHAUER (Arthur)
Le Fondement de la Morale
Librairie Générale, 1991

SFEZ (Lucien)
La Décision
Que Sais-je?
PUF, 2004

SHAPIRO (Ian)
Democratic Justice
Yale University Press, 1999

SHAPIRO (Ian)
The Moral Foundations of Politics
Yale University Press, 2003

SHAPIRO (Ian)
The State of Democratic Theory
Princeton University Press, 2006

SHILLER (Robert J.)
Finance and the Good Society
Princeton University Press, 2012

SICARD (Didier)
Travaux du comité consultatif national d'éthique
20e Anniversaire
PUF, 2003

SINGER (Peter)
Morality, Reason and the Rights of Animals
in *Primates and Philosophers*,
pp. 140 *et seq.*
Princeton University Press, 2009

SMIRNOV (A)
Understanding Justice in an Islamic Context
in *Philosophy East and West,*
vol. 46, 3, pp. 337-350,
University of Hawaii Press, 1996

STARR (Ross M.)
General Equilibrium Theory
An Introduction
Cambridge University Press, 2007

STIGLITZ (Joseph E.)
Freefall free Markets and the Sinking of the Global Economy
Penguin Books, 2010

STIGLITZ (Joseph E.)
The Price of Inequality
Penguin books, 2012

STRANGAS (Johannes)
Kritik der kantischen Rechtsphilosophie
Ein Beitrag zur Herstellung der Einheit der praktischen Philosophie
Böhlau, 1988

STUCKE (Maurice E.)
Does the Rule of Reason Violate the Rule of Law?
in UC DAVIS Law Review,
vol. 42, pp. 1375-1490 (2009)

SWEET (Alex)
All Things in Proportion?
American Rights Doctrine and the Problem of Balancing
Faculty Scholarship Series,
pp. 30 *et seq.*
Yale Law School, 2010

THIBAULT (P.)
Histoire universelle
De la révolution française au monde contemporain
Larousse, 1998

THOMSON (David)
England in the Twentith Century
Penguin Books, 1981

TREVELYAN (G. M.)
A Shortened History of England
Penguin Books, 1987

TSAKYRAKIS (Stavros)
Proportionality:
an Assault on human Rights?
in International Journal of Constitutional Law,
vol. 7, pp. 468-474 (2009)

TULLOCK (Gordon),
BUCHANAN (James M.)
The Calculus of Consent
Liberty Found Indianapolis, 2004

VALDEZ (Stephen),
MOLYNEUX (Philip)
An Introduction to Global Financial Markets
Palgrave Macmillan, 2010

VAN EFFENTERRE (H.)
Histoire universelle
des origines à la fin des grands empires
Larousse, 1998

VANDIER-NOCOLAS (Nicole)
Confucius
in *Histoire de la philosophie*
I vol. 1,
pp. 274-280
Gallimard, 1969

VAUCLAIR (Jacques),
DEPUTTE (Bernard)
Se représenter et dire le monde: du langage chez les primates
in *Aux origines de l'humanité, Le propre de l'homme,*
pp. 293 *et seq.*
Fayard, 2003

VENARD (Marc),
PIETRI (Luce)
Le monde et son histoire
La fin du Moyen Âge et les débuts du monde moderne
Robert Laffont, 1971

VON NEUMANN (John),
MORGENSTERN (Oskar)
Theory of Games and Economic Behavior
Princeton and Oxford University Press, 2007

WALZER (Michael)
Sphères de justice
une défense du pluralisme et de l' égalité
Seuil, 1997

WEINBERG (Steven)
Le rève d'une théorie ultime
Odile Jacob, 1997

WHITE (D. J.)
Decision Theory
Aldine Transaction, 2006

WIJAYARATNA (Môhan)
Les entretiens de Bouddha
Seuil, 2001

WILSON (Edward O.)
Sociobiology the new Synthesis
Harvard University Press, 2000

WILSON (Edward)
The Social Conquest of Earth
Liveright Publishing Corporation, 2012

WITTGENSTEIN (Ludwig)
Tractatus Logico-Philosophicus
Routledge, 2005

WITTGENSTEIN (Ludwig)
Tractatus Logico-Philosophicus
suivi de

Investigations philosophiques
Gallimard, 1961

WITTGENSTEIN (Ludwig)
Philosophical Investigations
Blackwell, 2001

WORMS (Frédéric)
Droits de l'homme et philosophie une anthologie 1789-1914
Presses Pocket, 1993